Van Gogh's Untold Journey

Revelations of Faith, Family, & Artistic Inspiration

by William J. Havlicek, Ph.D.

First Edition

Published by
Creative Storytellers
Publishers of Books & Digital Media
Keizersgracht 62-64
1015 CS Amsterdam
The Netherlands

Printed in Belgium by Bigger Dot and Die Keure, Brugge.

ISBN 9780982487211

Proceeds from the sale of this book are donated to PROGENY—an international organization dedicated to the rescue, safety, treatment, and rehabilitation of exploited and endangered children, and the pursuit of justice on their behalf.

For more information, please visit www.EndangeredChildren.org

A dynamic, interactive, digital version of this book is available with links to vibrant imagery, online video, audio, and other interactive resources. To obtain the digital version of this book, please e-mail the publisher using the message form at the following Internet address:

www.CreativeStorytellers.com

Please note: Citations and credits for all text quotations, sources, and images used in this book may be found in the appendices.

Van Gogh's Untold Journey

Revelations of Faith, Family, and Artistic Inspiration

William J. Havlicek, Ph.D.

Creative Storytellers

*I dedicate this work to my dearly departed
father and mother, John and Mary Havlicek, for their
lifelong devotion and loving example.*

Publisher's Note:

Creative Storytellers considers the publishing of this book to be a great privilege because its message, and the underlying principles of its author, Professor William J. Havlicek (as well as those of the inimitable Vincent), remind us that kindness, compassion, and generosity of spirit—together with action—will always enable us to overcome the moral and ethical dilemmas of our time. Both author and publisher have committed more than half of the net proceeds from the sale of this book to PROGENY, a global organization dedicated to the plight of disavowed, exploited, and endangered children around the world, and to their rescue, safety, and rehabilitation. Your purchase of this book means that you, too, are playing a significant part in giving just one lost child a real chance for recovery, a normal life, and the opportunities they deserve. Thank you!

Please visit: www.EndangeredChildren.org

CONTENTS

Please note: The Van Gogh Museum in Amsterdam has created an excellent online resource to Vincent van Gogh's letters, paintings, drawings, and sketches. This may be accessed at www.VanGoghMuseum.com.

ACKNOWLEDGEMENTS

I am deeply grateful to all of the following without whose help the publication of this book would simply not have been possible: my wife Jeanne, for her love, patience and support when days were long; my late mother-in-law Bobbie Rackliffe, whose unfailing support meant so much to me during my demanding doctoral days; the pastors and congregation of South Shores Church in Dana Point for their inspiration and kind support; the directors and staff of the Norton Simon Museum in Pasadena; the Van Gogh Museum in Amsterdam for their help and extraordinary online resources; my cousin John Barnett (JB); neighbor Margaret Sebold; the late and revered Professor David Nye Brown; Dr. John K. Roth, my doctoral committee chairman, for his steady unswerving support; the late Dr, Ralph Ross; the late Fr. Winance; and Dr. Frances K. Pohl and Dr. Patricia Easton for their untiring insight and investment of time in this project. I am also very grateful to my late childhood friend, James F. Daly, and his brother Mike, and my other Iowa friends Steve Alt, Mike S. Ryan, and his wife Judy; to Matthias and Kris D'Autremont; to my brothers Jack, Bob and Tim, sister Jean, and my dear nieces and nephews; our family pastor Fr. Blocklinger; my former students Julio and Candace Reyes; Brian and Lauren Scott; former fellow students George Bedell, Rob and Robin Vance; and Quentin Van Eyck from my year in Holland from 1967-1968. Deep appreciation also goes to the staff and faculty at the Laguna College of Art and Design, among them President Dr. Dennis Power, Vice President Dr. Hélène Garrison, European Study Director and colleague Professor Betty Shelton, Liberal Arts Chairman Professor Grant Hier, colleague Scott Angus, and staff members Mark B. Murray, Jennifer Daniels, and Kerri Redeker. And finally to David Glen, my publisher, colleague and friend, and his wife Jeanie, and the talented, dedicated staff at Creative Storytellers. Thank you all.

—William J. Havlicek
Dana Point, California

PREFACE

It seems fitting that more than half the profits from the sale of this book are committed to the plight of forsaken and endangered children worldwide. Anyone familiar with Vincent Van Gogh knows how devoted he was to the welfare of children. When I came across a publisher who had founded a charity for endangered children, I knew "Vincent's Untold Journey" was in precisely the right hands.

Throughout his life Vincent was convinced that one was gauged not by personal gain but by how much one can bestow on others—the true measure of what one has attained in life. This is a Gospel principle best known universally as "love thy neighbor as thyself." And it was the underlying hope that Vincent had for his art and life, and a hope that is shared by this author and his publisher—the hope that it will bless and offer forsaken children a real chance for safety, recovery, love, and compassion, and the opportunities in life they fully deserve.

However imperfect human endeavors are, effort must nonetheless be made to alleviate suffering where it is found. This innate ability resides in each of us. Vincent had in mind a very high ideal (shared by Charles Dickens whom Vincent deeply admired and imitated throughout his life) which was to make the plight of the abandoned and neglected better known. Both of these men had experienced some degree of neglect and abandonment, experiences they never forgot, and like a curse turned to blessing, they transformed the curse into a cure. Their art was used like a balm to sooth and staunch suffering first for themselves therapeutically, and then for others. Good art is always like that; based on real need and intended for real good. It is honest, directed and selfless in the best sense of those terms however idealistic that may sound. In fact, in the case of Vincent and Charles Dickens, it is their idealism married to a gritty realism that gives their art its steady radiance. Both men were generous and charitable to a fault.

I would like to paraphrase Vincent who once wrote that in order to know God one needed to love many things, for God created all things and by loving many things one comes to know their Creator. Such inverse logic also applies to this book—in knowing the many things that Vincent created one comes to love him, and through that love to love his Creator, the Creator of the Universe. I dedicate this work to that ideal, and to the many people in this world who still share this hope.

PRELUDE

"A person like Vincent is hard to replace. The amount he knows and the clarity of his views on the world are unbelievable. Therefore, I am sure that he will make a name for himself while he still has a certain number of years to live. Through him, I came in contact with many painters, among whom he was well thought of. He is one of the champions of new ideas; as there is nothing new under the sun, it is more correct to say, of the upheaval of old ideas which have degenerated or have lost their value through the hum-drum of our time."
—Theo van Gogh

In many ways, Vincent's work marks a permanent spiritual landmark in Western art. He captures the spiritual yearnings that crisscross the pages of humankind's spotted and tormented history. But while it is Vincent's vision that is examined in this present work, what makes his vision so potent is that it is a vision saturated not only with a timeless spirituality but also with the specific cultural spirit of his time, and in a real sense our time as well. His work is timeless—he gave expression to the public world at large even as he gave utterance to his personal and private place in that world. His work is a fusion of the private realms that make up every person's cultural identity. We can learn a great deal about ourselves as we study Vincent's writings, and we can learn to see how human existence is given meaning by devotion to a higher purpose.

One could say that Vincent is a contemporary man, and his 19th century existence feels oddly familiar to anyone with an eye to read between the lines. This is not hard to do because the late 19th century was a world undergoing massive seismic shifts and rumblings much like our own troubled times. Many of the same questions and doubts that haunted the 19th century still trouble us today. We sense the probing and throbbing questioning and convulsive churning of minds and hearts looking for answers. We can understand why throughout his life Vincent sought consolation in Victor Hugo's *Les Miserables*, and the novels of Charles Dickens. We seek it in the Bible, inspirational poems, music, and sacred works of art. Vincent's work is both heartbreaking and moving because it was spawned from a heart that had repeatedly been broken.

Vincent has been positioned, along with Paul Gauguin and Paul Cezanne, as one of the three key innovators of the Post-Impressionist Movement: Vincent representing the expressionist branch of the movement; Gauguin marking the symbolist branch; and Cezanne providing the conceptual innovations that led to Cubism. Picasso was directly influenced by all three of these artists but especially by the expressive aspects of Vincent, so much so that he referred to Vincent as his artistic father. Similarly, in the same way that Picasso borrowed from Vincent, Vincent borrowed from his own artist mentors: Rembrandt, Millet, Daumier, and many others. This is the way art evolves.

Vincent was less reactive and cutting edge than it may seem. He reached back into the past for aesthetic and moral direction as much as he leaned forward. I believe Vincent would have said that his work was a bridge linking the present to the past. In considering the moral concerns that link our cultural present to the 19th century, we discover hidden insights into ourselves as we traverse Vincent's bridge.

The first time I was to cross that bridge was in 1967 when as a twenty year old American art student living in Holland I saw the Vincent collection for the first time. One drawing in particular, "The Reaper with a Cap, Moving to the Right", staggered me. It was a heavily-worked, charcoal drawing where gritty marks gave massive form to a grimly focused reaper. Black pools of shadow flooded the folds of his garments as he lurched forward, swinging a sickle. This brooding worker was the literal and graphic embodiment of all the unknown miners smeared with coal dust that Vincent had seen as a missionary in the bleak mining community of the Borinage in 1879.

Yet the sum of it was much more than an experience of illusion and movement. It was also evidence of an intense effort on Vincent's part in making this drawing to show humankind's endless cycles of toil tangible. The powerful drawing made an anonymous man and his private exertion visible. Many consider this drawing, a significant part of the Van Gogh Collection in Amsterdam to be one of the most convinc-

The Reaper with Sickle, Vincent van Gogh

ing depictions of labor in the history of art.

I have long been interested in what motivated an artist like Van Gogh. Writing a book on Vincent was one way to find out. Being a painter myself was another way. It was through both of these ways that I found answers to my question about artistic motivation. It was a journey that took me into the heart of human motivation and the wells of spiritual, cultural and natural power that feed artistic life.

My personal involvement in visual art began very early with an uncle (whose birthday I shared) who gave me my first set of oil paints, along with deeply craved encouragement. It was also about the same time that one of my brother's friends gave me a book on how to draw. Those seeds of encouragement were planted in eager soil, and by high school my drawing skill was well developed. It was also in high school that a passion for reading, writing and painting were kindled by inspired teachers.

My family added a cultural foundation to all of this as my father was a Czech immigrant who brought with him rich European traditions along with my Babi's (grandmother) cooking and peasant stories. Among the family ancestry was the well known writer and moral activist Karel Havlicek Borovsky, to whom I am told I bear an uncanny resemblance, and from whom some of my idealism and passion for writing may emanate.

I was told by my maternal grandmother, who was the family's archivist, of a rich gallery of ancestors including Harriet Beecher Stowe, author of Uncle Tom's Cabin, Andrew Jackson, and (rather ominously) two of her own brothers who served life sentences for murder for their part in the Great Train Robbery! As a child I felt that I had inherited two complementary worlds staged in the United States and Europe. My maternal grandmother had been a homesteader and nurse in the Wild West in Cripple Creek, Colorado. Coincidentally, I too would later live in Colorado and obtain military medical training as a psychiatric orderly at Fitzsimmons Army Hospital, in Denver.

I also recall a particularly well-shaped reading chair that ended up in my boyhood bedroom and which became my transportation vehicle in late night reading expeditions during freezing Iowa winters and rain-drenched spring weekends. Iowa, with its dramatic and colorful seasonal changes, would also play a central part of my love for landscape painting and was another of the things that linked my personal aesthetic with that of Vincent. This landscape absorption would be amplified when I lived in Holland as a Junior Year Abroad Student in art school.

Preceding all of this was my introduction to religion as a student at a Catholic grade school and altar boy. There was a fusion of natural and supernatural thought that stimulated my childhood in ways that would later blossom into a lifelong interest in the Bible and sacred experience. These interests and motivations were also shared by Vincent and would be one of the strongest links that I would forge with him. The unity of the natural and spiritual aspects of Vincent's art and life would become a central theme of his letters, and of this book.

The landscape is a living thing to those whose lives are dependent upon it, a lesson I would learn in the summers in Iowa when I worked as a hired hand to farmers willing to pay a high school kid a minimal wage. Later this rural connection too would deepen when I rented a farmhouse in Kalona, Iowa, while in graduate school at the University of Iowa. Isolated as I was in a century old wooden farmhouse surrounded by fields and cattle, my vision as an artist became permanently immersed in things of nature. That unity of nature and spiritual life was to take me appreciably closer to Vincent. The power, presence and intensity of the seasons were never stronger and more real to me as when I had to literally dig my station wagon out of snow drifts, herd cattle, mend fences and witness animal birth and death—all set under the unbending power of nature. I recall on an early spring day, as the snow was beginning to melt, seeing a white object at the bottom of a stream. It was the carcass of a ewe who had drowned trying to ford the stream in a blinding blizzard, and whose frozen wool had acted like a sponge, dragging her to the bottom.

I had another experience parallel to Vincent's life while working as a psychiatric orderly in Hawaii during the Vietnam War, and witnessed first hand the shadowlands that Vincent had traversed of violence, exhaustion, delusion, mental breakdowns, and the brighter upsurge of hope and self-recovery.

All of this combined with a stimulating masters program at the University of Iowa's art and art history department located a stone's throw from the famed Iowa's Writers' Workshop helped me unify these experiences and embody these ideals into painting, writing, and exhibiting. Following graduation I moved to California and began to show my paintings and to receive a measure of success and much appreciated encouragement. I soon had affiliations with a number of well-respected Los Angeles galleries and museums, and received several large-scale private commissions. By 1990, I was exhibiting in Europe and on the east coast of the United States.

Vincent's moral universe was always beckoning to me, and in 1996, I returned to my scholarly roots by reigniting a doctoral program in philosophy at the Claremont Graduate University, in California. My doctoral program was centered on Vincent's personal letters, and my plan was to divide the letters into themes that would reveal the deep foundations of his world view, and that would become my doctoral thesis and the origin of this book. I had previously been a museum curator at the Riverside Art Center and Museum. Prior to that, I had been an assistant professor of studio and art history at Loma Linda University.

Vincent's world view was rich and complex, made up of his early memories of life in rural Brabant in The Netherlands. Crucial to this was that he was both son and grandson of two of the most effective welfare activists in Europe—pastors and missionaries to the poor. His letters were to unveil an extraordinary vision borne from his innate powers of observation and strong empathy with all humanity. The letters are ardent and hopeful, passionate and determined, spiritual, and at times, despairing. They are philosophical, poetic, lyrical, analytical—and nearly always beautiful. Vincent's letters are in many ways like a Dickens novel, reflections of the human condition as it tries to make sense of a world full of complexity and contradiction. The letters can rival the descriptive powers of any first-rate novelist. Judy Sund, in her important 1992 study *True to Temperament: Vincent and French Naturalist Literature*, makes the following comment regarding this literary dimension of Van Gogh:

"Vincent's affinity for the written word is both undeniable and under-acknowledged. He was a prolific letter writer whose collected correspondence now fills multiple volumes, and a voracious reader who claimed 'a more or less irresistible passion for books'. His letters are replete with references to and appraisals of books and authors; more than two hundred books are mentioned by title, and many others are alluded to in less obvious ways."

— Sund, 1992

16

Vincent himself wrote,

"I just can't believe that a painter should have no other task and no other duty than painting only. What I mean to say is, whereas many consider, for instance, reading books and such things what they call a waste of time, on the contrary, I am of the opinion that, far from causing one to work less or less well, rather it makes one work more and better to try to broaden one's mind in a field that is so closely allied with this work—that at any rate it is a matter of importance, which greatly influences one's work, from whatever point of view one looks at things, and whatever conception one may have of life."

It is these under-acknowledged aspects of Vincent that this book explores: his identification with the outsider, the marginalized, the afflicted; his support of other artists; his deeply held moral and ethical views; his use of literature as a catalyst for his art; his profound understanding and strikingly near-parallel life with that of Charles Dickens. There is also the remarkable synthesis between his painting and his nursing of atrociously injured miners from firedamp explosions in coalmines, and long treks into the night under starry skies to the bedside of a dying friend.

I saw a neglected dimension of Vincent, the untold journey of an unknown, adventurous, deeply compassionate man whose essence seems to have been lost in the dramatic and often apocryphal stories surrounding his illness and early death. My effort is to resurrect an unknown aspect of Vincent—one that is even heroic and certainly praiseworthy, and profoundly religious in the best sense of the word.

"Women Miners Carrying Coal", 1882. This is one of the earliest we have of Vincent van Gogh's paintings. Women coal miners shuffle in the snow weighted down under bags of heavy coal. Vincent had no formal art training at this time yet the work succeeds in spite of this. He provided insight into his intended meaning when he wrote: *"Now, with the snow, the effect is like black characters on white paper—like pages of the Gospel."* The crude painting has the aura of Pieter Bruegel, the late medieval master of peasant life. The pages of the Gospel graphically come alive illustrating the promise of Jesus to lift humankind's heavy burdens.

EPISODE ONE

FAMILY & EARLY AESTHETIC INFLUENCES

JOHANNA
THE FAMILY VAN GOGH
THE INSPIRATION OF CHARLES DICKENS
SORROWFUL BUT ALWAYS REJOICING

JOHANNA

*"...In thought I am living wholly with Theo and Vincent, oh, the infinitely
delicate, tender and lovely [quality] of that relation. How they felt for each
other, how they understood each other, and oh, how touching Vincent's
dependence at times - Theo never let him feel it, but now and then he feels
it himself, and then his letters are very sad - often I wept over them.
My darling - my dear - dear Theo - at every word, between every two lines,
I am thinking of you - how you made me part of yourself in the short time
we were together - I am still living with you, by you. May your spirit go
on inspiring me, then everything will be all right with our little fellow.*

Who will write that book about Vincent?..."

—Johanna van Gogh-Bonger, 1892

On the evening of July 27, 1890, Vincent Van Gogh walked into
a field near Auvers-sur Oise, in France, and shot himself with a revolver.
He lingered until the morning of July 29, his beloved brother Theo at his
side. He was only 37 years old. His last words to Theo were, "La tristesse
durera toujours" (the sadness will last forever). Six months, later, Theo
too died at just 33 years of age.

Left behind, and with the awesome task of preserving a legacy
virtually unmatched in the history of art, was one of the least celebrated
souls in the extraordinary and tragically brief life of Vincent Van Gogh—
his sister-in-law, Johanna van Gogh-Bonger. Had it not been for this
remarkable woman, virtually nothing of the illustrious Vincent we know
of today would remain, for she became heir and keeper of his immense
collection of over two thousand paintings, sketches, and illustrations.
Moreover, she was to preserve and chronicle at least 900 hand-written
letters without which we would never have come to understand the
devoted relationship and inter-dependency Vincent had with his brother
Theo, nor the remarkable beneficence that lay at the very core of the
Van Gogh family as a whole. Most importantly, we would never have
come to know the uncommon genius that was Vincent van Gogh. The

*Opposite: Johanna van Gogh-Bonger, Vincent's sister-in-law, and wife to
Theo van Gogh. The baby in the photo was also named Vincent.*

letters, publicly exhibited for the first time at the Van Gogh Museum in Amsterdam in November, 2009, were also to prove crucial in dispelling many of the apocryphal stories that were later to surround the artist's life—stories that crassly portrayed him as some madman whose art betrayed his fractured and frenzied soul rather than the highly intelligent man he in fact was.

Johanna had realized that Vincent's letters to Theo were crucial to our understanding of Vincent yet she did not want their powerful message to eclipse his art, withholding them from public scrutiny for nearly twenty-four years until Vincent's reputation as an artist was safely established. Johanna's astute concern, care, and dedication to preserving the very essence of Vincent Van Gogh were manifested in a way of which he would have approved: through action.

In 1914, while living in Amsterdam, she wrote of how she had first discovered the letters:

"When as Theo's young wife I entered in April, 1889, our flat in the Cité Pigalle in Paris, I found in the bottom of a small desk a drawer full of letters from Vincent, and week after week I saw the soon familiar yellow envelopes with the characteristic handwriting increase in number. After Vincent's death Theo discussed with me the project of publishing these letters, but death took him away ere he could begin to execute this plan. Nearly twenty-four years passed after Theo's death before I was able to complete their publication. Much time was necessary to decipher the letters and to arrange them; this was the more difficult because often the dates failed, and much careful thought was needed before these letters were fitted into their place. There was another reason, however, which kept me from making them known earlier. It would have been an injustice to Vincent to create interest in his personality ere the work to which he gave his life was recognized and appreciated as it deserved. Many years passed before Vincent was recognized as a great painter. Now it is time his personality was known and understood. May the letters be read with considera-tion."

Johanna's prudence in her handling of Vincent's letters and art was born from her understanding of the complex motives which drove her passionate and gifted brother-in-law, and the close, committed relationship between Vincent and Theo. But she was also astutely aware of the importance of Vincent's work in that he had bequeathed to posterity not just a phenomenal body of paintings and drawings but also a message—almost an appeal—of kindness and compassion for one's fellow man. This concept was not Johanna's alone; it is self-evident when one reads Vincent's erudite exchanges between Theo, Johanna, members of the Van Gogh family, and all those who were touched by his soul. Writing to a friend, Johanna once said:

"The letters have taken a large place in my life already, since the beginning of Theo's illness. The first lonely evening which I spent in our home after my return I took the package of letters. I knew that in them I should find him again. Evening after evening that was my consolation after the miserable days. It was not Vincent whom I was seeking but Theo. I drank in every word, I absorbed every detail. I not only read the letters with my heart, but with my whole soul. And so it has remained all the time. I have read them, and reread them, until I saw the figure of Vincent clearly before me. Imagine for one moment my experience, when I came back to Holland—realizing the greatness and the nobility of that lonely artist's life. Imagine my disappointment at the indifference which people showed, when it concerned Vincent and his work...Sometimes it made me very sad. I remember how last year, on the day of Vincent's death, I went out late in the evening. The wind blew, it rained, and it was pitch-dark. Everywhere in the houses I saw light and people gathered around the table. And I felt so forlorn that for the first time I understood what Vincent must have felt in those times, when everybody turned away from him, when he felt 'as if there were no place for him on earth...' I wished that I could make you feel the influence Vincent had on my life. It was he who helped me to accommodate my life in such a way that I can be at peace with myself. Serenity—this was the favorite word of both of them, the something they considered the highest. Serenity—I have found it. Since that winter, when I was alone, I have not been unhappy— 'sorrowful yet always rejoicing,' that was one of his expressions, which I have come to understand now."

Vincent had always longed for a close family. This became a tangible reality twice in his life: once when he had taken in, along with her two illegitimate children, the poor and abandoned Sien Hoornik, a Dutch woman from a criminally-minded family encouraged by her own mother to practice prostitution; then, at end of his life, with his brother Theo, Johanna and his little nephew and namesake. His role in these familial relationships, and the strong bonds that emerged from them, were significant. They have also been the source of much speculation by historians and biographers. What made the latter of these relationships especially complicated was that the adults were enmeshed in a precarious web of finan-

cial interdependency just as Theo and Johanna's child arrived. Vincent relied almost entirely on Theo's monetary support, and sought to earn it with the prolificacy of his art.

Despite this, and on the eve of an intense and risky childbirth (which by some estimates lasted 14 hours), Johanna wrote a deeply touching, rarely quoted letter to Vincent. She had been told that the birth would come at a real risk to her life. She was at the time just twenty-eight years old, and was a petite, delicately framed woman, and the infant was situated awkwardly in her womb. Her doctor may have even suggested that she put her final affairs in order in case she didn't survive the ordeal. This was no doubt very disturbing for poor Johanna considering that this was not only her first child…it might well be her last. Johanna had only been married to Theo a little over a year at this point. Nevertheless, her letter demonstrated that she was an integral part of their symbiosis, and she was clearly a person of great sensibility.

Above: Sien Hoornik, from a drawing by Vincent Van Gogh

Wednesday Night [January 30, 1890]

Dear Vincent,

Ever since Christmas it has been my intention, day after day, to write you—there is even a half-finished letter to you in my writing case—and even now, if I should not make haste to write you this letter, you would get the news sooner that your little namesake had arrived. Before this moment, however, I want to say good night to you. It is precisely midnight—the doctor has gone to sleep for a while, for tonight he prefers to stay in the house—Theo, Mother and Wil are sitting around the table with me—awaiting future events—it is such a strange feeling—over and over again that question, will the baby be here by to-morrow morning? I cannot write much, but I so dearly wanted to have a chat with you...Tonight—and all through these days for that matter—I have been wondering so much whether I have really been able to do something to make Theo happy in his marriage—he certainly has me. He has been so good to me, so good—if things should not turn out well—if I should have to leave him—then you must tell him—for there is nobody on earth he loves so much—that he must never regret that he married me, for he has made me, oh, so happy. It is true that such a message sounds sentimental—but I cannot tell him now—for half of my company has fallen asleep, he too, for he is so very tired. Oh, if I could give him a healthy sweet little boy, wouldn't that make him happy! I think I shall stop now, for I have attacks of pain every now and then which prevent me from thinking or writing in an orderly way. When you receive this all will be over. Believe me,

Yours affectionately,

Jo.

The dire circumstances under which this letter was written and the poignant message it conveyed must have been the source of great anxiety for Vincent. Prior to his own birth, an older brother—also named Vincent Willem Van Gogh—had been stillborn and now, upon receiving Johanna's letter, it must have seemed to him that birth and death had ominously convened again.

Still, it is a measure of Johanna's respect for the devotion between the two brothers, as well as her own solicitude for Vincent, that she wrote this letter four months before she had actually met him, and just six months before his death. In fact, Johanna was to only meet Vincent face-to-face twice, once on May 17, 1890, and again on June 10. She later described that first encounter, and the impressions she had of Vincent.

"I had expected to see a sick man, but here was a sturdy, broad-shouldered man, with a healthy color, a smile on his face, and a very resolute appearance; of all the self-portraits, the one before the easel is most like him at that period...Then Theo drew him into the room where our little boy's cradle was; he had been named after Vincent. Silently the two brothers looked at the quietly sleeping baby—both had tears in their eyes. Then Vincent turned smilingly to me and said, pointing to the simple crocheted cover on the cradle, "Do not cover him too much with lace, little sister." He stayed three days, and was cheerful and lively all the time. St. Remy was not mentioned...The first morning he was up very early and was standing in his shirtsleeves looking at his pictures, of which our apartment was full. The walls were covered with them..."

Vincent's letters and the testimony of Johanna portray a very different story than the popular tale of the mad artist who cuts off his ear. What emerges instead is a story of selfless loyalty, the epitome of the Gospel's sacred counsel—"love one another".

This was the core not only of Vincent's ethics; it was also the foundation of his aesthetic stance. Tangible expression of such transcendental themes appeared in his first masterpiece *The Potato Eaters* completed at the very beginning of his career. We find these themes with even greater validity in his late paintings, such as *The Starry Night*, of 1889, and *The Resurrection of Lazarus*, of 1890. One senses a soaring spirituality rounded with human and divine love.

This understanding of Vincent does not overtly appear in many accounts of his life, nor is its traditional sensibility something that seems familiar in our own times. In the early 1900s, when the previous century was being documented, there was a significant erosion of a belief in morality. Bear in mind that Johanna first published Vincent's letters in 1914 at the outset of the First World War, and when the world was facing great despair. It is easy to understand why in the ensuing years many historians, in telling Vincent's story, would neglect elements of his life that spoke of faith and commitment. Such values were enshrouded

by the horrific carnage and devastation on a scale never before seen in human history. People's minds were just elsewhere.

However, the strong moral outlook of Vincent's letters, found too in Johanna's memoirs written decades after the artist's death, spoke strongly to the very human spirit that was in dire jeopardy in those dark times. Perhaps our own private forebodings—fueled by the crises and moral dilemmas of our times today—can find sustenance in the innate and profound compassion of Vincent van Gogh.

Top left: One of the only—and controversial—photos of Vincent van Gogh (see notation in the Appendix). Lower left: Theo van Gogh, Vincent's brother. Lower right: Johanna van Gogh-Bonger, Theo's wife.

THE FAMILY VAN GOGH

"'When he came back to them of his own will, they received him with
so much love and tried everything in their power to make him comfortable...'
[His father wrote] 'We approved of his staying here for some time to make
studies. He wanted the mangling room fitted up for him...We had a nice stove
put in; as the room had a stone floor we had it covered with boards and made
it as comfortable as possible; we put in a bed on a wooden stand, so that it
might not be too damp...I proposed having a large window made in it but
he did not want that. In short, we undertake this experiment
with real confidence, and we intend to leave him perfectly
free in his peculiarities of dress, etc.'"

—Johanna van Gogh-Bonger, 1914

Throughout his life, Vincent was provided for by a number of people, among them his father, brother, uncles, friends, doctors, and Protestant clergymen. Their singular concern for him, clearly evident in Johanna's writings, does not concur with suggestions by earlier Van Gogh scholars many of whom have propagated the notion that Vincent's upbringing was abnormal, and was a major cause of his instability. Van Gogh biographer, M.E. Traulbaut, even proposed a Freudian hypothesis that Vincent's mother had rejected him in favor of her first-born son (also named Vincent) who had been still-born. Johanna attests to just the opposite—that in losing the first Vincent, it was imperative for the family to cherish and nurture the second.

Vincent van Gogh was born into an important Dutch family whose members, over the centuries, had been involved in a variety of vocations: theology, government, the military, sculpture, painting, crafts, and book-binding. Three at least were astute and adept in the business of selling art.

Vincent's grandparents had eleven children—two daughters

Opposite: Van Gogh's painting of his mother, Anna Cornelia Carbentus.
He never painted his father which he deeply regretted later in life.

and nine sons. Both daughters married military officers of high rank in the Dutch Armed forces, while six of the sons held notable administrative and business positions in what we now call The Netherlands. Vincent's Uncle Johannes, a handsome and powerful man, was Vice-Admiral and Commandant of the Dutch Navy—its second-highest ranking officer.

Three other sons became art dealers. One in particular was to have a powerful impact on Vincent and Theo in their decisions to pursue careers in art. Also named Vincent, but known as Uncle Cent, he was well-read, highly successful, and very influential. According to Johanna, he had opened a gallery in Den Haag (The Hague) that enjoyed prestige throughout Europe. She described Uncle Cent as a "gifted, witty, and intelligent man, and held great authority in the world of art at that time." Johanna told how Goupil & Cie., the renowned international art dealers and print publishers in Paris, offered him a partnership, and "achieved its highest renown only after Vincent (the uncle) joined it." There was, therefore, a well established set of vocational choices within the Van Gogh family.

Johanna, writing in her memoirs, provided a lucid understanding of the family Van Gogh:

"The family name, Van Gogh, is probably derived from the small town Gogh on the German frontier, but in the sixteenth century the Van Goghs were already established in Holland. According to the Annales Genealogiques by Arnold Buchelius, a Jacob Van Gogh lived at that time in Utrecht, "in the Owl behind the Town Hall." Jan, Jacob's son, who lived "in the Bible under the flax market," sold wine and books and was Captain of the Civil Guard. Their coat of arms was a bar with three roses, and it is still the Van Gogh family crest.

In the seventeenth century we find many Van Goghs occupying high offices of state in Holland. Johannes Van Gogh, magistrate of Zutphen, was appointed

High Treasurer of the Union in 1628; Michel Van Gogh—originally Consul General in Brazil and treasurer of Zeeland—was a member of the Embassy that welcomed King Charles II of England on his ascent to the throne in 1660. In about the same period Cornelius Van Gogh was a Remonstrant clergyman at Boskoop;...

...David Van Gogh, who settled in The Hague, was a gold-wire drawer. His eldest son, Jan, followed the same trade, and married Maria Stalvius; both belonged to the Walloon Protestant Church. David's second son, Vincent (1729-1802), was a sculptor by profession, and was said to have been in Paris in his youth: in 1749 he was one of the Cent Suisses. With him the practice of art seems to have come into the family . . . .

...Johannes was at first a gold-wire drawer like his father, but he later became a Bible teacher and a clerk in the Cloister Church at The Hague. He married Johanna van der Vin of Mallines, and their son Vincent (1789-1874) was enabled, by the legacy of his great-uncle Vincent, to study theology at the University of Leiden. This Vincent, the grandfather of the painter, was a man of great intellect, with an extraordinarily strong sense of duty. At the Latin school he distinguished himself and won all kinds of prizes and testimonials..."

Johanna, who had named her own child Vincent Willem Van Gogh after her charismatic brother-in-law, also drew attention to the recurring use of the name "Vincent" in the family line: an uncle, great-uncle, grandfather, and great-grandfather bore the name, and they included a sculptor, a Bible teacher, a gold-drawer and jeweler, an acclaimed theologian, and an art dealer in the person of "Uncle Cent".

It is clear from the letters of both Johanna, Theo, and others, that Vincent's parents were, despite his foibles and peccadillos, remark-ably accepting and generous throughout his life. This is amply demon-strated by the fact that Vincent was allowed back into their home repeatedly, even after he had attained the age of thirty years, and after he had provoked and confounded his cousins and the extended family by his conduct. This forgiveness and compassion of his parents most

Above: "The Parsonage at Nuenen" 1885, by Vincent van Gogh. Van Gogh Museum.
Van Gogh had an uncanny ability to render the massive reality of architectural objects. Here he
summons up the brown brick two story presence of the parsonage provided by the parish his fa-
ther officiated over. Vincent's sisters most likely are shown in the walkway.

likely accounts for the constant theme in his art and letters concerning
having his own home, marriage and children, and the domestic life he
yearned for.

    This kind of nurturing was very unusual in the nineteenth century.
Men were required to be self-supporting at fourteen to sixteen years of
age. Even in the era of the First World War in Holland, the Dutch-American
painter, Willem de Kooning, was gainfully employed, and providing for
his mother and siblings at the age of twelve. As noted by Stevens and
Swan in *De Kooning: An American Master* (2004): "In 1916, his pay was
one guilder a day. His mother took what he earned and gave him an
allowance, the usual practice of the time".

    Nevertheless, at great expense, and considering their modest
retirement savings, Vincent's parents remodeled part of their house into
a studio for him despite the fact that he was in his early thirties at the
time, and notwithstanding his unusual behavior. He would read in isola-

tion for long periods, dress as a peasant or farm laborer (belying his being a prominent, middle-class clergyman's son), and often refusing to eat with the rest of the family. Vincent's father, Theodorus, deserves far more credit than most historians have noted for helping his quirky and often exasperating son at various points in his life. Both Johanna and Theo have written that Vincent was not always an easy person with whom to get along.

Theo later reported:

"It seems as if he were two persons: one marvelously gifted, tender and refined, the other egotistic and hard-hearted. They present themselves in turns, so that one hears him talk first in one way, then in the other, and always with arguments on both sides".

Johanna tells of numerous, critical times when his father came to Vincent's aid, demonstrating a consistent and unusually tender concern for his son. Johanna believed that Theodorus's generosity and treatment of Vincent probably inspired her husband Theo to maintain this support following the father's death.

This familial solicitude is an important issue to clarify. Several early historical accounts have claimed that Vincent's parents were rigidly pious and austere; that there were continual quarrels between Vincent and his parents, some of the most intense to do with Vincent's love of his widowed second cousin, and his rage at her refusal to marry him. But the emergence of Vincent's vast body of letters, and the memoirs of Johanna van Gogh-Bonger, refute much of this wrong-headed speculation. We get a truer sense of the parents' behavior for the most part towards their peculiar son from a scene narrated yet again by Johanna:

"In one of many instances, he sought a way to reconcile his mother and wife after Vincent had been boxed on the ears for some misbehavior by the grandmother: "The tender-hearted mother was so indignant at this that she did not speak to her mother-in-law for a whole day, and only the sweet-tempered character of the young father succeeded in bringing about a reconciliation".

Johanna consistently paints a very different picture of Vincent's childhood than many early historians. Instead of uncompromising rigidity, it is one of tolerance and permissiveness by parents unwilling to be overly punitive with their children—Vincent in particular.

Vincent's father's constant efforts to hold the family together and support his son's artistic efforts were, however, not necessarily common in those times. In contrast to the parental support Vincent received, Henri Matisse, one of the foremost painters of the twentieth century, was disowned by his father when he became an artist. Hilary Spurling, in her *The Unknown Matisse* (1998) reports:

"It would be hard to exaggerate the shock of Matisse's defection in a community which dismissed any form of art as an irrelevant, probably seditious and essentially contemptible occupation indulged in by layabouts, of whom the most successful might at best be regarded as a kind of clown. Henri was already well known in Bohain as an invalid, a failure who had proved unfit to take over this father's shop. Now he had failed as a lawyer too, and was about to become a public laughing stock. 'The announcement of his departure was a scandal for Matisse's parents,' wrote a contemporary who grew up hearing the gossip in Bohain during the painter's youth: 'They felt their son's folly to be a catastrophe that brought shame on the whole family.'

'My father told me a few days ago, very angry and humiliated, that everyone took me for an imbecile, and yet I wasn't one,' Matisse wrote to Jean Biette on 31 July [1903]. 'The worst of it is that he held me responsible.' The conflict between the two had reached a crisis point. More than forty years later, as an old man in his eighties, Matisse could be moved to tears by memories of his father, 'to whom he had caused a great suffering, and who had never had confidence in him.'"

Considering the ethos of the late nineteenth century that caused Matisse's community and parents to reject and denounce him, Vincent's parents emerged as nothing short of beneficent.

Over the years, some have discredited Vincent's father in his efforts to have his son sent to a sanitarium, echoing Vincent's violent out-rage at the attempt. This psychiatric intervention was in fact consistent with his father's steady compassion for his son. Later, after his own self-confinement at San Remy Asylum, in 1889, Vincent stated that his father's earlier efforts to have him confined were justified, and regretted that his father's wish had not been carried out. Vincent later realized that early intervention might have prevented the extremes his illness was ulti-mately to take. And he later became convinced that his prior excessive behavior, compounded by substance abuse and a poor diet, caused the extreme form of epilepsy with which he battled in the final months of his life

There is therefore ample documented evidence to show that Theodorus was a major influence in stabilizing and nurturing his troubled son. It was he who rescued Vincent when he became seriously ill as a lay missionary; it was he who supervised Vincent's care and recovery; and it was his father's Bible that Vincent painted, in loving remem-brance, open and bathed in Rembrandt-like golden light, following his father's untimely death.

Vincent's mother, Anna Cornelia Carbentus, was born in 1819 in Den Haag (The Hague). She was the daughter of a bookbinder who, according to Johanna, had the honor of binding the first Constitution of Holland, thereby earning the title of "book-binder to the King". Johanna goes on to say:

"One of her qualities, next to her deep love for nature, was the great facility with which she could express her thoughts on paper; her busy hands, which were always working for others, grasped eagerly, not only with needle and knitting needle, but also the pen". Vincent's mother lived to be 87 years old: and "after having lost her husband and three grown sons, still retained her energy and spirit and bore her sorrow with rare courage".

Anna in turn described her daughter-in-law Johanna as "a re-markable, lovable woman" possessing "a cheerful, lively spirit". Van Gogh biographer and family friend, M.E. Tralbaut, writing about Vincent's mother, mentioned her "deep love of nature, especially for flowers and plants", and described her love of letter writing which may have directly inspired Vincent's own passion for the same.

Vincent's relationship with his brother Theo is well known, but in the following passage, Johanna provides glimpses into his relationships with the rest of his siblings:

"The two brothers were strongly attached to each other from childhood, whereas the eldest sister, recalling their childhood, spoke of Vincent's teasing ways. Theo remembered only that Vincent could invent such delightful games that once they made him a present of the most beautiful rosebush in their garden to show their gratitude. Their childhood was full of the poetry of Brabant country life; they grew up among the wheat fields, the heath and the pine forests, in that peculiar sphere of a village parsonage, the charm of which remained with them all their lives. It was not perhaps the best training to fit them for the hard struggle that awaited them both; they were still so very young when they had to go out into the world, and during the years following, with what bitter melancholy and in-expressible homesickness did they long for the sweet home in the little village on the heath."

According to Johanna, Vincent's sisters had said that at times he could be "absolutely dull and unsociable". He apparently practiced self-flagellation as a teenager. His teacher, Dr. Mendes da Costa, was to elaborate on this:

"...whenever Vincent felt that his thoughts had strayed further than they should have, he took a cudgel to bed with him and belabored his back with it; and when-ever he was convinced that he had forfeited the privilege of passing the night in his bed, he slunk out of the house unobserved at night, and then, when he came back and found the door double-locked, was forced to go and sleep on the floor of a little wooden shed, without bed or blanket. He preferred to do this in winter, so that the punishment, which I am disposed to think arose from mental masochism, might be more severe."

The compassionate sheltering of Vincent by his parents, however, could not curb the criticisms of their rural neighbors. The village priest, for instance, was convinced that the fledgling painter was responsible for getting a local peasant woman pregnant—a claim vehemently denied by Vincent.

Yet, even with the consistent support of his caring family, Vincent seemed to have an uncontrollable need to expend his powerful life-force to the point of collapse and utter exhaustion. Eventually, this hyperactive, intense activity combined with excessive alcohol, nicotine and caffeine consumption, and malnourishment, inevitably was to lead to mental illness.

That Vincent was able to stave off utter physical collapse for most of his life was mostly due to his underlying belief system in which he viewed complete diligence and hard work as essential components of a meaningful existence; he believed that applying himself to his work to the point of sheer exhaustion for the cause of his art would make his life worthwhile.

This heightened work ethic—this relentless drive—was woven deeply into the disposition of the Van Gogh family as a whole, sometimes with dire consequences. Vincent's father died early in life, as did Theo, and at least one sister, all of whom pursued their brief lives with dogged determination. The Van Goghs ardently believed in devotion and self-immolation as a virtue, as it was for many medieval saints such as St. Francis of Assisi who had exhausted himself by the age forty-five.

Understanding this family trait of the Van Goghs explains why Vincent believed he could reform Sien Hoornik, the disavowed and pregnant prostitute who lived with him for a year and a half. Vincent had the idea that she could be made into a dependable wife through diligent efforts. "Sien loves me and I love Sien; we can and will live together on what I should otherwise have lived on alone", Vincent wrote to Theo, underscoring the basic respect Vincent had for their father and his opinions. This esteem did not ignore his father's weaknesses, for Vincent mentions in at least one letter his father's capacity for rage, but he does not say what situations caused the rage, or how often it flared up. And despite her great love of Vincent's positive qualities, Johanna's sensitive account of the family dynamics in her memoirs makes it clear that he almost always precipitated his father's rage with angry, irrational behavior himself.

Johanna further elucidates this in her recount of Vincent's determined attempts to have a relationship with his recently widowed cousin Kee. This single event was to haunt him for the rest of his life, and caused enormous damage to his relationship with his extended family. Vincent exhibited an uncontrollable love and passion for his cousin which truly frightened the young woman. In Johanna's words:

"The thought of a more intimate relation did not occur to her, and when Vincent at last spoke to her of his love, a very decided no was the immediate reply...Vincent could not abide her decision, and with his innate tenacity he kept on persevering and hoping for a change in her feelings for him. When his letters were not answered, he accused both his and her parents of opposing the match..."

Vincent's excessiveness and irascibility caused senior members of the family to intercede in order to protect the young woman, which caused Vincent to react in a violent manner. But Vincent's father was also the town pastor, and Kee one of his flock. Her family brought pressure to bear on him in this capacity. Strong family values were part of the fabric of Dutch middle-class life in the nineteenth century, and disruptive behavior affected the entire community. Vincent's father, placed in a decidedly awkward position, was forced to ask his errant son to leave the family's home.

It's important to keep in mind that Johanna was herself raised in the patriarchal culture of nineteenth century Holland. She identified with Kee, and understood perfectly why Vincent would have been an unsuitable husband; he was unemployed, living at home, and unable to support the young woman and her child. Johanna's own experience later as a widow with her own child (following Theo's death in 1891) was to give her, on reflection, a clearer understanding of Kee's anxiety over the affair.

The intervention by his father and Uncle Stickler (Kee's father and one of Holland's most famous theologians) was seen by Vincent as unwarranted meddling. And because he had earlier been fired as an evangelical lay pastor in the mining communities, his mistrust of the clergy was all the more inflamed by his uncle's attitude.

It was of course Theo who was to exemplify the Van Gogh family's constancy through his unerring devotion and sustenance of his eccentric brother Vincent. It was Theo, perhaps more than anyone, who recognized that beneath the quirky foibles, there was in Vincent a clear manifestation of genius, and that this needed to be nurtured by the family, especially by Theo himself, in order for it to emerge in all its splendor. As we read from Johanna's memoirs:

"...oh, the infinitely delicate, tender and lovely [quality] of that relation. How they felt for each other, how they understood each other, and oh, how touching Vincent's dependence at times - Theo never let him feel it, but now and then he feels it himself, and then his letters are very sad..."

Such dedication was to take an enormous toll on the family as a whole. Theo was most like his father in excessive devotion to the needs of others, and to his own neglect. Perhaps bearing the same name had some effect on his own choices and actions. Both were to succumb to illness and early death, the father only five years before Vincent's own death in 1890, and Theo just one year later in 1891.

Despite, however, the inordinate tension Vincent created within the family, we know from Johanna's later accounts that the Van Gogh ethos—one which embodied compassion above all else—was pervasive. This resounded in Vincent who, notwithstanding all the agony and ill-feeling he may have engendered by his behavior, retained an abiding love for his father, and deeply regretted the fact that he had never painted his portrait. He was later to pour his regrets by painting (in almost ritualistic deference to his father's memory) a series of look-alikes. One in particular, his portrait of Patience Escalier, bore a striking resemblance to Theodorus van Gogh.

In the last days of his life, Vincent became more and more like his father. It is possible that the portrait of Patience Escalier not only revered his father; in essence it was a self-portrait of Vincent himself at the end of his journey. The urge to paint his parents seemed to speak of his need for redress—his way of seeking reconciliation from his remaining family members for his excessiveness and lack of fair treatment of others earlier in his life. He was to repeatedly maintain that love was not merely a feeling; real love had to be demonstrated with action.

From her own perspective as a young widow, Johanna has provided us with remarkable insight into the complexities of the Van Goghs. By sheer necessity, she had to quickly grasp the mindset of this extraordinary family in order to understand her own husband Theo, and his role in the whole dynamic. This understanding evolved even further over the quarter century following his death, with her reading, oversee-ing, translating and publishing the Van Gogh letters.

What has clearly emerged from Johanna's careful consideration of those letters, and what is so enduring about the family Van Gogh, regardless of the stresses and strains imposed to almost breaking point by its unconventional son, is how its members remained true to their core principles and spiritual beliefs—imbued and evident in the genius of Vincent himself.

Opposite: Vincent's "Portrait of a Peasant (Patience Escalier)", painted in August 1888, bore an uncanny resemblance to his father, and in many ways was how Vincent saw himself.

The Inspiration of
Charles Dickens

*"Scrooge was better than his word. He did it all, and infinitely more;
and to Tiny Tim, who did not die, he was a second father. He became as good
a friend, as good a master, and as good a man, as the good old city knew, or
any other good old city, town, or borough, in the good old world. Some people
laughed to see the alteration in him, but he let them laugh, and little heeded
them; for he was wise enough to know that nothing ever happened on this
globe, for good, at which some people did not have their fill of laughter in
the outset; and knowing that such as these would be blind anyway, he
thought it quite as well that they should wrinkle up their eyes in grins,
as have the malady in less attractive forms. His own heart laughed:
and that was quite enough for him."*

—From "A Christmas Carol" by Charles Dickens, 1843.

Vincent van Gogh and Charles Dickens never met. But throughout his life, Vincent held Dickens in the highest regard using him as a creative example and moral compass. This important spiritual connection with Dickens had been kindled by Vincent's avid reading of all Dickens's published works. And Vincent had read the reflections of many of Dickens's close friends and colleagues concerning his philanthropy and his Christian beliefs, and how he put these beliefs not just into his writing but (and most important for Vincent) through actual deeds of benevolence.

Dickens funded homes for destitute women. He was an activist in areas of social reform and workers' rights. He worked tirelessly at bettering the lives of orphans, the abandoned, and the destitute. Dickens's *Christmas Carol*, and its transformation of the fabled "Scrooge", addresses such themes: unreasonable working hours, poor wages, greed, appalling

*Opposite Page: Charles Dickens, 1812-1870. From a daguerreotype
by Jeremiah Gurney, circa 1867-1868.*

conditions, the horrible neglect of crippled children, all as part of the moral obligation incumbent upon those who claim to celebrate the kindness, generosity, and munificence of Christian ethics. Dickens's *Christmas Carol* —indeed the vast majority of his works—embraced all these Christian mores in fictional accounts that continue to speak even today. Vincent's love of this story and of the intrinsic meaning of Christmas was celebrated as an integral part of the Van Gogh family's moral code. When Vincent's excessive behavior caused his eviction from his parents' home on Christmas Eve, it was a devastating experience for all concerned.

Vincent, himself the son and grandson of welfare activists, was like Dickens committed to bettering the lives of those around him, sharing his own limited food and resources with the needy. The two men shared an extraordinary parallel in their deep compassion for others and an unrelenting desire to offer money, time, talent, help, and encouragement to those less fortunate than themselves. And while the two men were from different cultures, both shared virtually identical moral and aesthetic views.

Vincent found much inspiration in Dickens, and emulated him in many ways. And even though Dickens enjoyed a great deal of public success and notoriety, there was no envy on Vincent's part; it went far deeper than that. For he was, like Dickens, deeply concerned with the plight of the poor and the neglected—especially abandoned and abused women and children.

Although Vincent was born in 1853 and Dickens in 1812, it has been said that Vincent, in his general sentiments, was more a man of the earlier 19th century than of the latter part. He seemed formed by that era, and a steady diet of Dickens's stories provided imaginative nourishment for Vincent. His absorption in the values of those earlier decades can be seen in the timeless themes he chose to depict: families at table, farmers in fields, sunrises, sunsets, fields of corn or wheat, empty chairs and objects of daily use. Like Dickens, he clung to the Golden Rule in an industrialized age rapidly becoming immune to the plight of the less fortunate. His love of physical matter, as noted, was tied to moral values in unique ways, often consistent with those of Dickens. We know

*Above: "Applicants for Admission to a Casual Ward" by Sir Samuel Luke Fildes (1844-1927).
After seeing Fildes's work, Charles Dickens commissioned him as an illustrator. Here, too, there is a
'struggle for existence'. Fildes shows homeless people waiting outside a police station in wintry weather
for tickets that will admit them to the casual ward of a workhouse for overnight shelter. Another version of
this painting may be seen in the Tate Gallery, London.*

*Above: This watercolor study of a public lottery shows Vincent's strong admiration for the work of
Dickens's illustrator Fildes. Not only was the subject matter similar but Vincent attempted to use
many of the same colors and textures as did Fildes. Unfortunately, Vincent never produced a
satisfactory finished painting of this theme. He was to concede in his failure the extraordinary
mastery of the illustrious Fildes.*

*"The Empty Chair" by Sir Samuel Luke Fildes, appeared in the Christmas edition of
The Graphic in 1870, and poignantly shows Charles Dickens's desk and chair ominously
abandoned in his study after the writer's death.*

for instance that Vincent was upset when renovation projects in Old London destroyed many of the quaint, tottering brick buildings, meandering
streets, narrow alleyways, and colorful shop signage—the very backdrop of Dickens's novels. Van Gogh felt that the charisma of his favorite
era was being thoughtlessly swept away. He was also convinced that a
major moral force in the century disappeared when Dickens died in
1870. Vincent wrote poignantly about an illustration by Fildes entitled
"The Empty Chair" that appeared in an issue of *The Graphic* of 1870. We
see Dickens's desk and chair sitting abandoned in his study after the
great writer's death. Vincent wondered who would now fill the moral
void Dickens had left behind in that room. Vincent seemed to be asking
this question constantly in the course of his career. He painted empty
chairs many times, and recalled weeping when he saw the empty
chair his father had sat in moments after he departed from a lengthy
visit,

The subject matter of Vincent's art, especially that produced
between 1878 and 1886, was drawn from his personal experiences but
amplified by Dickens. When Vincent was a missionary to the miners in

the bleak Borinage region of Belgium, he read and reflected on workers' lives through the gritty depictions in Dickens's *Hard Times,* a stirring novel based on the horrendous lives of men and women lost in the unregulated, dismal, and desolate industrial towns of England at that time.

Dickens expressed his wrath at the moral indifference of his era, the inability of newly formed labor unions to curtail the long hours, and inequities in pay and working conditions. He wrote of maimings, ghastly diseases, and the death of children and young adults, all ground like grist in the throats of churning steel mills and quarries. Vincent witnessed such things firsthand, appreciating Dickens's poignant portrayals, and empathizing with the moral outrage he voiced. Vincent took all of this to heart and took action on behalf of the miners, helping to save lives, nurse burn victims, and champion better conditions for victims. And he faithfully documented these unfortunate people in the dozens of charcoal and pencil drawings he created between 1878 and 1885 featuring laborers, diggers, miners, cloth-weavers, and peasants, and illustrating welfare shelters for street children, abandoned women, and the least-fortunate of society. Vincent illustrated the very people of whom Dickens wrote.

Vincent continued to dream well after the writer's death that one day he might illustrate books like those of Dickens. In readying himself for this, he began to collect hundreds of illustrations found in the pulp-piles of discarded magazines of the era. Whenever possible, he purchased back issues at auctions, pasting the illustrations onto mat boards. He knew his collection so well he could retrieve examples of the top British and American illustrators on demand and with ease.

In a very short time he became an expert, all the while continuing to passionately read and reread all of Dickens novels, knowing the characters intimately by name. At the same time, he polished his own writing style by sending letters on an almost daily basis to whomever would take the time to read them. Literally thousands of such letters were written over his brief life; most were lost, carelessly tossed into the trash bins and stoves of the 19th century.

Correlations between painter and writer extend into many aspects of their upbringing. It is well known that Dickens experienced years of hardship in his childhood—as a child bootblack, for instance, while his father was in debtors' prison. Vincent also suffered episodes of extreme peer abuse as a boy at boarding school which may have stimulated (as a means of escape) his own reading and writing abilities—an emotional lifeboat. Many letters from his early teens shed light, for example, on the pain of departure, so often a subject of his life, letters and art. These are all themes that are the essence, too, of Charles Dickens.

Vincent was able to extract a gritty realism from Dickens that he described as a form of "resurrection", his interpretation being that Dickens did not create characters as much as he brought them to life. His was both illustrative writing and writing that transcended into illustration. The motif of resurrection that Vincent applied to Dickens's characters connects us with something even more profound—that both Dickens and Van Gogh held to the Christian belief in the literal transformation of the body into resurrected form after death. Their conviction of this remained strong even after their involvement with the established church waned. Their belief in the renascence of the corporeal being had a profound impact on their understanding of art. Resurrection deals with the reuniting of the body and spirit; in an artistic sense, it is taking dead matter and investing it with an artist's spirit, emotion and vision. The artist's physical media is charged with energy and becomes a resurrection in and of itself.

Vincent hoped to use his illustrative skills to give visual support to novels such as those of Dickens. He believed that if black letters on a white page can ignite one's imagination, so too can a black and white drawing. Echoing the German philosopher Hegel, Vincent thought that all artistic efforts—literary or otherwise—linked the unbounded, inner world of the mind and imagination with the outer world of finite reality. Effectively, the artist or novelist was a mediator between the infinite and finite realms, with the ability to illuminate life's unseen mysteries.

Dickens's friend and biographer, John Forster, informs us that Dickens had unusually vivid memories of his early childhood which may have included the memory of his younger brother dying at six months of age of "water on the brain". It is possible that Dickens, a little over two years old at the time, found some childish satisfaction in his brother's demise since it resulted in renewed attention for himself. Strong evidence exists that Dickens later suffered from unresolved guilt associated with his brother's death and his lack of normal feelings about it. This may explain the images of dead infants that often appear in his stories.

That irrational guilt that haunted Dickens finds its parallel in Vincent's early childhood. In Tralbaut's (1969) biographical study of Van Gogh, he also notes an early death; eleven months after Vincent's parents were married, their first son, Vincent Willem, was stillborn. A year later on the exactly the same day (March 30, 1853), the Van Goghs, still in mourning for the first son, gave birth to their second who was given the same first and middle name: Vincent Willem.

The similarities between Vincent and Dickens are unmistakable, in particular the dynamics of guilt and creativity. In a sense, guilt forced them to be acutely aware of their environments and the conditions in which they found themselves. The precariousness of their existence was dependent on unseen forces—the same forces that took their deceased brothers. In Dickens, this awareness was trained on themes and images of death and desolation, dank alleyways, old and worn steps descending into darkness, funereal scenes and grave sites—the same themes and images one finds in Vincent's letters and paintings.

As Ackroyd noted in his exhaustive biography of Dickens (1990):

"The atmosphere of the cathedral and of the ruined castle cast their own shadow; 'frowning walls, says Alfred Jingle,—tottering arches—dark nooks—crumbling staircases—Old cathedral too—earthy smell—pilgrims' feet worn away the old steps...'. Thus in his first book; and thus also in his last when, in 'The Mystery of Edwin Drood', Dickens describes the ancient city in just such terms ...In his beginning is his end but, in the years between, Dickens constantly sees Rochester in similar terms as reflecting 'universal gravity, mystery, decay and silence' and as thus reflecting upon his own precarious existence: '...what a brief little practical joke I seemed to be, in comparison with its solidity, stature, strength, and the length of life.' Age; dust; mortality; time. These are the images of Rochester drawn from him again and again, and is it too much of a hyperbole to leap from the adult Dickens to the child once more and to suggest that this low, mournful note was one that sounded for him throughout his childhood?

We recall that in Dickens's *Christmas Carol*, Scrooge was confronted with an eerie scene in which he witnessed his own death and its aftermath. It featured street peddlers bickering over Scrooge's clothes and bargaining for his bed sheets. He wrote in the following scene how a city of departed souls, secret crimes, and untold deeds are hinted at by discarded things:

"Far in this den of infamous resort, there was a low-browed, beetling shop, below a pent-house roof, where iron, old rags, bottles, bones, and greasy offal, were bought. Upon the floor within, were piled up heaps of rusty keys, nails, chains, hinges, files, scales, weights, and refuse iron of all kinds. Secrets that few would like to scrutinize were bred and hidden in mountains of unseemly rags, masses of corrupted fat, and sepulchers of bones. Sitting in among the wares he dealt in, by a charcoal stove, made of old bricks, was a grey-haired rascal, nearly seventy years of age; who had screened himself from the cold air without, by a frousy curtaining of miscellaneous tatters, hung upon a line; and smoked his pipe in all the luxury of calm retirement."

In the following letter, we note how similar Vincent's words and images are to those in the Dickens story. This again amply demonstrates how alike the two men were in their outlooks—of how the sacred journey fused the extremes of life and death:

"Well, today I went to visit the place where the dustmen dump the garbage, etc. Lord, how beautiful that is...Tomorrow I shall get some interesting objects for this Refuse Dump—including some broken street lamps—rusted and twisted—on view—or to pose for me, if you like the expression better. The dustman will bring them around. That collection of discarded buckets, baskets, kettles, soldiers' mess kettles, oil cans, iron wire, street lamps, stovepipes was something out of a fairy tale by Andersen. I shall probably dream of it tonight, but you may be sure I shall work on it this winter...How beautiful the mud is, and the withering grass! With a handshake in thought, Ever Yours, Vincent."

Between Dickens and Van Gogh there is a profound embrace of destitution and human suffering, a theme that Dickens used so effectively in *A Christmas Carol*, where Scrooge confronts his own mortality as he witnesses his clothes callously bargained for. While residing in London, Vincent made some of his strongest, most sympathetic comments about Dickens; his identification with the writer and his characters strengthened by the particulars of the city itself. Yet London was not the only link between these two artists. They were both interested in populist themes which they described in startling ways. Dickens often placed his characters in earlier periods of British history dating back to his childhood. Vincent always remained interested in earlier eras while being fully engaged, at the same time, with contemporary circumstances. Dickens's main characters are more often than not found in the lower stratus of society; Vincent similarly identified with the lower classes. Dickens described things with an uncanny perception making connections between realms of experience far from the ordinary. Vincent had this visionary quality as well, and routinely transformed the everyday into symbols of timeless meaning.

Van Gogh and Dickens have remained two of the most popular artists of all time, perhaps because they use a common language, a focus on daily existence and the whole of human experience with which we readily identify. Their timeless themes can be discovered throughout their work. Vincent wrote:

"It is a sad and very melancholy scene, which must affect everyone who knows and feels that one day we too have to pass through the valley of the shadow of death...What lies beyond is a great mystery which only God comprehends, but He has revealed absolutely through His Word that there is a resurrection of the dead"

What allowed Dickens and Vincent to look into the shadowy regions of death was their conviction that it was only the temporary obscuring of an eternal reality. For each of them, life and death comprised a whole, since each of them were born following the demise of another. Haunting as the circumstances of their births were, this drove their unshakable belief in Resurrection. For them, birth and death were inseparably linked. Death seen through resurrection becomes a second birth; mortality transformed into immortality.

This fusion of the corporeal world and spirituality will have a profound impact on their aesthetic outlook. Both Dickens and Vincent came to believe that aesthetic thought is the transformation of words and images into spiritualized vision—art a kind of figurative resurrection.

Van Gogh and Dickens each found their own way to merge the literal and the literary. They express an overt need to paint or put into words the reality of life in order to acknowledge its fragility and, at the same time, to render it—at least temporarily—permanent through the tangible substance of art.

We see Dickens in an old photo holding an antique writing quill of the sort used centuries earlier by William Shakespeare. While fountain pens existed at the time the picture was taken, Dickens loved the feel and romance of this venerable tool when drafting his novels.

There are other details revealed in the photo that offer more in-

sight into this remarkable man. We note his body language as he leans purposefully into his task, lost in thought; his impeccable velvet jacket, indicating the great regard shown for his vocation; the efficiency of his writing desk; the poise of his quill pen in readiness for those legendary flights of imagination.

From Ackroyd's biography, we discover that Dickens kept long lists of odd names such as Blackpool or Copperfield, revealing his attraction for composite names that brought unlikely things together such as black and pool, copper and field. This is unitary vision, like Van Gogh's, that fuses together the extremes of human experience.

The scene reveals a highly organized man who understood perfectly his own creative urges and needs. Highly efficient, he had arrived at a point in his life where nothing curtailed his creative flow. We know from Ackroyd's research how fanatically Dickens tested, pushed, and plumbed his own depths and skills in order to harness his artistic life in the same relentless manner. He was ever-searching for the kinds of tools and imaginative props he needed to keep that creative flow running at almost fever pitch—one that eventually was to destroy his health. Vincent, too, was to conduct his life at this same intensity, to the detriment of his own health.

In setting the photo of Dickens alongside Vincent's portrait of himself *Self-Portrait at the Easel*, we see some remarkable similarities between these two very influential men in their facial features, the cropped beards, smallish ears and noses, strong foreheads, resolute, focused eyes, strong shoulders, and an intense aura of thought and nervous energy. Like Dickens, Vincent portrayed himself in a traditional manner; he holds an equivalent to Dickens's venerable quill with the time-honored pallet and brushes, and the stout wooden canvas stretcher seen from behind. The entire painting depicts a stolid, character, like a heavy wooden boat.

Van Gogh and Dickens both were known for their love of old things. While Dickens prefered his quill to fountain pen, Vincent preferred to use, rather than the more modern drawing pencils that were available to him, raw chunks of soft lead—the sort Dutch masons and carpenters had used for centuries. This love of simple elemental things was true for all his art media. He collected antique items from garbage dumps, and saved old discarded pots, lamps, torn coats, and threadbare jackets to be used as props. Above all, he loved these things because they roused his sympathy and fired his imagination. He would often wear in public some cast-off treasure he had found, much to the discomfort of his respectable parents, And he loved common wisdom in the same way as he loved old well tempered things. He and Dickens were creative soul mates in such matters.

For Van Gogh and Dickens, old clothing seemed back-lit with light, beams of sunlight streaming though the holes beckoning to thoughts of immortality. In the Gospel, Jesus likened old garments to old wine skins that can no longer stretch as new wine ferments and expands. This image is part of a larger parable or colorful story Jesus tells about redemption. The thesis, taken up later by St. Paul (in *Romans*), is that death and disintegration must be ended eternally. Mortality must clothe itself in immortality—the resurrection of the flesh. Both Vincent and Dickens saw the promise of immortality shadowed in old, discarded clothing and its direct bond with its one-time owner...where regeneration is most apparent, it is also most needed. This idea is perfectly expressed by Vincent in the following passage from his letters in which he begins to resurrect the meaning of the lives associated with a cast-off magazine illustration. He talks about a longtime friend of Dickens, Thomas Carlyle.

In typical Van Gogh manner, he stacks meaning on top of meaning as he then speaks of Jesus, Dickens, art, redemption, resurrection, all in the space of a few lines:

"Do you have the portrait of Carlyle—that beautiful one in The Graphic? At the moment I am reading his Sartor Resartus—'the philosophy of old clothes.' Among the 'old clothes' he includes all kinds...; it is beautiful—and faithful to reality—and humane. He—Carlyle—has learned much from Goethe—but still more, I believe from a certain man who did not write books, but whose words, though he did not write them down himself, have endured—namely Jesus...who, long before Carlyle, included many forms of all kinds of things among the 'old clothes' too...There is no writer, in my opinion, who is so much a painter and a black-and-white artist as Dickens. His figures are resurrections."

At the end of his life, Vincent descended into the darkness of delusion and disorientation, constantly struggling toward the light which, in his own words, he saw as sanity. Long before this, while in a deep mine shaft in Belgium's Borinage, he said he saw daylight from over a thousand feet under the earth...it seemed the size of a star. Luster and light were, to Vincent, the materials of sanity and stability. He tried to focus his mind upon sanity just as a miner, in the very bowels of the earth, was anxious to return to the light of day.

Vincent compared daylight and starlight using the phrase "like pages of the Gospel." Here, the light of the gospel was a moral imperative—ethical light. In using these comparisons, he was referring to the New Testament and Jesus's call to love one's neighbor as oneself, demonstrated by his self-sacrificing love, charity and compassion for the poor and outcast. But Vincent also found his contemporary application of the timeless call of the Gospel in Dickens who expressed these same themes and admonitions in his novels.

The tenor of a Dickens novel was deeply spiritual even as secular positivism began to erode and discourage many who lived in those times. Neither Vincent nor Dickens were immune to the tensions of their times; they were objective people troubled and plagued with all of the doubts and tensions that haunted humanity. That both Dickens and Vincent each personally experienced suffering is well documented. That they were able to distill value from their suffering provides us with poignant examples by which we too can live. Even considering that Vincent did in the end despair and take his own life, in examining the circumstances and his state of mind at the time, we see that in his last hours he came back to center, sharing his final moments with his brother Theo in a last embrace. This sentiment remained even on his death bed and, like Dickens's "Little Nel" or the laborer "Blackpool", we are left with heroic figures who cling to their values even as they descend into darkness believing that there is always light somewhere above.

We can all do well to reflect on the meaning, messages and moral imperative that Dickens and Vincent left for us to ponder. Here we begin to see that their art was one facet of a larger sentiment for humanity. If these men had been unfeeling and uncommitted to the needs of others, we would doubt the truth of their art. When all of the pieces are put together, some stunning conclusions appear which shed light on why these two creative individuals continue to haunt the western mindset and to inspire us to this day. The world view of either of these artistic twins perhaps intensifies not just our understanding of them but of fundamental truths within ourselves.

Opposite: Van Gogh's chair, with his pipe resting on it, was one of a set of locally hand-made rustic wooden chairs he used to furnish his studio in his famed "Yellow House" in Arles. With woven seats and heavy braces, these chairs were simple and unadorned, appealing to Vincent's love of all things natural. He once said that he preferred that his art be shown in a farm kitchen rather than in an upscale gallery. Like the things found in a farm house, he believed that good art should be honest, well made and free from affectation. Vincent's chair is simple in contrast to the elegance of Dickens's chair. Both, however, are shown empty, reminding us of their departed owners, and that life itself is fleeting.

Sorrowful But
Always Rejoicing

*Now I am looking across the vast expanse of meadows, and everything
is very quiet; the sun is disappearing again behind the gray clouds, but sheds
a golden light over the fields. These first hours after our parting—which you
are spending in church, and I at the station and on the train—how we are
longing for each other and how we think of the others, of Theo and Anna
and the other little sisters and the brother....On the steamer I thought often
of Anna—everything reminded me of our journey together. The weather
was clear, and the river was especially beautiful, and also the view, seen
from the sea, of the dunes, dazzling white in the sun. The last I saw of
Holland was a little gray church spire.—Vincent van Gogh, 1883*

The Resurrection had been an important motif throughout the
history of Flemish art, appearing in the fifteenth century religious works
of Bouts, Memling, and others. But Vincent's ideas of resurrection were
also in the tradition of the seventeenth-century landscaper painter,
Jacob Van Ruisdael, who depicted it occurring in nature. We can also
see this in the Revelation of St. John where he says, "Then I saw a new
heaven and a new earth, for the first heaven and the first earth had
passed away...(Revelation 21:1, NIV). Here, "passed away" means transformed or resurrected from temporal to immortal matter. Natural resurrection symbolism in Dutch art is particularly meaningful because of
Holland's eternal battle with the sea. For the Dutch, the idea of resurrecting
the earth has always been absolute—concrete and tangible. It is about
using windmills to drain sea-soaked pastures, constructing dikes, digging
canals, desalinating the land, and making it bountiful. It is about taking
what was uninhabitable or devastated by disaster and converting it into

*Opposite: This painting (now in the Rijksmuseum, Amsterdam) was by one of the foremost
landscape painters of all time, Jacob van Ruisdael, who was also very likely a medical doctor.
as his name appears on a list of doctors active in the 17th century in the vicinity of Haarlem
where he lived and died. He is buried in St. Bavo Church seen here dominating the horizon.*

the vital and useful. This reclamation mentality added content to every activity—for Van Ruisdael, for instance, labor was understood as a sacred activity, one by which the land could be sustained through vigilant maintenance of their dikes. As Michael S. Ryan, a gifted Iowa landscape painter, puts it, these are "signs of man's hand on the land."

It is therefore understandable that Vincent's art, and his personal edification and spiritual growth, are linked to labor and the hard work of building a civilization dike-by-dike, brick-by-brick. Like the Dutch, there was for him no separation between personal piety and daily life; they were an inseparable reality as found in every plot of man-handled soil in Holland. This earthy spirituality helps us understand why Vincent could not separate history and the land itself from a call to ministry, the Gospel themes of redemption, compassion, and action directed at the people and their land. It also explains why he sees his artistic vocation as a divine calling.

One of Vincent's lifelong favorite sayings was taken from St. Paul, "sorrowful but always rejoicing". In the face of such profound imagery, what one notices is that literary media becomes a tool of the imagination in the same way as a brush. Painters and poets must both visualize things in order to render them in words or graphical images. Vincent did not believe there was any real difference between these modes. As Judy Sund demonstrates in her thoughtful analysis of the literal and visual arts, "...when both ocular and literary thinking are united the strongest expression results." This is why Vincent insisted that Dickens was a great black and white painter—he evoked visual images in his novels. Vincent was in his turn a "poet-painter"—he tells stories in painted words.

The word "illustrate" is derived from the Latin infinitive *illustrare*— to shed light upon a subject. Van Gogh and Dickens illuminate their vision as artist and writer, directing the "light" into the minds of their respective audience. The best painting or drawing achieves nothing for the unimaginative onlooker. It comes to life and light only by effort on the part of a viewer to meet it with equal intensity and willing receptivity. Both making and responding to works of art require enlightened imagination. This is how Vincent's aesthetic outlook applies equally to both his letter writing and his drawing and painting—they comprise a singular, integrated message. Understanding this aesthetic principle may, for the 21st century art connoisseur, require expanding one's concept of art itself not merely as entertainment alone but as a form of enlightened edification.

Vincent first achieved this as a writer well before he ever painted a picture. He uses the process of writing as a reflective state of mind to gather together, reflect upon, and record his complex range of observations. This gives depth to Vincent's use of the phrase "like pages of the Gospel". He writes as a means of weaving together the strands and fibers of his daily experiences. This gathering of meaning is, according to John Roth (1997) "...a sacred attitude—a focused, intense, gathering of the pieces of life into a perceived unity or sense of wholeness. A sense of wholeness is another way of defining the word sacred."

Mark Roskill (1963) enlarged on Vincent's sacred thought process. He described it as rapid and fluid—connecting a past memory as he comes upon a fresh impression: "Another most suggestive analogy between the letters and the paintings involves the interplay of past and present. One can look for correspondences in the comparative importance of their roles at different times and in the ways in which they were brought into synthesis with one another."

Vincent's perceptions are both inward and outward-looking—they move Vincent forward. His inimitable way of writing serves to knit together the purpose of his existence. Like a weaver on a loom, his imagination must work the shuttle forward and back, again and again. In writing a letter, he prefers to narrate the events of a full day, reflecting on their collective impact. This weaving together of life and of destiny is given expression in his work: shifting currents of daylight, the intensities ranging from dazzling radiances to dark, fateful, silent elements as they serve to mirror his emotions. He symbolizes his life in the passing of the day, as a light rising and gradually diminishing. It is his sacred way of visualizing existence—without light there can be no vision. Light has often been a universal symbol of divine illumination, a vision that allows one to glimpse the mysterious contours of eternal realms.

"The path of the righteous is like the first gleam of dawn, shining ever brighter till the full light of day". (Proverbs 4:18 NIV)

Even in the early stages of Vincent's life, this forward and back-ward moving process had begun, and would become permanent features of his thought and art: reflecting upon experiences, and forming and fusing these reflections into a whole, expressed in charged graphic words and literary images. At a later point, he would add another level to this process by fashioning drawings and paintings in which this complex activity was piled up in paint and plunging perspectives.

This gathering together of experiences appears again in the letter he wrote to his parents from Ramsgate, where he linked his present journey to an earlier one with his sister: "...everything reminded me of our journey together." His meaning is especially rich when he relates, "The last I saw of Holland was a little gray church spire." Here he weaves into his letter a complete love of the very things that have given his short life meaning: Holland, home, land, family, faith.

Church spires appeared repeatedly over the next two decades in many of Vincent's drawings and paintings. There is one, for example, centrally placed in *The Starry Night* of 1889, one of his last and most important paintings. In looking back on that early letter from Ramsgate, it is clear how unified and consistent Vincent's sacred vision remained all of his life. It demonstrated how literal his "pages of the Gospel" was for him.

Vincent was undoubtedly reminded here of many Dutch seven-teenth-century landscapes that feature church spires, as found in numerous paintings by Jacob van Ruisdael. In the flatness of Dutch countryside, church spires could be seen for miles. Van Ruisdael's landscapes, like those of many Dutch 17th century paintings, were based on local views. Often these paintings were small, meant for the wall of a modest room, yet they succeed in conveying the vastness of a mural.

This link between Vincent and Van Ruisdael is an important

one. Like the memories of his own childhood, they were also an integral part of Holland's collective memory. Vincent was able to recall these images at any moment for he had an extraordinary visual memory. And he had been raised in a family trained in theology and involved in art sales and distribution. The Van Gogh home was replete with many prints and paintings provided by Goupil & Cie., the art dealers managed by Vincent's uncle. Vincent was surrounded by Dutch heritage in vast, visual form.

Vincent's letters were spawned from the Van Gogh family's propensity for writing. We know that his mother, a pastor's wife, was a prolific letter writer known for issuing several letters a day. The Ramsgate letter previously mentioned was written from the busy English seaside community in 1876:

> *Dear Father and Mother,*
> *Ramsgate 17 April 1876*
>
> *You have probably received my telegram, but you will be glad to hear some more particulars. On the train I wrote down a few things, and I am sending them to you, so that you will know all about my journey.*
> *Friday.*
> *In thought we will stay together today. Which do you think is better...the joy of meeting or the sorrow of parting? We have often parted already; this time there was more sorrow in it than there used to be, but also more courage because of the firmer hope, the stronger desire, for God's blessing. And didn't nature seem to share our feelings, everything looked so gray and dull a few hours ago.*
> *Now I am looking across the vast expanse of meadows, and everything is very quiet; the sun is disappearing again behind the gray clouds, but sheds a golden light over the fields. These first hours after our parting—which you are spending in church, and I at the station and on the train—how we are longing for each other and how we think of the others, of Theo and Anna and the other little sisters and the brother. Just now we passed Zevenbergen [boarding school]; I thought of the day you took me there, and I stood on the steps at Mr. Provily's,*

looking after your carriage on the wet road; and then of that evening when my father came to visit me for the first time. And of that first homecoming at Christmas!

Saturday and Sunday.

On the steamer I thought often of Anna—everything reminded me of our journey together. The weather was clear, and the river was especially beautiful, and also the view, seen from the sea, of the dunes, dazzling white in the sun. The last I saw of Holland was a little gray church spire. I stayed on deck until sunset, but then it became too cold and rough.

At dawn the next morning on the train from Harwich to London it was beautiful to see the black fields and green meadows with sheep and lambs and an occasional thorn bush and a few large oak trees with dark twigs and gray moss-covered trunks; the shimmering blue sky with a few stars still, and a bank of gray clouds at the horizon. Before sunrise I had already heard the lark. When we were near the last station before London, the sun rose. The bank of gray clouds had disappeared and there was the sun, as simple and grand as ever I saw it, a real Easter sun. The grass sparkled with dew and night frost. But I still prefer that gray hour when we parted.

Saturday afternoon I stayed on deck till the sun had set. The water was fairly dark blue with rather high white-crested waves as far as one could see. The coast had already disappeared from sight. The sky was one vast light blue, without a single cloud. And the sunset cast a streak of glittering light on the water. It was indeed a grand and majestic sight, but still the simpler, quieter things touch one much more deeply."

In the first paragraph of this letter, we note that Vincent referred to this trip as a "journey", probably inspired by Bunyan's *Pilgrim's Progress*, a popular 19th century inspirational work he frequently quoted. The word appeared quite often in his letters. Under the Friday entry in the third paragraph, Vincent noted that the weather, gray and overcast, reflected the family's mood. The journey began with pangs of departure, Victorian in intensity, words, images and experiences fused with intense passion as was Vincent's way. And yet, "still the simpler, quieter things touch one much more deeply."

Between the lines, we sense his desire for permanence, family, and stability; he is haunted by the inevitability of leave-taking, and of life's impermanence. Such longings will remain strong currents in Vincent's life. The fourth paragraph evokes the impression of a "vast expanse of meadows" and, following his contemplation about his family, these lines carry the idea of distance, the pulling away of what is, to what will be. "...the sun is disappearing again behind the gray clouds, but sheds a golden light over the fields" suggests that separation in time and space are blessed and luminous, and while difficult deepen the bonds of love.

Distances, gray weather, and separation coalesce as Vincent recalled a childhood memory evoked by something he passed while on the train: "I stood on the steps at Mr. Provily's, looking after your carriage on the wet road." He blends another image: the rain-soaked road half seen though tear-blurred eyes. A pang of abandonment surfaces telling us of his love for his father. In later letters, we learn more about this childhood memory, and an unmentioned horror which took place at a boarding school named Zevenbergen. There is good reason to believe that he was abused there, and this may help explain his life-long identification with Charles Dickens's abandoned children, and both Van Gogh's and Dickens's lifelong need to protect the defenseless.

Clearly, even in childhood, Vincent linked the conditions of the weather with human emotions, merging the inner and outer realms of experience into emotionally charged vision and detail. We see this in his letter where he makes the connection between the gray clouds and the sadness of departure. This strongly evoked memory is the key feature of his aesthetic outlook and his potent and emotionally charged art. Vincent's letters are literally a door that opens onto the workings of his mind. They reveal the ways in which he wove emotional reaction with perception. He was, like Charles Dickens, a master of observation and description.

Looking back at the letter from Ramsgate, Vincent's memory was like an inventory of centuries of Dutch art: black fields, green meadows, sheep, lambs, thorn bushes, oak trees, gray moss-covered trunks, stars shimmering in dark blue skies, banks of gray clouds on distant horizons, sunrises, larks, the grass sparkling with dew and night frost, and especially the sun, "as simple and grand as ever I saw it, a real Easter sun." All of these things are illuminated in a dense atmosphere melded with recollections of home and family.

The letter ends: "At dawn the next morning...I had already heard the lark." This was a recurrent theme in Vincent's life—waiting for light—an indication that his spiritual quest had unseen promises. This was further conveyed by his unmistakable reference to the Resurrection in the phrase "a real Easter sun" and expressed in his numerous paintings of blazing yellow suns. He continued to conjoin his earliest religious experiences with Christ's Resurrection, reminding us that what he understood about nature he first understood in the Bible, fusing sacred perception with personal conviction.

As mentioned previously, in comparing Vincent's letters to paintings he created within the same timeframe, one is struck by the way the qualities of light he described coincided with his progress through life. Sunrise was the central motif: dawn, a real Easter sun. In his letters a decade later, midday or high noon were mentioned more often, and appeared even more regularly in his paintings. In the last period of his life, he often evoked the setting sun, troubled skies, starlight and moonlight. Vincent would, as in the Ramsgate letter, make a habit of describing an entire day as he moved from one location to another. With its emphasis on the dawn, this early letter shows how Vincent saw the early day as the literal dawning of his adult life.

Vincent would later become a landscape painter and he was to produce works like those described in the "early dawn" Ramsgate letter. His paintings would be pregnant with meaning—death, suffering and a hard-won resurrection. For the lowlands of Holland were indeed haunted by memories of struggle and sacrifice in each rain-swept mile, fought for, and resurrected not only from the ocean, but also from centuries of domination by Spain and invasion by France. Later, having gained freedom and respite, the bounty and beauty of the land provided a quiet peace after the untold suffering of foreign occupation. Vincent identified readily with his own family of 17th century patriots who considered themselves chosen people planted in a "Promised Land" following a long and arduous journey. The many church spires—upturned nails on a flat horizon—were reminders of safe passage. Vincent made these rich evocations palpable first in his mind, then in his writings, and ultimately in his art.

Vincent probably knew from his study of Forster's early biography of Charles Dickens that the famous writer had often vacationed with his family in Ramsgate. Dickens died in 1870, just six years before Vincent arrived for a teaching assignment in the seaside town. The letters he was to write while in Ramsgate betray strong Dickensian elements—his description, for instance, of little boys' pathetic moon-lit faces staring out to sea from dark windows. Nearly identical scenes can be found in Dickens's novels such as *Great Expectations* or *Oliver Twist*.

The Ramsgate letter of April 1876, rooted in the dislocated lives of home-sick children, reminds us of how strong Vincent's ties remained to his own home and country—the very opposite of fictional accounts of him as fundamentally a loner, self-absorbed, and disaffected. Those family ties would be tested severely in the years that were to follow his sojourn in England, and in some cases (and by Vincent's own account) were to become irreparably broken. Despite or because of these fractures, however, his need for reconciliation and forgiveness remained as terrible pangs in his emotional life. This desire for reunion would eddy beneath the forward-slanting characters of his handwriting, and later break into streams of painting. It would compel him to live with peasants and rural cloth-weavers, sharing their stolid existence as consolation for an apparently lost home life. His desire for family would make the subject of domesticity a central motif in his literary choices, and later as the subject matter of his art.

We learn more from the letter when we consider the circumstances of that journey, and the rich range of historical and familiar things to which Vincent made reference. He wrote the letter in parts, slowly, and in response to his observations and experiences, first from the train, and then aboard the steamship that took him across the English Channel where he had been awarded a teaching contract at a boys' school in Ramsgate.

This was not his first trip to England. He had previously lived in London between 1873 and 1875 as an employee of Goupil & Cie., the international art dealers. Vincent's "Uncle Cent" (another Vincent) was one of the senior advisers and investors in Goupil. Vincent's work performance had plummeted, however, due to the heart-wrenching rejection of a woman with whom he had been passionately in love. In an effort to help the young man, his seniors had given him a fresh start by transferring him to the Goupil Gallery in Paris where he worked from 1875 to 1876. It was this branch of the company his brother Theo was eventually to manage. When Vincent's performance failed to improve, he was fired. As a member of an otherwise successful family, his dismissal deeply affected his morale.

His move to England as a teacher was therefore something of a reprieve. He retained strong associations with London from a previous visit...memories of love, elation and heavy rejection. And it was to be Charles Dickens's benevolent and erudite portrayal of London's orphans, and the wretched misery of the city's poor that would rub off on Vincent and have a marked influence on his approach to his own art and writing.

The literary realm (and the role Dickens played in it) was to become a key element of Vincent's world view. Much recent research has been devoted to this subject, such as in *True to Temperament: Vincent and French Naturalist Literature* (Judy Sund, 1992) in which Sund explains how Vincent's love of literature was transferred into visual art. This is not the usual path for the artist who more often than not begins his or her career by drawing from nature...not by reading. In offering an explanation, Sund cites Vincent's own account of the process; he frequently said that for him there was no difference between writing and painting. Vincent's unified experience—that all art forms whether written or drawn are part of an imaginative whole—was cultivated not just from his admiration for Dickens's words but also from his sensitivity to the plight of the people he so aptly described.

Dickens, in his *American Notes* of 1842, wrote:

"Ramsgate Sands" by William Powell Frith, another illustraor much admired by Vincent.

"The return of day is inseparable from some sense of renewed hope and gladness; but the light shining on the dreary waste of water, and showing it in all its vast extent of loneliness, presents a solemn spectacle, which even night, veiling it in darkness and uncertainty, does not surpass. The rising moon is more in keeping with the solitary ocean; and has an air of melancholy grandeur, which, in its soft and gentle influence, seems to comfort while it saddens. I recollect, when I was a very young child, having a fancy that the reflection of the moon on the water was a path to Heaven, trodden by the spirits of good people on their way to God."

When we read Vincent's thoughts from that period, we recognize how clearly his views resembled those of Dickens:

"It always strikes me, and it is very peculiar, that whenever we see the image of indescribable and unutterable desolation of loneliness, poverty and misery, the end or extreme of all things, the thought of God comes into our minds. At least it does with me, and doesn't Father also say, 'There is no place I like to speak better than a churchyard, for we are all standing on equal ground; furthermore, we always realize it.'"

This passage demonstrates how Vincent was able to express himself in a stylistic sense very much like Dickens. More importantly, it shows how much in common their imaginative and spiritual outlooks allowed them to weave together strands of time, eternity, mortality, and immortality. In their sacred vision, desolation and extreme sadness lead to their exact opposites; to hope, and where death is a glorious path to eternal life—a bridge of light to resurrected glory. For Vincent, extreme desolation quickened thoughts of consoling transcendence. Similarly, Dickens spoke of a sad beauty that was comforting. The underlying ideas were identical, arising from a common belief in an unseen spiritual world.

Later, in 1878, while living and working as a missionary in the Borinage mining camps of Belgium, Vincent said that the pages of the Gospel were written all over the landscape, and recorded, like the paragraphs of a tragic story, in the dark lines etched on the faces of starving women and children.

This level of meaning refuses to separate aesthetic experience from the larger meanings of life—antithetical to current ideas that art is for art's sake...that a work of art can be enjoyed simply because it seems beautiful in some nebulous sense. For Van Gogh, Dickens, and other 19th century artists motivated by moral and ethical principles, it was considered immoral to detach beauty from deeper moral and ethical content.

Vincent wrote another letter in April, 1877, from Etten in which we see starlight and redemption like shining words breaking through clouds of desolation. This letter takes us into the very soul of his art. Here again we find the Bible's ethical words literally covering the land and filling the heavens. This letter recorded a strenuous, all-night, forced march—a mission to a friend's deathbed that took Vincent by starlight through dark forests and shrouded meadows, and over ancient pathways, to a night vigil in a church graveyard. The letter reads like a sacred mystery play, and in a very real sense it is. Vincent's splendidly painted words allow us to literally walk into a painting such as *The Starry Night* which he actually painted several years later. This letter's almost ecstatic vision showed how steady and unshakable his artistic themes, forms and manner of thinking remained throughout his artistic career. Vincent would quote his father (and Charles Dickens) in saying, "There is no place I like to speak better than a churchyard, for we are all standing on equal ground." This is certainly not "art for art's sake". For Vincent, death and art were both a graphic reality that could not be denied.

We see Vincent's real view of art in the letter from Etten:.

Dear Theo,
Etten
3 April 1877

I must send you another letter; as you see, I am writing from Etten.
Yesterday morning I received a letter from home in which Father wrote that Aerssen was dying and that he had been to see him, as Aerssen had expressed the wish that father should visit him. At this news my heart was drawn so strongly toward Zundert that I longed to go there also. . . .

Today I received a postcard from Anna, saying she arrived safely; may she do well. Has it struck you, too, that something has come over her that makes you think of the woman who loved Jesus; of whom the Bible speaks? And think-ing of her, I am reminded again and again of Beranger's words: In the Palaces and under the thatch, The Virgin says, I have prepared With my own hands the honey and balsam For human sufferings.

And how sweet she was with that family at Welwyn, sharing their happiness and misfortune, and never withholding any help or comfort that was within her; also in the days that child fell ill and died. I have seen so clearly how they all loved her. From the very beginning she exerted herself to the utmost, rising early in the winter to light the fire and with her own hands, even though the first days were not easy for her, and she wrote she often thought, "Without Thou, O Eternal Being, Ah, what would man be on this earth; Who is there in heaven but Thou; Nought delights me any more on earth but Thou." And how she looked forward to Communion, and went to it, and was fortified by it. And how Pa and Mother love her, as, indeed, we all do; ay, let us stay close together.

Saturday night I took the last train from Dordrecht to Oudenbosch, and walked from there to Zundert. It was so beautiful on the heath; though it was dark, one could distinguish the heath, and the pine woods, and moors extending far and wide...The sky was overcast, but the evening star was shining through the clouds, and now and then more stars appeared. It was very early when I arrived at the churchyard in Zundert; everything was so quiet. I went over all the dear old spots, and the little paths, and waited for the sunrise there. You know the story of the Resurrection—everything reminded me of it that morning in the quiet graveyard.

As soon as they had got up, Aerssen and Mientje told me that their father had died that night—oh! they were so grieved, and their hearts were so full. Hein also came very early in the morning. I was glad to be with them, and I shared their feelings, for I too loved the man.

The aunts send you their love, as well as Jan Doome, whom I also visited. From there I walked with Hein to Rijsbergen and spent about an hour in the house; we read the Bible together. Woutje Prins had also sat up with Aerssen three nights, and had been with him to the last. His passing was peaceful. I shall never forget that noble head lying on the pillow: the face showed signs of suffering, but wore an expression of peace and a certain holiness. Oh! it was so beautiful, to me it was characteristic of all the peculiar charm of the country and the life of the Brabant people. And they were all talking about Father, how good he had always been to them, and how much these two had loved each other."

Following his friend's death, Vincent turned his thoughts to the promise of resurrection, a hope that had been given timeless, graphic expression three hundred years earlier by Jacob van Ruisdael in his soaring *View of Haarlem.* In the first paragraph of Vincent's letter from Etten, we notice the strong wording, "I must send you another letter," expressing his need to remain in close contact with his younger bother Theo. The "I must" of the letter was deeply felt, and appears many times in future letters. Vincent's need to write (and later to paint) would become compulsions, when the bonds between him and his parents would for a period of time be severely strained following a serious family breach of trust and propriety, a separation that would cause all concerned months of profound suffering.

Also in the Etten letter, we read a chain of reflections broader in scope than in the letter from Ramsgate; he now addresses primary existential issues: birth, illness, labor, healing, faith, life's purpose, the mystery of death and eternity, and in particular the hope of resurrection. Lit up by the evening star, his personal vision moved into and out of darkness as he rapidly marched in a race against death, contemplating his action, for soon he would summarize it in this letter to Theo. He wove into a single fabric his understanding of the greatest mystery of all—death. Like so many important letters drafted at critical periods of his life, the one from Etten chronicled a large span of time, and the changing light of the hours. It opened at twilight, moved through the blackness of night into a lilac-colored dawn, and yellow daylight—appropriate colors symbolically, considering that the theme of the letter was the entirety of a life culminating in eternity. In many ways, this letter was to portend Vincent's own life, including the way his deceased friend's head rested upon the pillow—precisely the way Theo was one day to describe Vincent's head and face at the moment of his death.

In the third paragraph, Vincent honors his sister for her steadfast care for the sick. He then quotes from memory a well-known Dutch poem: "...rising early in the winter to light the fire and with her own hands". This, like other poems from his childhood, demonstrated the Dutch moral ideal of love as action. He seemed also to have had in mind Proverbs 31:15 (NASB): "She rises also while it is still night and gives food to her household". His sister was clearly someone who took seriously the ideal of love as action. We are also reminded of Vincent's comment that he would not recognize love as anything but an action—feelings that are not given tangible expression are meaningless. This unswerving conviction grounded his art in an outward-bound core and helps explain why his art was and is always emotionally potent, beautiful, and—like the stars of which he was so enamored—brilliant.

Action taken on behalf of the sick and helpless was a natural thing for the Van Goghs. Vincent nursed many people over the course of his short lifetime. We are told by numerous sources how he heroically attended injured miners in Belgium as a lay evangelist and nurse. In describing the care Vincent gave his mother, Johanna tells us:

"Vincent, who had become an expert nurse in Borinage, helped to nurse his mother with the greatest devotion, and in every letter during that period they praised him for his faithful help. "Vincent is untiring, and the rest of the time he devotes to his painting and drawing with the greatest zeal." "The doctor praised Vincent for his ability and care." "Vincent proves an ideal nurse and at the same time he works with the greatest ambition."—Johanna van Gogh-Bonger.

The fourth paragraph in the letter from Etten contains a cluster of action themes. Like his sister, Vincent also made a life-long habit of rising before daybreak, and of working to the point of exhaustion. He would say, "I believe that the more one loves, the more one will act: for love that is only a feeling I would never recognize as love". The entire Van Gogh family embraced with zeal the social obligations of prayer and compassion, and devotion in assisting others. Vincent ended the paragraph with "And how Pa and Mother love her, as, indeed we all do; say, let us stay close together". Such strong comments underscored the strong ties the entire family had for one another and their need to act upon such ties.

The letter went on to describe Vincent's response to learning of the critical illness of Aerssen, a close family friend who resided in Vincent's boyhood home in Zundert, Holland. His immediate response was to embark on an exceedingly long foot journey home, not surprising considering all we know of his deep love for family and friends.

Of special interest in the letter is the reference in paragraph five in which he recounted his thoughts as he visited the graveyard where his elder brother (also Vincent but who had been still-born) was buried. We read into this Vincent's characteristic response to death—instead of fear, the promise of resurrection: "You know the story of the Resurrection—everything reminded me of it that morning in the quiet graveyard." This is a typical, life-long example of how he perceived death as a natural, and supernatural, step into eternity. Death and rebirth were seen as an

"The Raising of Lazarus" by Vincent van Gogh. In the collection of the Van Gogh Museum, Amsterdam.

intrinsic part of the cycle of seasons—sowing, growing, and harvesting.

Writing in paragraph six, Vincent was filled with awe at what could be a New Testament scene, like the account of the death and resurrection of Lazarus in the Gospel of John or the Acts of the Apostles. One is also reminded of another sacred painting by Jacob van Ruisdael— *The Jewish Cemetery*—with its graves shattered seemingly by a bridge of light—a rainbow. This work links death to Noah's ark and the rainbow covenant between Creator and man, promising humankind a reprieve from flood and inevitable death. It can be understood as a natural symbol of salvation and transcendence. In the Bible, God said:

"This is the sign of the covenant which I am making between Me and you and every living creative that is with you, for all successive generations; I set my bow in the cloud, and it shall be for a sign of a covenant between Me and the earth. It shall come about, when I bring a cloud over the earth, that the bow shall be seen in the cloud, and I will re-

"The Jewish Cemetery" by Jacob Isaaksz van Ruisdael, 1654-55

member My covenant, which is between Me and you and every living creature of all flesh; and never again shall the water become a flood to destroy all flesh. When the bow is in the cloud, then I will look upon it, to remember the everlasting covenant between God and every living creature of all flesh that is on the earth." (Genesis 9:12-17 NASB)

This covenant was especially meaningful to the Dutch who lived at or below sea level, open to constant flooding. Much as the rainbow falls where rain is not too heavy, giving joy because its appearance was a light-filled reminder that sunshine was on its way, Vincent believed that nature itself revealed the mind of a Creator.

In paragraph seven and eight of the Etten letter, Vincent described the face of the dead man, its look of holiness, and how death and life are conjoined because of the presence of living witnesses to his death—the family and friends who had come to witness the passing of this much loved man. It was a communion with death. "And they were all talking about Father, how good he had always been to them, and how much these two had loved each other." Most telling was the way Vincent noticed how this loss was an occasion for a higher gain, like the rainbow after the deluge.

Towards the end of his life, as Vincent was recovering from substance abuse and the debauchery of his time in Paris, he noted that his health always improved when he returned to the countryside, and painted the bright landscapes, especially those of Holland and his beloved Arles.

But before that, Vincent was to descend into the darkness of a sort of living hell—the desolation of Belgium's Borinage—where he would experience firsthand the dismal plight of the miners and peasant workers who struggled to survive in awful circumstances.

There, he would come to know—and tell of—dreadful loss and wretched human conditions. He would say that a careworn face was akin to old clothing. The story of life's stresses and strains was, to Vincent, left on both skin and cloth. Heavy use left heavy traces.

"Coal Mine in the Borinage" by Vincent van Gogh. Watercolor, pencil, transparent watercolor, on wove paper. Cuesmes-Wasmes: 1879. In the collection of the Van Gogh Museum, Amsterdam.

For Vincent, the events that were to unfold in the drudgery and squalor of the Borinage would unequivocally redefine him. He went there to minister to the poor workers and peasants of that horribly depressed region. But the terrible conditions he witnessed would cause his inner world to stand in stark contrast with the open spaces he had experienced until then. Far from family and all that was familiar, Vincent would be forced to re-examine his very soul and to re-assess his core beliefs. Like the miners who sacrificed their health to extract the precious coal from the bowels of the earth, so too Vincent would sacrifice a precious part of his own youth.

The lessons he was to learn in the bleakness of the Borinage were to forge a significant part of Vincent's fundamental fabric.

Opposite: "Le Moulin de la Gelette" by Vincent van Gogh.

EPISODE TWO

DESOLATION & EMERGENCE

BLEAK DAYS IN THE BORINAGE
A SPIRITUAL RENASCENCE

Bleak Days in the Borinage

*"Every human society has what is called in the theatres a third substage.
The social soil is mined everywhere, sometimes for good, sometimes for evil.
These works are in strata; there are upper mines and lower mines...The dark
caverns, these gloomy protectors of primitive Christianity, were awaiting
only an opportunity to explode beneath the Caesars, and to flood the human
race with light. For in these sacred shades there is latent light. Volcanoes are
full of blackness, capable of flashing flames. All lava begins at midnight.
The catacombs, where the first mass was said, were not merely the cave
of Rome; they were the cavern of the world."*

—*Victor Hugo, Les Miserables, 1862*

The Great Exhibition of 1851 was symbolic of man's progress up
to that time in the Industrial Revolution. The extraordinary Crystal Palace
was constructed in London using prefabricated iron and glass modules.
The colossal ice-like apparition embodied all the inventiveness, skill,
engineering prowess, and romanticism of the period. Vincent was born
in 1853, just two years after the opening of the Great Exhibition, and in
many ways he was to become an archetype of those times with his combination of complicated and contradictory urges. He lived in a far more
modern world than we might imagine.

There were many advances, for example, in the design and
construction of ships which effectively brought the era of sail to a close.
In 1836, the 703-ton steamer *Sirius* sailed with 100 passengers from London
to New York, and within a few hours of her arrival, another steamer
twice her size, the 1,440-ton *Great Western*, also arrived in New York
after a crossing of only fifteen days from Bristol, England. The year of
Vincent's birth saw many impressive achievements in engineering including the first railroad tunnel cut right through the Alps—the Vienna-Trieste
Line. In the following year, the first steel street pillars were erected in

*Opposite: "Peasant Burning Weeds" by Vincent van Gogh. Oil on panel. October, 1883.
Private Collection.*

Berlin by Ernst Litfass. Then, in 1855, the first iron Cunard steamer crossed the Atlantic in just nine-and-a-half days. In 1856, the Black Forest railroad opened with forty tunnels. By 1859, the construction of the awesome Suez Canel got underway. And by 1865, the first railroad sleeper-cars, designed by George M. Pullman, were in use in the United States. Fifty thousand new miles of railway were laid in Europe alone between 1850 and 1870 to augment over 15,000 miles already built prior to that time.

As a consequence of these great achievements, there was an explosion in coal extraction and steel manufacturing, with its resultant wide-spread pollution. Coal production was to rise sharply, particularly in the Ruhr area, continental Europe's first great industrial zone. But the extraction of coal from the earth was hazardous to the health of the miners who toiled in dreadful conditions, breathing the treacherous black dust. Charles Dickens was among those who questioned the price in human lives for each ton of coal. And the dire conditions of people in the mining communities were to be the subject of some of Vincent's first drawings in which he attempted to capture the lives he saw destroyed

in the coal mining camps.

When he had first arrived in the Borinage to minister to its people, the youthful and idealistic Vincent tried sharing the glowing words of the Gospel with the coal miners, hoping they would find solace in the light of revelation through Christ's example, in particular His self-sacrificing nature. Vincent's hopes were soon to be crushed, however, when he discovered that the sick and starving folk were not interested in light and revelation—they first needed food, water, and warm clothing. He quickly responded to this in a way that was to become the hallmark of his ethos; he gave away everything he had (including his own clothing), ripped up his bedsheets for bandages, and slept on straw. And by such actions, he won the admiration and respect of the workers, and was able to convert some of them. Writing in 1878, Vincent tells us:

"When I was in England, I applied for a position as evangelist among the coal miners, but they put me off, saying I had to be at least twenty-five years old. You know the roots or foundations, not only of the Gospel, but of the whole Bible is "Light that rises in the darkness," from darkness to light. Well, who needs this most, who will be receptive to it? Experience has shown that the people who walk in darkness, in the center of the earth, like the miners in the black coal mines, for instance, are very much impressed by the words of the Gospel, and believe them, too. Now in the south of Belgium, in Hainaut, near Mons, up to the French frontiers—aye, even far across it—there is a district called the Borinage, which has a unique population of laborers who work in the numerous coal mines. I found the following about them in a little geography: 'The Borins (inhabitants of the Borinage, situated west of Mons) find their employment exclusively in the coal mines...groups of working men, worthy of our respect and sympathy, daily descend into them. The miner is a type peculiar to the Borinage; for him daylight does not exist, and he sees the sunshine only on Sunday. He works laboriously by the pale, dim light of the lamp, in a narrow tunnel, his body bent double, and sometimes he is obliged to crawl. He works to extract from the bowel of the earth that mineral substance of which we know the great

Opposite Page: "The Miner's Return" by Vincent van Gogh. Post 1881. Pencil, pen, & brush. Kröller-Müller Museum, Otterlo, The Netherlands.

utility; he works in the midst of thousands of ever-recurring dangers; but the Belgian miner has a happy disposition, he is used to the life, and when he goes down into the shaft, wearing on his hat a little lamp to guide him in the darkness, he entrusts himself to God, Who sees his labor and protects him, his wife and children.'"

Some of Vincent's traits were remembered vividly. When the miners of Wasmes went to the pits, they pulled vests made of old sacking over their linen work clothes, using them like pea-jackets to protect themselves from the freezing water that spurted from the cracked walls of the mine shafts as they descended in the clanking cages of the elevators. On one occasion, Vincent saw the word "fragile" stenciled on the sackcloth on a miner's back. This touched him deeply.

An eyewitness to Vincent's life in the Borinage, later wrote to Johanna:

"An epidemic of typhoid fever broke out in the district. Vincent was destitute himself, having given everything he owned, including money and clothes, to the poor. An inspector of the "Evangelization Council" came to the conclusion that Vincent's "exces de zele" bordered on the scandalous, and shared his opinion the church council in Wasmes. On learning of this, Vincent's father went from Nuenen to Wasmes, only to find his son lying on a sack filled with straw, exhausted, and emaciated. In the room where he lay, lit dimly by a single hanging lamp, some miners—their faces pinched with starvation and suffering, were crowded around Vincent.

Vincent had made a significant number of converts among the Protestants of Wasmes. His deeds were legion. People talked of the miner whom he went to see after an accident in the Marcasse mine. To paraphrase Johanna's account of this event, the man was a habitual drinker, "an unbeliever and blasphemer," according to the people who told the story. When Vincent entered his house to help and comfort him, he was received with a volley of abuse. He was called a 'macheux d'capelets' [a rosary chewer], being mistaken for a Roman Catholic Priest. But Vincent's evangelical tenderness won the man over."

However, one of the hardest lessons Vincent was to learn from his time in the Borinage was that humankind can be capable of blind indifference to, or at least apathy toward, the suffering of others. He would fall victim to this mentality himself when he was abandoned by the organized church—by a synod committee of tradition-bound clergymen who fired him as a missionary because he did not dress and preach eloquently. It did not seem to matter to them that he literally poured out his life in sacrifice and service on behalf of the diseased and destitute. In one case, he spent over forty days devoting himself to saving the life of a horribly burned, disfigured miner who had been given up for dead.

His greatest acts of mercy were, however, to be rejected by those he firmly believed would value them the most. He revered his pious parents, wanting to emulate their example, but he never once imagined that his hard-earned efforts would be dismissed because of non-conformity with traditional religious mores and methods. This crushing rejection caused him to become disoriented, and even undergo a temporary loss of faith. But in the long term it would prepare him to withstand further rejection in his strenuous efforts to become a painter.

The Church, however, saw things differently. In its 1879-80 report of the Union of Protestant Churches in Belgium, chapter "Wasmes" [twenty-third report of the Synodal Board of Evangelization (1879-80)] it stated:

"The experiment of accepting the services of a young Dutchman, Mr. Vincent Van Gogh, who felt himself called to be an evangelist in the Borinage, has not produced the anticipated results. If a talent for speaking, indispensable to anyone placed at the head of a congregation, had been added to the admirable qualities he displayed in aiding the sick and wounded, to his devotion to the spirit of self-sacrifice, of which he gave many proofs by consecrating his night's rest to them, and by stripping himself of most of his clothes and linen in their behalf, Mr. Vincent would certainly have been an accomplished evangelist.
Undoubtedly it would be unreasonable to demand extraordinary talents. But it is evident that the absence of certain qualities may render the exercise of an evangelist's principal function wholly impossible. Unfortunately this is the case with Mr. Vincent. Therefore, the probationary period—some months—having expired, it has been necessary to abandon the idea of retaining him any longer.

The evangelist, M. Hutton (sic), who is now installed, took over his charge on October 1, 1879."

The irony of the phrase which Vincent loved to associate with aiding miners—"light that rises in the darkness"—is that his ardent effort to spread light plunged him into a darkness of anger and despair. He used his letters to rage, revile, and to dig himself out of the pit of disillusion and disappointment he felt over his dismissal, and was forced to re-examine his views of God, finding some comfort in Christ's parables about blindness: "If you were blind, you would have no sin, but since you say, 'we see', your sin remains." John 9:41.

In 1888, he was to write:

"I must tell you that with evangelists it is the same as with artists. There is an old academic school, often detestable, tyrannical, the accumulation of horrors, men who wear a cuirass, a steel armor, of prejudices and conventions; when these people are in charge of affairs, they dispose of positions, and by a system of red tape they try to keep their protégés in their places and to exclude the other man. Their God is like the God of Shakespeare's drunken Falstaff...these evangelical gentlemen find themselves with the same point of view on spiritual things as that drunken character (perhaps they would be somewhat surprised to discover this if they were capable of human emotions). But there is little fear of their blindness ever changing to clear-sightedness in such matters.

A caged bird in spring knows quite well that he might serve some end; he is well aware that there is something for him to do, but he cannot do it. What is it? He does not quite remember. Then some vague ideas occur to him, and he says to himself, 'the others build their nests and lay their eggs and bring up their little ones'; and he knocks his head against the bars of the cage. But the cage remains, and the bird is maddened by anguish. 'Look at that lazy animal,' says another bird in passing, 'he seems to be living at ease.'

Yes the prisoner lives, he does not die; there are no outward signs of what passes within him...But then the season of migration comes, and attacks of melancholia...'But he has everything he wants,' say the children that tend him in his cage. He looks through the bars at the overcast sky where a thunderstorm is gathering, and inwardly rebels at his fate. 'I am caged, I am caged, and you tell me I do not want anything, fools! You think I have everything I need! Oh! I beseech you liberty, that I may be a bird like other birds!'

A certain man resembles this idle bird. And circumstances often prevent men from doing things, prisoners in I do not know what horrible, horrible, most horrible cage. There is also—I know it—the deliverance, the tardy deliverance. A justly or unjustly ruined reputation, poverty, unavoidable circum-

stances, adversity—that is what makes men prisoners...Do you know what frees one from this captivity? It is every deep, serious affection. Being friends, being brothers, love, that is what opens the prison by some supreme power, by some magic force. Without this, one remains in prison. Where sympathy is renewed, life is restored."

The caged bird of the 1880 letter stands in sharp contrast with his 1878 letter, with its image of descending light. Now it was Vincent who was caged, a prisoner, a man with an "unjustly ruined reputation." He compared the prejudices of the evangelical brotherhood that dismissed him to a cage, metal bars, steel armor, and tradition-bound blindness, and compares himself to the canary victim.

He now knew that the Gospel was not always easy to share especially if those in authority did not heed its message. When, in addition to starvation, disease and the diabolical explosions of the mines, an evangelist had to deal with compromised union officials, red tape, rule-bound committees, and indifference, the light was not only eclipsed but contradicted and discredited by the very men one would hope heeded it the most.

However strong his condemnation of the Synod of Elders, Vincent did not believe that all professional clergy were corrupt: "I must tell you that with evangelists it is the same as with artists. There is an old academic school, often detestable...". He did not class the good Reverend Pietersen, who had helped and encouraged him, as detestable. In fact, throughout his later life he will be shown kindness, concern and be aided by several pastors. This is important to bear in mind because it has been suggested by some historians that, after the Borinage, Vincent no longer believed in God which was not the case. From that time forward, Vincent was to acknowledge his belief in God but harbor strong misgivings about power-blinded institutions, religious, artistic or otherwise. And from Vincent's angry response, it is clear that he had not fully absorbed all of the lessons he should, especially lessons about humility and correction. Perhaps his wrath was not entirely misplaced when we consider how the miners themselves admired and trusted him because of his acts of true compassion.

Despite the disappointments arising from his dismissal, and just at the moment of his greatest need, there came a guide to help him find his way. The Reverend Pietersen, a kind pastor and painter, stood up for Vincent, and took a fatherly interest in him, patiently encouraging him. Reverend Pietersen had good reason to be impressed by the intensity and empathy he felt for Vincent's efforts, and asked him for a sketch. It would be more than a year before Vincent transformed himself from pastor to serious painter, but the seed had been sewn by the kindly Pietersen in those bleak days in the Borinage. Vincent recorded his thoughts at the time:

"Lately I have been at a studio again, namely at the Reverend Mr. Pietersen's who paints in the manner of Schelfhout or Hoppenbrowers and has good ideas about art. He asked me for one of my sketches, a miner type. Often I draw far into the night, to keep some souvenir and to strengthen the thoughts raised involuntarily by the aspect of things here."

Pietersen was a living bridge linking religion and art, embodying art as a sacred calling. Before Vincent could clamber over this bridge, however, he had to exhaust his role as the epitome of a 19th century missionary. What he did not realize, as he moved along the narrow tunnels of the mines amid the stench of misery, was how similar in many ways his mission as a sacred artist would become. Artists venture into lesser known places and, like missionaries, are often harassed by those closest to them who view their career choice as vapid, and discourage them on the basis of financial uncertainty.

For Vincent, the choice of art as a career was far more complicated. His personal expectation had been to emulate his pastor father. But his failure in the eyes of the Church had shattered that cherished dream. The descent into the mines was equally a descent into his own naked humanity. Forced to surrender his identity as a provider to the unfortunate, he saw in art a way to emerge from all the confusion and darkness. His drawings and paintings would come to portray human suffering with a radiant glow of authenticity gleaned from real, empirical experience—its simple truth engraving the hearts of those who came in sight of it. His life in itself would become an honest journey, stripped of pretense and false expectations, and forged from a deep understanding of humankind.

The Borinage mining episode was also, for Vincent, a transition into adulthood—an important step for his innately dependent personality, even though it took a significant physical toll on him. For some months after his work ended in the Borinage, he suffered from what seemed to be a nervous breakdown. But from then on, he began to think and act out of inner conviction rather than on the expectations of others. A transformed and enlightened Vincent emerged with a more worldly view, yet no less Gospel-minded. His vocation had evolved from preacher to painter, but his motivation to serve humankind remained intact.

"Surely there is a mine for silver and a place where they refine gold. Iron is taken from the dust and copper is smelted from rock. Man puts an end to darkness, and to the farthest limit he searches out the rock in gloom and deep shadow. He sinks a shaft far from habitation, forgotten by the foot; they hang and swing to and fro far from men...He hews out channels through the rocks, and his eye sees anything precious. He dams up the streams from flowing, and what is hidden he brings out to the light." Job. 28:1-11

"The Iron Mill in The Hague" by Vincent van Gogh. Christie's. Gouache, watercolour, wash, pen and India ink and pencil on paper. Executed in The Hague in July 1882. Painted just four years after his calamitous mining dismissal this scene of a barge next to a churning iron factory undoubtedly evoked memories of the Borinage. It also must have reminded him of Dickens' novel Hard Times and its legendary "Coketown," a city of hellish furnaces and smoke stacks with their strangling, choking smoke.

A SPIRITUAL RENASCENCE

"...I often read in Uncle Tom's Cabin these days. There is so much slavery
in the world, and in this remarkably wonderful book that important question
is treated with so much wisdom, so much love, and such zeal and interest in the
true welfare of the poor oppressed that one comes back to it again and again,
always finding something new...I still can find no better definition of
the word art than this, "L'art c'est l'homme ajoute a la nature"
[art is man added to nature]—nature, reality, truth, but with a
significance, a conception, a character, which the artist brings
out in it, and which he gives expression, "qu'il degage," which he
disentangles, sets free and interprets...in Uncle Tom's Cabin
especially, the artist has put things in a new light; in this book,
though it is becoming an old book already—that is, written
years ago—all things have become new..."

—Vincent van Gogh

The abject misery of the time he spent in the Borinage had a profound impact Vincent's approach to his life and art. He was to undergo a spiritual renascence. He had been so sure of his purpose when he first had arrived in the Borinage. But reality had not lived up to his expectations which were largely constructed from the moral underpinnings of his family and their religious premises. Vincent's state of mind at that moment in his life was described in his own words:

"Not long ago I made a very interesting expedition, spending six hours
in a mine. It was Marcasse, one of the oldest and most dangerous mines in the
neighborhood. It has a bad reputation because many perish in it, either going
down or coming up, or through poisoned air, firedamp explosion, water seepage,
cave-ins, etc. It is a gloomy spot, and at first everything around looks dreary
and desolate. Most of the miners are thin and pale from fever; they look tired

Opposite: "Backyards of Old House in Antwerp in the Snow" by Vincent van Gogh.
Oil on Canvas, Antwerp, Belgium. December, 1885. In the collection of the
Van Gogh Museum, Amsterdam

and emaciated, weather-beaten and aged before their time. On the whole the women are faded and worn. Around the mine are poor miners' huts, a few dead trees black from smoke, thorn hedges, dunghills, ash dumps, heaps of useless coal, etc....

...The mine has five levels, but the three upper ones have been exhausted and abandoned; they are no longer worked because there is no more coal. A picture of the maintenages would be something new and unheard of—or rather, never before seen. Imagine a row of cells in a rather narrow, low passage, shored up with rough timber. In each of those cells a miner in a coarse linen suit, filthy and black as a chimney sweep, is busy hewing coal by the pale light of a small lamp. The miner can stand erect in some cells; in others, he lies on the ground ...The arrangement is more or less like the cells in a beehive, or like a dark, gloomy passage in an underground prison, or like a row of small weaving looms, or rather more like a row of baking ovens such as the peasants have, or like the partitions in a crypt. The tunnels themselves are like the big chimneys of the Brabant farms.

The water leaks through in some, and the light of the miner's lamp makes a curious effect, reflected as in a stalactite cave. Some of the miners work in the maintenages, others load the cut coal into small carts that run on rails, like a streetcar. This is mostly done by children, boys as well as girls. There is also a stable yard down there, 700 meters underground, with about seven old horses which pull a great many of those carts to the so-called accrochage, the place from which they are pulled up to the surface...The villages here look desolate and dead and forsaken; life goes on underground instead of above. One might live here for years and never know the real state of things unless one went down in the mines.

People here are very ignorant and untaught—most of them cannot read—but at the same time they are intelligent and quick at their difficult work; brave and frank, they are short but square shouldered, with melancholy deep-set eyes. They are skillful at many things, and work terribly hard. They have a nervous temperament—I do not mean weak, but very sensitive. They have an innate, deep-rooted hatred and a strong mistrust of anyone who is domineering. With miners one must have a miner's character and temperament, and no pretentious pride or mastery, or one will never get along with them or gain their confidence.

Did I tell you at the time about the miner who was so badly hurt by a firedamp explosion? Thank God, he has recovered and is going out again, and is beginning to walk some distance just for exercise; his hands are still weak and it will be some time before he can use them for his work, but he is out of danger. Since that time there have been many cases of typhoid and malignant fever, of what they call la sotte fievre, which gives them bad dreams like nightmares and makes them delirious. So again there are many sickly and bedridden people—emaciated, weak, and miserable.

In one house they are all ill with fever and little or no help, so that the patients have to nurse the patients. "Ici c'est les maladies qui soignent les maladies" [here the sick tend the sick], said a woman, like, "Le pauvre est l'ami du pauvre" [the poor man is the poor man's friend]...

...Going down into a mine is a very unpleasant sensation. One goes in a kind of basket or cage like a bucket in a well, but in a well from 500-700 meters deep, so that when looking upward from the bottom, the daylight is about the size of a star in the sky.

It feels like being on a ship at sea for the first time, but it is worse; fortunately it does not last long. The miners get used to it, yet they keep an unconquerable feeling of horror and fear which reasonably and justifiably stays with them. But once down, the worst is over, and one is richly rewarded for the trouble by what one sees."

Vincent noted that the miners were prematurely aged, tired and ill, and he was horrified by the plight of the children, both boys and girls, many of whom were abused in the unsupervised isolation of their dismal underground world. He experienced firsthand the very settings depicted by Dickens. The miners, child-like themselves, were victims of greed and indifference, ignored and unprotected like "Little Nell" in *The Old Curiosity Shop*. Dickens's understanding of the abused and disavowed was based on his own experiences as a bootblack. Vincent's empathy may have come in part from being abused during his time at a poorly supervised boys' academy.

Vincent's moral emergence—his spiritual revival—fused lessons learned from literature with those gleaned from his experiences in the Borinage. He came to integrate the inspiring messages of Dickens's writing into his thought process. And he was to draw similar meaning from the writings of many other poets and essayists.

This state of suffocating darkness and despair so prevalent in those times was captured perfectly by Dickens in the following passage from *The Old Curiosity Shop*:

"There's an old well there," said the sexton, [to Little Nell] "right underneath the belfry; a deep, dark, echoing well...if you lower the bucket till your arms are tired and let out nearly all the cord, you'll hear it of a sudden clanking and rattling on the ground below, with a sound of being so deep and so far down, that your heart leaps into your mouth, and you start away as if you were falling in."

"A dreadful place to come on in the dark!" exclaimed the child, who had followed the old man's looks and words until she seemed to stand upon its brink. "What is it but a grave!" said the sexton. "What else! And which of our old folks, knowing all this, thought, as the spring subsided, of their own failing strength, and lessening of life? Not one!"

The dry well the sexton showed Little Nell was like the mine shaft Vincent described so powerfully. Wells, graves, or mines were used by Dickens to symbolize death. Little Nell, in the above passage, and later Stephen Blackpool in *Hard Times*, were both innocent victims whose fate was death. Little Nell was forewarned of her imminent and untimely death by looking into a well, while Blackpool died after falling into an abandoned mine shaft. The miners with whom Vincent identified were, in his estimation, doomed in just the same way as were Nell and Blackpool.

The workers in the Borinage were constantly reassured by their overseers that the mines were safe. But this was far from the truth. Vincent told of an explosion underground where a man was badly injured, suffering terrible burns, and Vincent was compelled to nurse him back to life. The mines were in fact a living nightmare for the workers, where life was regularly snuffed out like a candle by explosions, or by the collapse of tunnels and shafts.

The image of the shining star—hope eternal—was to appear

often in Vincent's letters and art : "...when looking upward from the bottom, the daylight is about the size of a star in the sky." His early letters described stars shimmering in black skies, eternity embodied in glowing points. This glimmering vision and its heavenly message was to reappear at the end of his life in one of his best-loved paintings *The Starry Night of 1889*. A star, too, transfigured the tragic Stephen Blackpool who, crushed and broken at the bottom of a mine shaft, was consoled by its glowing light above. Dickens likened it to the star of Bethlehem announcing the birth of Christ, the Light of the World.

Vincent's image of the cage was to become a symbol of impotence and rage in his later letters: "And circumstances often prevent men from doing things, prisoners in I do not know what horrible, horrible, most horrible cage."

Canaries were kept in small cages throughout the mines. They were highly susceptible to the toxic and volatile fumes that were the harbinger of regular explosions and the resultant human carnage. The tiny yellow birds quivering in the gloomy underworld were a surreal comfort to the tottering ghosts who toiled within the dripping caverns.

Wraith-like horses, crumpled, dejected miners in damp, sackcloth jackets, thorns, the frozen earth, snow, ashes, black dust, and ever-ominous shadows, were the potent images Vincent assimilated into the core of his being. Shared vicariously with Dickens, Vincent would, in some ways unwittingly, merge these somber yet powerful impressions into a personal epic that, through art, would rival the words of Charles Dickens who wrote:

"Everything in our lives, whether of good or evil, affects us most by contrast. If the peace of a simple village had moved the child [Little Nell] more strongly, because of the dark and troubled ways that lay beyond and through which she had journeyed with such failing feet, what was the deep impression of finding herself alone in that solemn building; where the very light, coming through sunken windows, seemed old and grey; and the air, redolent of earth and mould, seemed laden with decay purified by time of all its grosser particles, and sighed through arch and aisle and clustered pillars, like the breath of ages gone! Here

was the broken pavement, worn so long ago by pious feet, that Time, stealing on the pilgrims' steps, had trodden out their track, and left but crumbing stones."—Charles Dickens

Of this mysterious play of shadows and human destiny Dickens described, David Levin (1999) offers these reflections:

"There is a certain affinity between shadows and ashes. Like ashes, shadows are traces that can speak of evil—but also of the precariousness, the contingency, the fatal hidden doubt, of all our hopes. Philosophers with total visions of hope must be careful: those who avoid or deny the tracework presence tracery of shadows are likely to end up in Benjamin's words, as "seers whose visions appear over dead bodies," forever haunted by shadows that will relentlessly pursue them—shadows cast in ghostly forms from the realm of death. On friendly terms with death, indeed its messengers, shadows silently move through the world, touching things lightly and without violence—as if to remind us that accounts are due in the time of justice."

In describing the miners, Vincent described himself and his sympathy for their suffering:

"They are skillful at many things, and work terribly hard. They have a nervous temperament—I do not mean weak, but very sensitive. They have an innate, deep-rooted hatred and a strong mistrust of anyone who is domineering."

The passionate way that Vincent applied the ideology of *Uncle Tom's Cabin* to his own experience proved his link to the wisdom, faithfulness, love, humility, and simplicity he found in Harriet Beecher Stowe's book. It was words like these that helped Vincent to symbolically resurrect his missionary zeal through his art.

"A few days ago we had a very heavy thunderstorm at about eleven o'clock in the evening. Quite near our house there is a spot from which one can see, far below, a large part of the Borinage, with the chimneys, the mounds of coal, the little miners' cottages, the scurrying little black figures by day, like

ants in a nest; and farther on, dark pine woods with little white cottages silhouetted against them, a few church spires a way off, an old mill, etc. Generally there is a kind of haze hanging over it all, or a fantastic chiaroscuro effect formed by the shadows of the clouds, reminding one of pictures by Rembrandt or Michel or Ruysdael...I often read in Uncle Tom's Cabin these days. There is so much slavery in the world, and in this remarkably wonderful book that important question is treated with so much wisdom, so much love, and such zeal and interest in the true welfare of the poor oppressed that one comes back to it again and again, always finding something new.

I still can find no better definition of the word art than this, "L'art c'est l'homme ajoute a la nature" [art is man added to nature]—nature, reality, truth, but with a significance, a conception, a character, which the artist brings out in it, and which he gives expression, "qu'il degage," which he disentangles, sets free and interprets...in Uncle Tom's Cabin especially, the artist has put things in a new light; in this book, though it is becoming an old book already— that is, written years ago—all things have become new." —Vincent van Gogh

Uncle Tom's Cabin was, as Vincent said, an explanation of slavery, exploitation and death through the voice of a woman whose writing depicted the sordid practice in all of its vicious extremes. Harriet Beecher Stowe examined the ceaseless brutality of slavery with heart-rending compassion, trying to humanize what to many was perfectly acceptable. In telling the story of Uncle Tom's Cabin through the eyes of a slave rather than a slave owner, Stowe's message played a significant part in stemming the growth of slavery in America and positioned her among the greatest writers of all time, proving that art—in its many forms— could accomplish extraordinary things. She had with her pen achieved far more than did legions of politicians and pundits.

Stowe was not alone. The slavery issue was to a very large degree fought through literature. Charles Dickens was universally read. His books sold extremely well in America, although much to his dismay they were often sold without his royalties being paid. Nevertheless, Dickens made several trips to the United States, and was met by surging crowds in Boston and New York. The messages in his novels were clear: it was time for more humane treatment of one's fellow man. While Dickens's writing predated the Civil War in America, Harriet Stowe effectively emulated and amplified the same message which embraced so much of what civilized society needed to reform: pollution of the environment, political corruption, greed, the abuse of animals, and above all inhumanity and moral blindness, especially with regard to children. Dickens and Hugo had both been eminently vociferous as champions of the the destitute and the disavowed. So many had become mere phantoms, lost forever in the cultural quagmire left by the Industrial Revolution. Harriet Beecher Stowe, using the impetus of Dickens and Hugo, would propagate the same powerful message throughout America.

Perhaps this emergence—this connection between spiritual revival, religion, and art—prompted Vincent when he wrote:

"In our Brabant we have the underbrush of oak and in Holland, the pollard willows; here [in the Borinage] the blackthorn hedges surround the gardens, fields and meadows. Now, with the snow, the effect is like black characters on white paper—like pages of the Gospel."

Vincent wrote of his favorite author, "There is no writer, in my opinion, who is so much a painter and a black-and-white artist as Dickens. His figures are resurrections". Greatly influenced by Dickens, Vincent's notebooks and letters overflow with Gospel words, many of which will be transformed into paintings. Some images were taken directly out of the pages of the Gospel, as in *The Good Samaritan*, but in the early stages, his ideals were rooted in local hovels, fields, and hedgerows. We read of his early efforts:

"Though every day difficulties crop up and new ones will present themselves, I cannot tell you how happy I am to have taken up drawing again. I had been thinking of it for a long time, but I always considered the thing impossible and beyond my reach. But now, though I feel my weakness and my painful dependence in many things, I have recovered my mental balance, and day by day my energy increases."

He pictured lean miners and the forbidding mines they inhabited like so many ants in an anthill. In the early 1880s, the pages of his sketchbooks overflowed with passionate depictions of miners who were, as John K. Roth would say, "concrete universals", real people who embody real messages. They would soon be joined by other workers: reapers, diggers, field-hands, peasants, and an army of impoverished beings all in need of Vincent's graphic resurrection:

"I have sketched a drawing representing miners, men and women, going to the shaft in the morning through the snow, by a path along a thorn hedge: passing shadows, dimly visible in the twilight. In the background the large mine buildings and heaps of clinkers stand out vaguely against the sky..."

And if the identification with the Gospel in snow and thorns was not complete enough, he now used the image of childbirth:

" So you see I am in a rage of work, though for the moment it does not produce very brilliant results. But I hope these thorns will bear their white blossoms in due time, and that this apparently sterile struggle is no other than the labor of childbirth. First the pain, then the joy."

Vincent knew that the novels of Dickens and Hugo helped to force reforms for the poor. But the fact that Van Gogh actually assisted suffering people was to make his art all the more potent. His depictions of laborers have often been called the most convincing in the history of art. It was not reproductive skill that made his figures resonate with life; it was his passionate identification as a fellow being that would animate the bent bodies of fragile humankind, drawn in charcoal. As previously noted, the psychological parallels of Van Gogh and Dickens during their childhoods are unmistakable. They deepen graphically when we read from Peter Ackroyd's seminal biography of Charles Dickens:

"He had a surplus of energy, to be sure, more energy than most human beings possess, but he was employing it all the time. He seemed, through unhappiness or uncertainty (both of which qualities, to judge from his letters, he possessed extensively), to wish to tire himself, to occupy himself so much that he did not

have time to think or contemplate the course of his life; there was almost a need to punish himself. As his fictional hero, David Copperfield, puts it at a similar point in his own life: "I made it a rule to take as much out of myself as I possibly could, in my way of doing everything to which I applied my energies. I made a perfect victim of myself." And then again, in the same narrative, "I fatigued myself as much as I possibly could...".

Dickens, too, could not bear to relax.

All of this was true, too, of Vincent, as his own words would confirm time and again. This overwhelming urge to push beyond his physical limits occurred first in the mining camps. But therein lies a paradox: his passion to alleviate the fatigue of others did not extend to himself, exploiting his own health to an alarming degree—the very thing he tried to prevent in others. Van Gogh biographers A. M. Hammacher and Renilde Hammacher (1982) make the following observations about Vincent that are nearly identical to those made about Dickens:

"The known facts are too numerous for one not to agree with Vincent himself, who said that the output which, after ten years of preparation, he finally produced at speed in the space of ten years meant exhausting his physical and psychic strength and destroying his health. His psychological disposition—including his unconscious—possessed a reservoir of energy comparable to the fertile field which has to be plowed, sown, manured, and rained on, before its latent forces can be realized. Such forces included the sickness which could not fail to make itself felt after Vincent had whipped up all his nerves into a paroxysm in order to produce his work. Tensed beyond the limits, he could not be saved by any relaxation of tension. Relaxation became disorientation."

The forsaken region of Belgium where Vincent ministered was analogous with Dickens's "Coketown", his fictional city described in *Hard Times*, wherein was the home of the laborer Stephen Blackpool. Vincent saw clearly how this fictional character was the portrait of any of the thousands of real, nameless men, women and children he met in the Borinage.

"...among the multitude of Coketown, generally called "the Hands"—

a race who would have found more favor with some people if Providence had seen fit to make them only hands, or, like the lower creatures of the seashore, only hands and stomachs—lived a certain Stephen Blackpool, forty years of age.

Stephen looked older, but he had had a hard life. It is said that every life has its roses and thorns; there seemed however, to have been a misadventure or mistake in Stephen's case, whereby somebody else had become possessed of his roses, and he had become possessed of the same somebody else's thorns in addition to his own. He had known, to use his words, a peck of trouble. He was usually called Old Stephen, in a kind of rough homage to the fact.

A rather stooping man, with a knitted brow, a pondering expression of face, and a hard-looking head sufficiently capacious on which his iron-grey hair lay long and thin, Old Stephen might have passed for a particularly intelligent man in his condition. Yet he was not. He took no place among the remarkable "Hands," who, piecing together their broken intervals of leisure through many years had mastered difficult sciences and acquired a knowledge of most unlikely things. He held no station among the Hands who could make speeches and carry on debates. Thousands of his compeers could talk much better than he, at any time. He was a good power-loom weaver, and a man of perfect integrity. What more he was, or what else he had in him, if anything, let him show for himself."—Charles Dickens, in Hard Times

Note how easily one can transition from Stephen Blackpool to a description of Van Gogh at that time who found in Dickens's fiction a person who was so "characteristic," so much like himself. Vincent was comforted to find so much of his own immediate reality in Dickens. In fact, Blackpool's physical description could have been of Vincent himself; Blackpool was forty, but looked much older, with stooping posture, knitted brow, and pensive expression, all very much like Vincent's own traits. The name Blackpool may be synonymous with someone lost in a dark pool of ignorance and indifference, leading perhaps to the darkness of death itself. Both men, in their fictional as well as their real personas, were dedicated to giving of themselves in order to improve the lives of the downtrodden.

Vincent did not seek reward for his actions; he aspired to illuminate needy people through his art. Like Dickens, he would bring their troubling reality before us, demanding our acknowledgment. As a missionary, Vincent quickly discovered that he could not save the many Blackpools of nameless origin who were victims of greed and indifference. As an artist with a mission, Vincent could only try to give graphic form to their silent struggle in an unseeing, uncaring world.

"They walked, and in their talk of the beauty of the earth do not notice the frail little beggar girl tripping after them". (Chekhov 1947)

"There seemed however, to have been a misadventure or mistake in Stephen's case, whereby somebody else had become possessed of his roses, and he had become possessed of the same somebody else's thorns in addition to his own."

Dickens's character Stephen Blackpool would die as a result of his fall into an abandoned coal mine known as "Old Hell Shaft." Vincent had also descended into the Marcasse mine, one of the most dangerous in Europe. The name is evocative since its French meaning suggests a wild boar (marcassin). Old Hell Shaft was perhaps like a wild boar who it attacks and harms those who fall victim to its rage. Stephen's final words, spoken in a humble dialect, expressed the cry for all who fell prey to the hideous place that was the Borinage.

"I ha' fell into th' pit, my dear, as have cost, wi'in the knowledge o' old fo'k now livin', hundreds and hundreds o' men's lives—fathers, sons, brothers, dear to thousands an' thousands, an' keeping 'em fro' want and hunger. I ha' fell into a pit that ha' been wi' th' fire-damp crueler than battle. I ha' read on 't in the public petition, as onnyone may read, fro' the men that works in pits, in which they ha' pray'n and pray'n the lawmakers for Christ's sake not to let their work be murder to 'em, but to spare 'em for th' wives and children that they loves as well as gentlefo'k loves theirs. When it were in work, it killed wi'out need; when 'tis let alone, it kills wi'out need. See how we die an' no need, one way an' another—in a muddle—every day!" —Charles Dickens.

Dickens's Blackpool said everything essential about mines in both a metaphorical and actual sense. The lawmakers and unions were called upon to stop the needless death of innocent people, countless thousands of whom had by then lost their lives. The general indifference to their fate was too much for Vincent, and in the end it crushed him emotionally.

Dickens relates how as Blackpool lay dying outside Old Hell Shaft, he looked up and said:

"'If Mr. Bounderby had ever know'd me right—if he'd ever know'd me at aw— he would'n ha' took'n offence wi'me. He would'n ha' suspect'n me. But look up yonder, Rachel ! Look above!

Following his eyes, she saw that he was gazing at a star. 'It ha' shined upon me,' he said reverently, 'in my pain and trouble down below. It ha' shined into my mind...wi' it shinin' on me—I ha seen more clear, and ha' made it my dyin' prayer that aw th' world may on'y coom toogether more, an' get a better un- nerstan'in' o' one another, than when I were in 't my own weak seln.'

The bearers being now ready to carry him away, and the surgeon being anxious for his removal, those who had torches or lanterns prepared to go in front of the litter. Before it was raised, and while they were arranging how to go, he said to Rachel, looking upward at the star: 'Often as I coom to myseln, and found it shinin' on me down there in my trouble, I thowt it were the star a guided to Our Savior's home. I awmust think it be the very star!'

They lifted him up, and he was overjoyed to find that they were about to take him in the direction whither the star seemed to him to lead.
'Rachel, beloved lass! Don't let go my hand. We may walk toogether t'night, my dear!'

'I will hold thy hand, and keep beside thee, Stephen, all the way.'

'Bless thee! Will somebody be pleased to coover my face!
They carried him very gently along the fields, and down the lanes, and over the

wide landscape; Rachel always holding the hand in hers. Very few whispers broke the mournful silence. It was soon a funeral procession. The star had shown him where to find the God of the poor; and through humility and sorrow, and forgiveness, he had gone to his Redeemer's rest." —Charles Dickens

Mines appear as a central motif in the Dickens novel working as powerful symbols of stifling social convention—pits from which painters, among others, try to ascend and escape. For Vincent, the mining experience not only symbolized broader public themes; it also allowed him to personally understand how humanizing moral beliefs could be expressed through an artistic and religious vocation. There could, in his view, no longer be a separation. Consoling words and comforting deeds would now become embodied in transforming images. This is so evident that when a passage is read, such as "the effect is like black characters on white paper—like pages of the Gospel" one realizes how thorns, snow, landscape, and desolate mines can be given visibility, all taking part in a sacred whole that is redeemed and resurrected within the Gospel. This can also be graphically evident in redemptive stage plays, like Victor Hugo's *Les Miserables*: ..."passing shadows, dimly visible in the twilight".

As the French philosopher Maurice Merleau-Ponty put it in discussing words and meaning in *The Visible and the Invisible*, "the whole landscape is overrun with words" (using nearly the same words as Vincent's). Here there is no ambiguity between language, art and image; signified and signifier—they are both "an expression of experience by experience":

"And, in a sense, to understand a phrase is nothing else than to fully welcome

Opposite: "Snowy Landscape with Arles in the Background", February 1888. Oil on canvas. Private Collection.

it in its sonorous being, or, as we put it so well, to hear what it says (l'entendre). The meaning is not on the phrase like the butter on the bread, like a second layer of "psychic reality" spread over the sound; it is the totality of what is said, the integral of all the differentiations of the verbal chain; it is given with the words for those who have ears to hear. And conversely the whole landscape is overrun with words as with an invasion, it is henceforth but a variant of speech before our eyes, and to speak of its "style" is in our view to form a metaphor. In a sense the whole of philosophy, as Husserl says, consists in restoring a power to signify, a birth of meaning, or a wild meaning, an expression of experience by experience, which in particular clarifies the special domain of language."
—Merleau-Ponty

We are reminded here again of what Mark Roskill (1991) said about Vincent's thought:

"The coalescence that he made between the visible aspects of experience and their internal or philosophic meaning was supremely intense.".

Kathleen Powers Erickson (1998) has carefully reported these connections and their impact on Vincent's artistic visions:

"Vincent's genius lies not so much in the originality of his vision, but in his unique synthesis of the traditional and the modern, both in art and religion. Essential to the nineteenth-century Romantic aesthetic was the belief that art and religion are inextricably linked."

During his time in the Borinage, Vincent had nursed many men back to life, specifically those suffering from third-degree burns. Covered with perspiration, these men were caked with fine, black coal dust which, when ignited, turned them into terrifying human torches, their coal-soaked bodies aflame like candles in the dark. Vincent discovered that the charred limbs of those who survived needed to be softened and oiled in order to regain suppleness. He would administer cloth compresses soaked in olive oil to their blackened skin, a restorative balm

Victor Hugo
from a photogravure
by Comte Stanisław
Julian Ostroróg dit
Walery, 1875

that also helped stave off disease. Years later in his studio, he would soak chunks of charcoal in oil to make powerful composite drawings of anonymous laborers, finding his own graphic balm to wage war on the disease of human indifference, and to assuage his own anger at the things he had seen.

This concept of beauty falls far outside our traditional understanding of the word. But for Vincent, beauty was truth-telling first and foremost. Like a wound slowly healing, beauty was the outward proof of inner regeneration. Vincent could no longer view the miners as different than himself, nor could he think of their experience in any manner other than with compassionate solidarity. Having experienced public rejection as a missionary, he was now able to commiserate with them, and become one of them himself.

"The miners and the weavers still constitute a race apart from other laborers and artisans, and I feel a great sympathy for them. I should be very happy if someday I could draw them, so that those unknown or little-known types would be brought before the eyes of the people. The man from the depth of the abyss, de profoundis—that is the miner; the other with his dreamy air, somewhat absent-minded, almost a somnambulist—that is the weaver. I have been living among them for two years, and have learned a little of their unique character, at least that of the miners especially. And increasingly I find something touching and almost sad in these poor, obscure laborers—of the lowest order, so to speak, and the most despised—who are generally represented as a race of criminals and thieves by perhaps vivid but very false and unjust imagination."
—Vincent van Gogh

And then there was Gauguin. Paul Gauguin, the great Post Impressionist painter, recognized the symbolic power of Vincent's experiences in the mines, and the role it took in shaping his life and opinions. Gauguin was somewhat of a cynical extremist—self-promoting, egotistical and preoccupied with himself to an inordinate degree. We find in Gauguin's letters, and those of his wife, a real perspective of how he contrasted with Vincent. While there is still controversy over the reasons behind Gauguin's *Essais d'Art Libre*, *(Still Life)* was written in 1894, four years after Vincent's death. Nonetheless it reveals far more than it conceals:

"In my yellow room there was a small still life: this one in violet. Two enormous shoes, worn, misshapen. The shoes of Vincent. Those that, when new, he put on one nice morning to embark on a journey by foot from Holland to Belgium. The young preacher (he had just finished his theological studies to become, like his father, a pastor) was on his way to see those in the mines whom he called his brothers, like the simple workers, such as he had read of in the Bible, oppressed for the luxury of the great.

Contrary to the teachings of his instructors, the wise Dutchmen, Vincent believed in Jesus who loved the poor; his soul, entirely suffused with charity, desired by means of consoling words and self-sacrifice to help the weak, to combat the great. Decidedly, decidedly, Vincent was already mad.

His teaching of the Bible in the mines was, I believe, profitable to the miners below, but disagreeable to the authorities on high, above ground. He was quickly recalled, dismissed, and a family council convened that judged him mad, and advised rest at a sanatorium. He was not, however, confined, thanks to his brother Theo.

One day the somber black mine was flooded by chrome yellow, the fierce flash of firedamp fire, a mighty dynamite that never misfires. The beings who were crawling and teeming about in filthy carbon when this occurred bid, on that day, farewell to life, farewell to men, without blasphemy.

One of them, terribly mutilated, his face burnt, was taken in by Vincent. "And yet," the company doctor had said, "he is a finished man, barring a miracle of very costly nursing. No, it would be folly to attend to him."

Vincent believed in miracles, in maternity.

The mad man (decidedly he was mad) kept watch for forty days at the bedside of the dying man; he prevented the air from ruthlessly penetrating into his wounds and paid for the medications. He spoke as a consoling priest (decidedly he was mad). The work of this madman had revived a Christian from the dead.

When the wounded man, finally saved, descended into the mine again to resume his work, you could have seen, said Vincent, the head of Jesus the martyr, carrying on his forehead the halo and the jagged crown of thorns, red scabs on the dirty yellow forehead of a miner.

And me...I painted him—Vincent—who traced with his yellow brush on the suddenly violet wall: I am the Holy Spirit. . . sound of Spirit.

Decidedly, this man was mad."—Paul Gauguin

Having shared the famous Yellow House in Arles, France, with Vincent in 1889, Gauguin had many opportunities to discuss Vincent's early life with him. He noted in his essay the humble subject of discarded shoes, ripped, and as unappealing as blackthorn and sackcloth, the castoffs in an age of recycled things. In art history, these subjects are lower than the most humble still life of the French 18th century painter Chardin, for instance, with his focus on pots, pans, and kitchen items dented and stained with age. Gauguin was drawn to the shoes and their link with the mines as a place of devastation. The shoes were ruined by misuse like the miners themselves. Gauguin used the shoes as a metaphor for the mines as a place of destruction. He symbolized the danger of explosion as fire emitting a chrome yellow flame, which can be interpreted as redemption. Gauguin suggested that Vincent's life and work were important for the redemption of art itself, moving away from mere entertainment and back to real life-enhancing content, all in a way that Gauguin often did not emulate himself. But in tribute to Vincent, Gauguin's admiration of his compassionate nature is more than evident.

The overall thrust of Gauguin's essay carried many important

Portrait de l'artiste (Self-portrait) by Paul Gauguin, c. 1893-94. Oil on canvas

references to those experiences as part of Vincent's development. At the same time, Gauguin purposely began to contribute to the myth of Vincent as a mad and accursed artist.

Gauguin came across in his essay as a somewhat self-serving and duplicitous friend who, while claiming to applaud Vincent's work in the mines, and the art that resulted, also did not want to be sullied by his friendship with the Van Gogh brothers, especially after Vincent's suicide and Theo's descent into mental turmoil and subsequent death some months later. In the essay, he appeared to be distancing himself from them in claiming that all artists have a madness, in a general sense rather than a clinical one. He used Vincent's insanity metaphorically to elicit compassion for artists like himself. Vincent was quite aware of Gauguin's back-stabbing.

Victor Hugo also used the mine as a metaphor for layers of social stratification, as in a "social ladder," a phrase which Vincent used to describe the motives of Gauguin, the "schemer," the upward climbing man who was more than willing to use the Van Gogh brothers as long as they were advantageous to him:

"I feel instinctively that Gauguin is a schemer who, seeing himself at the bottom of the social ladder, wants to regain a position...at the same time very politic."

Gauguin was well-read, knowing that the theme of the mine was often used by the authors of the time, as an image of human degradation. Victor Hugo's novel *Les Miserables* was widely read, and Vincent, Gauguin, Bernard and others in their group used it almost as a muse. Gauguin gave Vincent a self-portrait, referring to himself as the main character in the novel, Jean Valjean. Gauguin, like Hugo, understood the layers of society signified by the cave and the mine, and one's acceptance or rejection within these complex and shadowy zones. Gauguin, in the third section of his essay, compared the social disconnection and scorn of those "authorities on high", with the isolation and neglect of the miners deep in the caves of the earth.

It was clear from Gauguin's essay that Vincent was not mad in a conventional sense but rather the reverse. The way Gauguin used madness is similar to the way in which Jesus speaks of blindness and sight: "If you were blind, you would have no sin; but since you say, 'We see,' your sin remains" (John 9:41 NASB).

To better understand the madness to which Gauguin alludes, one finds an answer in *Les Misérables* where Hugo considers the plight of the downtrodden, lost in the "caves" of society:

"This cave is beneath all, and is the enemy of all. It is hate universal. This cave knows no philosophers; its poniard has never made a pen. Its blackness has no relation to the sublime blackness of script. Never have the fingers of night, which are clutching beneath this asphyxiating vault, turned the leaves of a book, or unfolded a journal....

Of all things, including therein the upper saps, which it execrates. It does not undermine, in its hideous crawl, merely the social order of the time; it undermines philosophy, it undermines science, it undermines law, it undermines human thought, it undermines civilization, it undermines revolution, it undermines progress. It goes by the naked names of theft, prostitution, murder, and assassination. It is darkness, and it desires chaos. It is vaulted in with ignorance.

All the others, those above it, have but one object—to suppress it. To that end philosophy and progress work through all their organs at the same time, through amelioration of the real as well as through contemplation of the absolute. Destroy the cave Ignorance, and you destroy the mole Crime...

...Humanity is identity. All men are the same clay. No difference, here below at least, in predestination. The same darkness before, the same flesh during, the same ashes after life. But ignorance, mixed with the human composition, blackens it. This incurable ignorance possesses the heart of man, and there becomes Evil."
—*Victor Hugo*

120

One immediately sees the connection between Van Gogh, Hugo, Dickens, and even to some extent Gauguin. The literal and metaphorical aspect of the mines pertains not only to death but also to ignorance, hate, and neglect for all misunderstood and abandoned men—especially artists. Line by line, the Gauguin account resonated with irony, anger and incomprehension at the 19th century upper classes living thoughtlessly above the wasted souls beneath the earth. As Victor Hugo described it in *Les Misérables*, class can equally become caste. These themes were often the concern of Realist or Naturalist writers such as Hugo and Dickens. More than mere concerns expressed in words, they were bolstered by the actual experiences of these writers.

Dickens, Hugo, and Stowe with Uncle Tom's Cabin, had achieved what Vincent believed great art could also accomplish. He had studied, too, some of the best illustrators of the time including Samuel Luke Fildes, who had made Dickens's characters come so alive. Art could, in Vincent's view, disentangle the web of expediency that was so prevalent in those dark times, and to which he had been an eyewitness in the mining camps of the Borinage. He believed he could send the same message by appealing to the deepest sympathy of humankind through his art. And he clearly saw that his zeal and true interest in the welfare of others was the literal fulfillment of the Gospel's most demanding request that one love another as if that person were oneself.

"All lava begins at midnight," said Victor Hugo. Desolation leads to redemption, as Dickens, Hugo, and Van Gogh insisted. A star appeared in the night to lead the way for Vincent in his darkest hours. And later in life, his horrible mental suffering and confinement in the Hospital of San Remy would give way to the elegiac *Starry Night*. The fragile, sackclothed land of suffering would overflow with words and white-blossomed drawings, spread over blackthorn hedges that twisted and entwined human existence. His art would blanket the landscape like a snow-stormed invasion of healing Gospel pages, flowing like lava at midnight.

Vincent's moral actions in the mining camps were to provide sustenance for his spiritual renascence. And the lessons of the Borinage, and the wisdom learned from kindred spirits in the literary realm, would forge Vincent's transformation into an artist with an intensity of compassion and purpose seldom seen in the history of mankind.

Opposite: "Still Life with Bible", Vincent van Gogh, 1885. Oil on Canvas. In the collection of the Van Gogh Museum, Amsterdam. Painted only a few weeks after the death of his father, Vincent portrays the family Bible, bathed in light reminiscent of a Rembrandt. This was Vincent's way of honoring his father's spiritual legacy.

Episode Three

A Calm Ardor for Work

Healing Themes
Domestic Dreams

HEALING THEMES

"Though every day difficulties crop up and new ones will present themselves, I cannot tell you how happy I am to have taken up drawing again...If I stay in good health, well, then I shall fight my battle quietly in this way and no other—by calmly looking through my window at the things of nature and drawing them faithfully and lovingly...And the old Dutch pictures and drawings prove clearly enough that those things do not stand in the way of painting and drawing. The mixture of studio and family life is no drawback, especially for a painter of the figure. I remember perfectly interiors of studios by Ostade—small pen drawings, probably of corners of his own house—which show clearly enough, the Ostade's studio looked very little like those studios where one finds Oriental weapons and vases and Persian rugs, etc."

—Vincent van Gogh

Following his dire but formative time spent in the Borinage and his subsequent emotional collapse, the twenty-eight year old Vincent slowly recovered his equilibrium. His relentless energy began to flow in the direction of his art. He started to draw daily, calmly, and with patient deliberation. He needed healing and said:

"It may be feverishness, or nerves, or something else, I don't know, but I don't feel well....one feels one's resistance ebbing, and is overcome by a pervading feeling of weariness....it suddenly seemed as if all my troubles crowded together to overwhelm me and it became too much for me because I could no longer look clearly into the future".

Perhaps for the first time, the nurturing that he had given to others he applied to himself. He had a good deal of healing to do in mind and body. But a very important insight into Vincent needs to be drawn from this outlook which offers a rare view into his artistic mindset. In counter-balance to the hard-driven aspect of his personality, there was

Opposite: "Bowl With Peonies And Roses" by Vincent van Gogh. 1886 - Oil on Canvas. In the collection of the Kröller-Müller Museum, Otterlo, The Netherlands.

a tender, gentle side. Johanna spoke of this with a sense of awe, reiterating how Vincent patiently and tenderly nursed his mother for weeks on end following a serious injury. What she noted above all was his sensitivity to the healing process. Vincent had become an accomplished nurse in the Borinage caring for burn victims.

Vincent continually mentioned in his letters the consoling influences of the landscape and the healthful effects of working outdoors. He was convinced that the making of art was in itself a restorative. The therapeutic qualities of painting and drawing combined with a robust home life induced an entirely different Vincent. *The Potato Eaters* of 1885, for instance, depicted a family of peasants huddled around a table eating a frugal meal. Family, nature and nurture were all given graphic expression in every aspect of this work. It deliberately depicted the rustic crudeness of the peasants' dwellings. Vincent said his intention was to evoke the smell of coffee, boiled potatoes, bacon grease, and dung in this portrayal of simple reward for a hard day's work: a meal, and quiet rest at the end of an exhausting day. The heavily-piled paint, the somber earthen pallette, and above all the spareness of the peasants themselves succeeded saying in paint what only a Dickens could achieve in words. Visually evoking smell was typical of Vincent; he always saw things from a unique perspective.

Van Gogh was extremely systematic in everything he did, and was a careful planner throughout his short life. Notwithstanding the (often spurious) aura that has come to surround him, he was in fact as inventive in technical matters as he was in visual imagination. He was not at all impulsive. He was by nature pragmatic and resolute. He brought all these traits to bear when he set up his efficient studio-apartment in The Hague. Serenity, art and healing convened in the cozy home he now furnished with a most improbable family.

"Last winter I met a pregnant woman, deserted by the man whose child she carried. A pregnant woman who had to walk the streets in winter, had to earn her bread, you understand how. I took this woman for a model, and have worked

with her all winter. I could not pay her the full wages of a model, but that did not prevent my paying her rent, and, thank God, so far I have been able to protect her and her child from hunger and cold by sharing my own bread with her. When I met this woman, she attracted my attention because she looked ill. I made her take baths and as much nourishing food as I could afford, and she has become much stronger. I went with her to Leyden, to the maternity hospital where she will be confined. (No wonder she was ill, the child was not in the right position, and she had to have an operation—the child had to be turned with forceps. However, there is a good chance of her pulling through. She will be confined in June.) It seems to me that every man worth a straw would have done the same in such a case."

He then shared his feelings about women and children:

"As for me, I do not feel strange in the company of the woman and the children, but more in my element, and as if we had been together a long time. Using my hands to do things which Sien is too weak to do, for instance making the beds or a thousand other things, is not unusual for me. I have often done things like that, either for myself or for sick people, etc. Once I nursed for six weeks or two months a poor miserable miner who had been burned. I shared my food for a whole winter with a poor old man, and heaven knows what else, and now there is Sien. But so far I have never thought all this foolish or wrong. I think it so natural and right that I cannot understand people being so indifferent to each other in general. I must add that if I were wrong in doing this, you were also wrong in helping me so faithfully—it would be too absurd if this were wrong. I have always believed that 'love thy neighbor as thyself' is no exaggeration, but a normal condition. So be it...".

Vincent's letter became a literary tour. The brothers had been perfecting their writing skills since childhood, trying to outdo one another with word pictures. In this, Vincent was perhaps more successful than Theo, though there are letters written by Theo that have great expressive force. But there is little doubt that Theo must have been moved by Vincent's words for they were as poignant as they were confident...just as well, for Theo needed reassurance that his financial support for Vincent was not being frittered away.

Theo was also the only family member corresponding with Vincent at this time. The family was shocked and bewildered that Vincent was living with a prostitute and had for the time being given up on him.

Theo consoled his father and mother. An expert negotiator, he eventually managed to get everyone speaking again. Soon little boxes began to arrive, tiny clothes for the infant, gloves, and one of Vincent's mother's expertly knitted scarves for the little girl. Then, dishes and silverware were lovingly sent by his parents. Vincent was greatly touched by the gesture, and wrote tenderly of it: "No mystical or mysterious studio but one that is rooted in real life—a studio with a cradle, a baby's crapper—where there is no stagnation, but where everything pushes and urges and stirs to activity".

In the end, Sien (whose name in English sounded like "sin") returned to her old lifestyle on the streets, abandoning Vincent. He was later to describe the heart-rending scene of their separation: Sien passed her two-year-old boy to Vincent already seated in a train car. The little boy played with the buttons of Vincent's corduroy coat. Suddenly a whistle blew and Vincent reluctantly passed the precious child back to Sien through the window. The train jerked forward, gradually pulling away as he leaned out of the window to wave until they were no longer visible. He never saw them again. He wept often, recalling tender moments with the toddler, and regularly mailed letters and money to Sien. But weeks later, the letters were returned unopened. Some years later, in all probability pregnant again, she leapt from a bridge into the dark water. Her seductive black dress pulled her under, and she was gone. Earlier Vincent had predicted it would one day happen. Severely ill himself, and prior to his hospitalization, he wrote:

"*Dear Theo,*

It is evening before I go back to the hospital, and I do not know what they will tell me there; perhaps I shall only be there for a short time, perhaps I shall have to stay in bed for days. Therefore, I am writing you once more from home. It is already late, and it is so quiet and calm here in the studio; but outside it is storming and raining, which makes the calm inside even greater.

How I wish you could be with me, brother, this quiet hour, how much I should have to show you. The studio looks so real, I think—plain grayish-brown paper, a scrubbed wooden floor, white muslin curtains at the windows, everything clean. And of course, studies on the wall, an easel on both sides, and a large white working table. A kind of alcove adjoins the studio, there I keep all the drawing boards, portfolios, boxes, sticks, etc., and also the wood engravings. And in the corner a closet with all the bottles and pots, and then all my books. Then the little living room with a table, a few kitchen chairs, an oilstove, a large wicker easy chair for the woman in the corner, near the window that overlooks the wharf and the meadows, which you know from the drawing. And beside it a small iron cradle with a green cover.

I cannot look at this last piece of furniture without emotion, for it is a strong and powerful emotion which grips a man when he sits beside the woman he loves with a baby in the cradle near them. And though it was only a hospital where she was lying and where I sat near her, it is always the eternal poetry of the Christmas night with the baby in the stable—as the old Dutch painters saw it, and Millet and Breton—a light in the darkness, a star in the dark night. So I hung the great etching of Rembrandt over it, the two women by the cradle, one of whom is reading from the Bible by the light of a candle, while great shadows cast a deep chiaroscuro all over the room. I have hung a few other prints there, too, all very beautiful ones—'Christus Consolator' [Christ our consolation] by Scheffer; a photograph of a picture of Boughton; 'The Sower' and 'The Diggers' by Millet; 'The Bush' by Ruisdael; beautiful large wood engravings by Herkomer and Frank Holl; and 'Le Banc des Pauvres' by De Groux.

Well, and then in the kitchen there is the strictly necessary, so that if the woman comes back before me, she will find everything she needs, and can prepare some dinner in ten minutes; so that she can feel that I have thought of her when she comes into a house with flowers in front of the window where she will sit. And up in the large attic, a large bed for us; and my old one for the child, with all the bedding neatly arranged. But you must not think that I bought all this at once; this winter we already started buying things bit by bit, though I did not know then how things would go and where we should have to live. And now, thank God, the result is that this little nest is ready for her and after all her pain. But we have been busy these days, her mother and I, especially the former. The most difficult thing was the bedding; we made and altered every-thing ourselves, bought straw, seaweed, bed-ticking, and filled the mattresses ourselves in the attic. Otherwise it would have been too expensive.

And now, having paid my old landlord, I shall have 40 guilders left out of what you sent me. It is true that tomorrow I shall have to pay 10 guilders to the hospital, but that gives me two weeks of food and medical treatment, so that I shall have enough money without your sending more than usual this month, though during it I had the expense of moving, of getting settled, and Sien's return after her confinement, and buying the cradle, etc. 'On est sur de perir a part, on ne se sauve qu' ensemble.' ('You are sure to perish alone, only together you can save yourself). I think this saying is true, and I base my life upon it; could this be wrong or a miscalculation? See, brother, I think of you so often, so very, very, often these days; in the first place, because all I possess, all that I really have belongs to you—even my own energy and love of life, for now with your help I can go forward, and I feel the power to work growing within me.

But there is another reason why I think of you so often. I know how only a short time ago I came home to a house that was not a real home with all the emotions connected with it now, where two great voids stared at me night and day. There was no wife, there was no child. I do not think there were fewer cares for all that, but certainly there was less love. And those two voids accom-panied me, one on either side, in the street and at work, everywhere and always.

There was no wife, there was no child.

See, I do not know whether you had that feeling which forces a groan or a sigh for us at moments when we are alone: My God, where is my wife: my God, where is my child? Is living worth while?

When I think of you, I suppose, I am not mistaken in believing something of the same melancholy is in you, though less passionately and nervously than in me, but at least to some extent and at some moments. And I do not know whether you approve of it or not, whether you think it right or wrong, when I tell you that I sometimes think of you this way. But this much, I believe about you, and this much I know of myself, notwithstanding my nervousness, that there certainly is a foundation of serenity in both our characters—serenity quand bien meme—so that neither of us is unhappy, because the serenity is based on our own true and sincere love for our profession and work, art takes a great place in our minds and makes life interesting. So I certainly do not want to make you melancholy, but only to try to explain my deeds and thoughts by means of something in your own temperament.

Now speaking of Father—do you think Father would remain indifferent and make objections—near a cradle? You see, a cradle is not like anything else—there is no fooling with it—and whatever there may be in Sien's past—I know no other Sien than the one of this winter—than that mother in the hospital whose hand pressed mine when we both felt tears in our eyes as we looked at the little baby for whom we had been working all winter. And just listen, entre nous soit dit—without preaching a sermon, it may be true that there is no God here, but there must be one not far off, and at such a moment one feels His presence. Which is the same as saying, and I readily give this sincere profession of faith: I believe in God, and that it is His will that man does not live alone, but with a wife and a child, when everything is normal. And I hope that you will understand what I have done, and take it as such, namely as a natural thing, and that you will not think of me as fooling or being fooled. And, brother, when you come, and I hope you will come soon—then see Sien only as a mother and an ordinary housewife, and nothing else. For that is what she really is, and I feel she knows this all the better for knowing the 'other side of the coin.' The last thing I bought was a few plates, forks, spoons and knives, for neither Sien nor I possessed them before; and I thought, another set for Theo or for Father when they come to visit me. So your place at the window and your place at the table are ready and waiting for you.

So I only want to ask—you will certainly come, won't you? I thought it wise and discreet of you not to have spoken to Father and Mother about it. Now that the confinement is over, the flowers are blooming again, and it was better to wait until now to tell Father and Mother. I mean, I thought it better to keep the thorns to myself and show them only a rose. Therefore, when Sien comes back and I am better, I want to tell it in the way I mentioned it to you, so when they ask you about it, you can just give a hint.

Adieu, good night.

Yours sincerely, Vincent.

Vincent's letter revealed so much. But above all it showed that his portrayals of everyday life—birth, nursing, sewing, family meals, soup kitchens, welfare centers, and prayer meetings—were far from arbitrary choices. He drew everything familiar with great affection and passion. He actually amplified his devotion to these themes by depicting them using unorthodox media: egg, coffee, milk combined with oil, watercolor, ink, and charcoal. He even discovered that bread could be used as an eraser. His descriptions of his studio showed how diligent he was with everything he tackled. He had easels set up on each side of the room, and carefully organized boxes, portfolios, bottles, linseed oil, charcoal sticks, pencils, and paints for maximum efficiency. He preoccupied himself with finding artistic uses for kitchen materials in general.

Vincent devised inventive solutions for controlling the flood of light in his studio:

"You know there are three windows in the studio. They let in far too much light, even when I cover them, and for a long time I have been thinking about how to remedy this...

...But now, after a new attack, I have six shutters and about six long boards.

Those shutters are sawed in two now, so that both the upper and lower halves can be opened or closed at will, and the light let in or shut out for either above or below...You understand that I can also shut one or two of the windows now, and so get one general light which will make the effects much stronger; they used to be neutralized by reflections or diffuse light."

He demonstrated great sensitivity to materials for the cultivation of his art down to the most humble of physical substances. He understood the innate properties of matter in the same way that he understood the mysterious light that played in the corner of his studio.

'But it occurred to me to make a drawing first with carpenter's pencil and then to work in and over it with lithographic crayon, which (because of the greasiness of the material) fixes the pencil, a thing ordinary crayon does not do, or, at least, does very badly. After doing a sketch in this way, one can, with a firm hand, use the lithographic crayon where it is necessary, without much hesitation or erasing. So I finished my drawings pretty well in pencil, indeed, as much as possible. Then I fixed them, and dulled them with milk. And then I worked it up again with lithographic crayon where the deepest tones were, retouched them here and there with a brush or pen, with lampblack, and worked in the lighter parts with white body color...

...On the back of the page you will find a sketch of the little churchyard. The coloring there is very unusual. It is very beautiful to see the real heather on the graves. The smell of turpentine has something mystical about it, the dark stretch of fine wood border separates a sparkling sky from the rugged earth, which has a generally ruddy hue—fawn—brownish, yellowish, but everywhere with lilac tones."

The lure of the heather, the other-worldly smell of turpentine amid churchyard graves, all reverberated with the mystery of death and resurrection and starlight on safe passageways. In stressing his

Gospel aesthetic of simplicity, he told us how he preferred a rough scrubbed floor to the popular Turkish carpets of upscale Parisian ateliers. He dulled his drawing with the simplest of washes—with milk taken from the pantry. As mentioned, the scent of turpentine, the traditional thinner for oil paint derived from pine resins, had religious associations for Vincent. And he delighted in the blackness of charcoal, graphite and ink, and deplored ostentation in the tools of his trade just as he did in people.

"If one wants to work with the pen and autographic ink, then I am of the opinion that one should in no case take a finer pen than an ordinary writing pen. Very fine pens, like very elegant people, are sometimes amazingly useless; and, as I see it, they often lack elasticity which the most ordinary pens just naturally have to a certain extent...

...This is how I reason about carpenter's pencil. What did the old masters use for drawing? Certainly not Faber B, BB, BBB, etc., etc. [calibrated professional artist's pencils of corresponding intensity] but a piece of rough graphite. Perhaps the instrument which Michelangelo and Durer used somewhat resembled a carpenter's pencil. But I was not there to see for myself, so I don't know; I only know that with a carpenter's pencil one can get effects quite different than those with thin Fabers, etc."

Vincent demonstrated his understanding of the use of all art media, the "fat'" or "lean" properties of substances (a term used by professional artists in applying oily over non-oily media) in everyday use, which either fused, or resisted adhering to one another. This fusion of form and content was made evident in his ink drawings of Sien's infant son which Vincent "demi-toned" by absorbing black pools of ink with breadcrumbs to lighten them. Similarly, Rembrandt was equally inventive, adding egg to his oil paint. Dutch painters preferred to use their homes as studios, unlike the Italian artists whose studios were usually in a commercial quarter of the city. This might explain their use of everyday things such as egg, milk and coffee, in their art—things that were ready at hand. The Dutch culinary tradition was carried into the nineteenth century at the RijkHBS Konig Willem II Upper School which Vincent attended in the 1860s. According to Silverman (2000), his drawing teacher Cornelius C. Huysmans's mission "was to reclaim his students so that they might 'learn how to see' and learn to integrate beauty into objects of daily use". Silverman goes on to note:

"One instance of Huysmans's pragmatic approach was his recommendation that students pour milk over their finished pencil drawings to 'preserve marks and remove the shine,' perhaps adding a little coffee to the milk as a 'varnish' to give the drawing 'the color of India paper'. Vincent himself would later pursue his own "kitchen craft" approach to the art of drawing and color, what he referred to as his cuisine de l'art."

Regarding the natural beauty of such substances and his delight in the natural origins of things Vincent wrote:

"Charcoal is good, but if one works at it too long, it loses its freshness, and one must fix it immediately to preserve the delicacy of touch. In landscape too, I see that draftsmen like, for instance, Ruysdael and Van Goyen, and Calame and Roelofs too among the moderns, used it to great advantage...

...One can do great things with charcoal soaked in oil, I have seen Weissenbruch do it; the oil fixes the charcoal and at the same time the black becomes warmer and deeper...Today I will send you by parcel post three studies which I hope are dry enough; however, if they stick to the sheet of paper I put over them as a precaution, sponge them off with tepid water. The paint on the smallest one especially has sunk in a lot. In a week or so brush it over with the white of an egg, or with a little varnish in a month, to restore the color. I send them to you to give you an idea of the work, which will be better as I go along, you know...

...I wrote Rappard about the crayon yesterday, because I had to write him about

various things concerning lithography; as I wanted to send him a few sketches done with it, I used it for some drawings of our baby, in different positions, and I found it is very well suited to sketching, too. One can bring in demitones by means of bread crumbs. Perhaps the very deepest shadows can't be done very well with it, but in many cases one can use lithographic crayon then, which is also very rich in tone."

Included in the storage cabinet was his collection of wood engravings:

"I must also tell you that I am getting on so well with my collection of wood engravings, which I consider yours, I only having the use of them. I now have about a thousand sheets—English (especially Swains), American and French ones."

Vincent had a large collection of prints, from Rembrandt and Millet to nineteenth century popular illustrators. He used these for copying, studying, and above all for inspiration. He was attracted by the direct, unpretentiousness of engravings and illustrations, which revealed the reality, perhaps starkness, of everyday life—very much like the descriptions of Dickens and Hugo. In related letters, Vincent elaborated on his engravings:

"I have finished cutting out and mounting the wood engravings from the Graphic [magazine]. Now they are arranged in an orderly manner, they show up ever so much better...I have a magnificent Giacomelli, a large sheet representing a 'Flight of Crows'."

We see how one of Vincent's last and most searing paintings, *Crows over Wheat Fields (1890)*, can be related to Giacomelli and to Vincent's early absorption in the elemental power and expressive subject matter of wood engravings. As Vincent's art matured, he embraced past and present styles, combining them to suit his own needs. His collecting was wide ranging and intense, and he once informed his artist friend Rappard: "I bought twenty-one volumes of the Graphic, namely 1870-1880.".

These engravings and illustrations were a continual reminder to Vincent of his life in the Borinage, and the harsh living conditions endured there, and also in Dickens's accounts of life at that time. He had been so affected by those visions of appalling human conditions that he kept the engravings of miners until his death, even replacing them when they were lost or given away.

Vincent always revered works with Gospel inclinations as in Frank Hol's *I Am the Resurrection and the Life*, and more so in Rembrandt's depictions of life, death and the Resurrection of Christ. He spoke reverently of Rembrandt's engravings of Christmas night, the Christ Child in the manger, and the Christmas star, relating them to healing and hope. More themes congealed in his quiet room: the faces of Millet's peasants laboring by the sweat of their brows. They too were reminders of Dickens's Blackpool, the forsaken miner, and the star seen from the mineshaft that comforted him, as it did Vincent in his own dark circumstances.

Vincent revealed his own essentially intellectual approach to his art career as he noted them in Rappard:

"Rappard has something which not everybody possesses, he reflects, and he cultivates his sentiment. He can make a plan, he can grasp a scheme in its entirety, he can stick to an idea. Many call reflection and concentration inartistic because they at least are not fit for sustained labor. It is a question of both dexterity and quickness and of perseverance and calm patience besides."

The characteristics that Vincent admired in Rappard were to be made real in his own life. In describing the cultivation of sentiment, he made it clear that its primary characteristics were reflection, thought, planning, and consistency—not frenzy. Vincent had brought Sien and her children into his life at a very significant time in his quest to conquer one of the summits of art—mastery of the human figure. The fruit of this sustained focus was *The Potato Eaters* which was, by his own estimation, his greatest painting.

All these things resonated for Vincent and being aware of such things was a gift he possessed; and revealing this gift to others through his art was his purpose. Dark revelations blossomed into his first successful paintings. He released a torrent of works a few months later in rural Drenthe. There he gave color to life-long memories and the intimation of a silver star in a cobalt night, the mysterious heath of Holland under an ivory moon, a huddled family before a glowing fireplace, and the violet repose of a deceased friend's face. All of these impressions and experiences were woven into a body of work filled with regret over the loss of his dreams of domestic life. He had effectively become the spiritual father of the dispossessed.

Opposite: "House in Auvers" by Vincent van Gogh, 1890. Oil on canvas. In the collection of the Museum of Fine Arts, Boston.

DOMESTIC DREAMS

"'M. Millet, it is plain,' wrote Theophile Gautier, 'understands the true poetry of the fields. He loves the peasants whom he represents. In his grave and serious types we read sympathy which he feels with their lives. In his pictures sowing, reaping, and grafting are all of them sacred actions, which have a beauty and grandeur of their own, together with a touch of Virgilian melancholy.'"

—Julia Cartwright

A letter from the French artist J.F.Millet to his friend and biographer Sensier, written in about 1850, influenced Vincent greatly. Millet was known for his piety and profound knowledge of the Bible. He became vitally important to Vincent; for not only did Millet's art convey Biblical messages in a natural unaffected way, he also was a family man, living in a rural environment. This was all the more significant for Vincent who increasingly wanted to return to his rural roots. Millet's painting was as simple and elemental as the book illustrators Vincent's so revered. Millet's solid way of portraying things resonated with the earthy reality that Dutch seventeenth-century art exuded.

The importance of Millet in Vincent's life cannot be over emphasized. Before Vincent's birth, Millet had shown how rural themes of painting and the Gospel message could be united. Sowing symbolized spreading the Word of God, for instance. In the Parables of Jesus, harvesting and reaping are used as symbols for death and eternal life. Millet's art and example as a letter-writing, laboring artist paralleled Vincent's own literary outlook and rural Gospel-based upbringing. Additionally, Millet was a painter and printmaker whose uncomplicated etchings were a major part of the illustrations Vincent had collected. Vincent studied how Millet transferred the engraved line and strong shading of the print into color, atmosphere, and brushwork in painting.

Millet's success as a printmaker broadened the availability of his art, for even those of modest means could afford a print.

Vincent's championing of the poor was expressed in many ways, among them his collection of *Graphic,* a magazine which was filled with the work of some of the most popular printmakers and illustrators of the day. The main purpose of the magazine was to rouse compassion and donations for the poor. It combined riveting portrayals of the needy with descriptions of their plight:

"I think it very noble, for instance, that no winter passed without the Graphic doing something to arouse sympathy for the poor. For example, I have a page [print] by Woodville representing a distribution of peat tickets in Ireland; another by Staniland called "Help the Helpers," representing various scenes in a hospital which was short of money; "Christmas in the Workhouse" by Herkomer; "Homeless and Hungry" by Fildes, etc. I like them better than the drawings by Bertall, or the like, for the Vie Elegante."

Coal miners remained important subjects to Vincent, especially after his immersion in their hard lives. In 1882, he tried to get a print of miners that was related to an article in *Graphic:* "I cannot get Renouard's 'The Miners' here. I have gone to all kinds of places..."

Vincent purposely imitated the healthy spirit and unembellished honesty of popular illustrations and their simple focus on the dignity of daily life. They became characteristics of his own art and in his choice of media and materials:

"Or take another sheet of Ridley's which I have, engraved soberly and austerely by Swain—"The Children's Ward in a Hospital"—there I feel the justification for what I've heard people who are supposed to be first-rate connoisseurs contemptuously refer to in these terms, 'Oh, well, that's the old-fashioned style.' And then we remember what Herkomer [Dickens's illustrator] wanted to say— that old style of engraving, that elaborate, honest, unembellished drawing, is by far the best...I assure you, every time I feel a little out of sorts, I find in my

collection of wood engravings a stimulus to work with renewed zest. In all these fellows I see an energy, a determination and a free, healthy, cheerful spirit that animate me. And in their work there is something lofty and dignified—even when they draw a dunghill."

Vincent explained how he admired "the striking, powerful, virile drawings." He respected the strength, clarity, stark line, directness and simplicity of prints. These formal properties were tied to moral and ethical issues such as honesty and truthfulness, moral sentiments that he cultivated in himself.

"But isn't it queer that in an artistic town like The Hague a man like me should be the highest bidder at a book auction? One would think that other buyers would turn up—but no! I really did not expect to get them...my brother helped me buy them—dirt cheap—a guilder a volume. However glad I am to have them, it makes me sad to think that so few take an interest in them. I think it's wonderful to find such a treasure, but I would rather see so lively an interest in them that I should not be able to get hold of them for the time being. Oh, Rappard—in many respects it's like this—much that has great value nowadays is ignored and looked down upon as worthless rubbish, garbage, waste paper. Don't you think there is something very dull about our times? Or am I imagining it? A certain absence of passion and warmth and cordiality ..."

He was so taken with Millet's published letters that he seems to have memorized whole passages from them. At Drenthe, Vincent's letters often recalled Millet's in form and content. Millet outlined his artistic doctrine in the following passage, and we will see just how much Vincent identified with and emulated it. And they both shared a tendency to dream amid the sights, sounds and pungent smells of rural existence.

Millet wrote:

"But, to tell the truth, peasant-subjects suit my nature best, for I must confess, at the risk of your taking me to be a Socialist, that the human side is what touches me most in art, and that if I could only do what I like, or at least attempt to do it, I would paint nothing that was not the result of an impression directly received from Nature, whether in landscape or in figures. The joyous side never shows itself to me; I know not if it exists, but I have never seen it. The gayest thing I know is the calm, the silence, which are so delicious, both in the forest and in the cultivated fields, whether the soil is good for culture or not. You will confess that it always gives you a very dreamy sensation, and that the dream is a sad one, although often very delicious. You are sitting under a tree, enjoying all the comfort and quiet which it is possible to find in this life, when suddenly you see a poor creature loaded with a heavy faggot coming up the narrow path opposite. The unexpected and always striking way in which this figure appears before your eyes reminds you instantly of the fate of humanity—weariness...In cultivated land sometimes—as in places where the ground is barren—you see figures digging and hoeing. From time to time, one raises himself and straightens his back, as they call it, wiping his forehead with the back of his hand— 'Thou shalt eat bread in the sweat of thy brow.' Is this the gay and playful kind of work that some people would have us believe? Nevertheless, for me it is true humanity and great poetry."

In another of Millet's artistic epistles, note how he insists that the artist must seek out the elemental aspects of nature and resist the conventional pressure to compromise for immediate success:

"A profound impression will always find out a way of expression, and naturally seeks how to declare itself in the most forcible manner. The whole of nature's arsenal has been at the disposal of men of might, and their genius has made them employ, not what we may think the most beautiful things, but the most suitable. Has not everything in creation its own place and hour? Who would venture to say that a potato is inferior to a pomegranate? Decadence set in from

the moment that Art, which was in point the child of Nature, became the supreme goal, and men took some great artist for their model, forgetting that his eyes had been fixed on the infinite. They talked of working from nature, but they approached her in a conventional form."

Millet's admonitions also paralleled Dickens regarding the importance of Nature, inspiration, and foundational moral commitments in art. Vincent cited, memorized and constantly noted the moral views of both Millet and Dickens; in fact, Vincent eventually sounded like both of them. Dickens warned British painters:

"Fellows, try to understand that your model is not your final aim, but the means of giving form and strength to your thought and inspiration. Look at the French...and see how much better they do it than you do."

Vincent made tangible use of Dickens's idea of giving form and strength to one's thought and inspiration; he describes "The broad-fronted houses...oak trees of a splendid bronze...in the cornfields, tones of inexpressible purity, on the wet trunks, tones of black." He gives "plastic solidity" to nature, describing its strong colors and deep contrasts: "The poor soil of Drenthe is just the same—but the black earth is even blacker still—like soot—not lilac-black like the furrows." One can see that he is describing this in the forceful ways Millet and Dickens enjoin. Van Gogh's sensitivity to the natural elements of moisture, lush soil, texture, and plant growth in Drenthe finds their parallel in his studio practices. His absorption in "the cuisine of the kitchen" and the domestic intimacy that it implies is now extended into the world of cottages, domesticated fields and waterways.

Vincent, on seeing Millet's art, reported:

"I don't know whether I have already written to you about it or not, but there has been a sale here of drawings by Millet. When I entered the hall of the Hotel Drouot, where they were exhibited, I felt like saying, 'Take off your shoes, for

the place where you are standing is Holy Ground.'"

Following Sien's departure, Vincent had moved to rural Drenthe. He wrote to Theo a letter that was like walking into a lifetime of his painting:

"Dear Brother,

I must tell you about a trip to Zweelo, the village where Liebermann stayed a long while, and where he made studies for his picture at the last Salon, the one with the poor washerwomen. Where Ter Meulen and Jules Bakhuyzen have also been a long time. Imagine a trip across the heath at three o'clock in the morning, in an open cart (I went with the landlord, who had to go to the market at Assen), along a road, or "diek" as they call it here, which had been banked up with mud instead of sand. It was even more curious than going by barge. At the first glimpse of dawn, when everywhere the cocks began to crow near the cottages scattered all over the heath and the few cottages we passed—surrounded by thin poplars whose yellow leaves one could hear drop to earth—an old stumpy tower in a churchyard, with earthen wall and beech hedge—the level landscapes of heath and cornfields—it all, all, all became exactly like the most beautiful Corots. A quietness, a mystery, a peace, as only he has painted it.

But when we arrived at Zweeloo at six o'clock in the morning, it was still quite dark; I saw the real Corots even earlier in the morning. The entrance to the village was splendid: enormous mossy roofs of houses, stables, sheepfolds, barns.

The broad-fronted houses here stand between oak trees of a splendid bronze. In the moss are tones of gold green; in the ground tones of reddish or bluish or yellowish dark lilac gray; in the green of the cornfields, tones of inexpressible purity; on the wet trunks, tones of black, contrasting with the golden rain of whirling, clustering autumn leaves—hanging in loose tufts, as if they had been blown there, and with the sky glimmering through them—from the poplars, the birches, the lime and apple trees.

The sky smooth and clear, luminous, not white but a lilac which can hardly be deciphered, white shimmering with red, blue and yellow in which everything is reflected, and which one feels everywhere above one, which is vaporous and merges into the thin mist below—harmonizing everything in a gamut of delicate gray. I didn't find a single painter in Zweeloo, however, and people said none ever came in winter.

I, on the contrary, hope to be there just this winter. As there were no painters, I decided not to wait for my landlord's return, but to walk back, and to make some drawings on the way. So I began a sketch of that little apple orchard, of which Liebermann made his large picture. And then I walked back along the road we had driven over early in the morning.

For the moment the whole country around Zweeloo is entirely covered as far as the eye can see—with young corn, the very, very, tenderest green I know.

With a sky over it of a delicate lilac-white which gives an effect—I don't think it can be painted, but which is for me the keynote that one must know in order to understand the keynotes of other effects.

A patch of earth—flat—infinite—a clear sky of delicate lilac-white. The young corn sprouts from that earth, it is almost moldy-looking with that corn. That's what the good fertile parts of Drenthe are basically; the whole in a hazy atmosphere. Think of Brion's "Le dernier jour de la creation"; yesterday it seemed to me that I understood the meaning of that picture.

The poor soil of Drenthe is just the same—but the black earth is even blacker still—like soot—not lilac-black like the furrows, and drearily covered with ever-rotting heather and peat. I see that everywhere, the incidentals on the infinite background: on the moors, the peat sheds; in the fertile parts, the very primitive gigantic structures of farms and sheepfolds, with low, very low little walls and enormous mossy roofs. Oak trees all around them.

When one has walked through that infinite country for hours and hours, one feels that there is really nothing but that infinite earth—that green mold of corn or heather, the infinite sky. Horses and men seem no larger than fleas. One is not aware of anything, be it ever so large in itself; one only knows that there is earth and sky. However, in one's quality of a little speck noticing other little specks—leaving the infinite apart—one finds every little speck to be a Millet.

I passed a little old church exactly, "The Church at Greville" in Millet's little picture in the Luxembourg; instead of the little peasant with his spade in that picture, there was a shepherd with a flock of sheep walking along the hedge. There was not a glimpse of the true sea in the background, but only of the sea of young corn, the sea of furrows instead of the sea of waves. The effect produced was the same. Then I saw plovers, very busy—a sandcart, a shepherd, road menders, dungcarts. In a little roadside inn I drew an old woman at the spinning wheel, a dark little silhouette out of a fairy tale—a dark little silhouette against a light window, through which one saw the clear sky, and a small path through the delicate green, and a few geese pecking at grass.

And then when twilight fell—imagine the quiet, the peace of it all! Imagine then a little avenue of high poplars with autumn leaves, imagine a wide muddy road, all black mud, with an infinite heath to the right and an endless heath to the left, a few black triangular silhouettes of sod-built huts, through the little windows of which shines the red light of the little fire, with a few pools of dirty yellowish water that reflect the sky, and in which trunks lie rotting; imagine that swamp in the evening twilight, with a white sky over it, everywhere the contrast of black and white. And in that swamp a rough figure—the shepherd— a heap of oval masses, half wool, half mud, jostling each other, pushing each other—the flock. You see them coming—you find yourself in the midst of them—you turn around and follow them. Slowly and reluctantly they trudge along the muddy road. However, the farm looms in the distance—a few mossy roofs and piles of straw and peat between the poplars.

The sheepfold is again like the silhouette of a triangle—dark. The door is wide open like the entrance to a dark cave. Through the chinks of the boards behind it gleams the light of the sky. The whole caravan of masses of wool and mud disappears into that cave—the shepherd and a woman with a lantern shut the doors behind them.

That coming home of the flock in twilight was the finale of the symphony I heard yesterday. That day passed like a dream, all day I was so absorbed in the poignant music that I literally forgot even food and drink—I had taken a piece of brown bread and a cup of coffee in the little inn where I drew the spinning wheel. The day was over, and from dawn till twilight, or rather from one night till the other, I had lost myself in that symphony.

I came home, and sitting by the fire, I felt I was hungry, yes, very hungry. But now you see how it is here. One is feeling exactly as if one had been to an exhibition of the Cent chef-d'oeuvres, for instance; what does one bring home from such a day? Only a number of rough sketches. Yet there is another thing one brings home—a calm ardor for work.

Do write soon, today is Friday, but your letter has not yet arrived; I am longing to get it. It also takes some time to get it changed, as I have to go to Hoogeveen for it, and then return here. We do not know how things will go, otherwise I should say, now the simplest thing would be perhaps to send the money once a month. At all events, write soon. With a handshake,
Yours sincerely, Vincent.

Vincent was totally absorbed by the rhythms of Drenthe—its farming landscape, people and pursuits. Earlier, his art had been influenced by book illustrations, most of which were in black and white, appealing to his love for drawing. As previously noted, he liked to create drawings using a limited pallette of colors. However, in Drenthe, the blue-grey soil, flaming autumn leaves, rain-drenched sky, and pools of water ignited his innate sense of color. He began to create a sacred romance out of the teeming soil with new vigor.

Vincent's first heavily layered oil paintings were created here in Drenthe—a world of black mud, yellowish-sand, and ripening corn. Textural penetration, artistic cultivation, and painterly weaving were embodied everywhere in his letter to Theo. It was as if he was seeing for the first time how the rich textural variations of nature—sand, rock, mud, water, sky, and grass—could be translated and woven into the language of paint and facture. And as if to underscore this earthy revelation, Vincent told us in the letter that the grand finale of the entire day was the coming home of the shepherd and his flock. "The whole caravan of masses of wool and mud disappears into that cave—the shepherd and a woman with a lantern shut the doors behind them. That coming home of the flock in twilight was the finale of the symphony I heard yesterday."

A few months later, he would purchase a spinning wheel to study as a still-life subject, setting up a new studio around it. He gave the spinning wheel a regenerative meaning much clearer than the iron cradle which was associated with his failed relationship with Sien. The spinning wheel had long been associated with Vincent's mother whom he felt he symbolically honored whenever he drew or painted the wheel. She was an expert knitter who amazed many with her blinding speed with the long needles—proud of how quickly she produced finished items. Perhaps it was her speed that Vincent emulated when he moved so rapidly over his canvases, often completing three paintings a day. The cradle and the spinning wheel appeared as central motifs in his art from the beginning to the end of his career. Humankind has long recognized the enduring meaning ot them, and of the cradle as a symbol of birth. There are also interesting ways that the two can be linked as in a rocking cradle where time and mortality are conjoined as they really are in all existence. In his last letter to his mother written two weeks before his death, we see that time and issues of fate were on his mind:

"Last year I read in some book or other that writing a book or painting a picture was like having a child. This I will not accept as applicable to me—I have always thought that the latter was the more natural and the best—so I say, only if it were so, only if it were the same. This is the very reason why at times I exert myself to the utmost, though it happens to be this very work that is least understood, and for me it is the only link between the past and the present."

Van Gogh's sojourn in Drenthe helped mold his identity as an artist, his roots sunk deeply in the steaming earth. It was another Brabant of sorts (his actual place of birth). But at Drenthe it was not so much a physical rebirth that occurred; it was instead the emergence of a painter of the soil.

As we read on in Vincent's letter, it is apparent that Millet's work had sharpened his own perceptions of color, both in the landscape and his art, as well as in his deepening awareness of people and their various trades. His time in the Drenthe countryside was a literal return home: "what does one bring home from such a day?" After his loss of home life with Sien, he found great respite in Drenthe's cottage life and a more reliable muse—a lifelong bond with nature.

Vincent's dreams of domesticity now extended to all rural life. The sight of "an old woman at the spinning wheel, a dark little silhouette out of a fairy tale, and a few geese pecking at grass..." touched him deeply.

The spinning woman was to Vincent the ultimate embodiment of motherhood. And in that mysterious spinner, his reverence for home and vocation were to merge. She spun away before the very landscape he painted as if she were a symbol of mother nature. In homage to her, he wove it all into strands of lush pigment, the lilac sky, a country lane, and geese flying overhead, all rendered on the dense carpet of his canvases.

Much of the Drenthe letter to Theo poignantly revealed Vincent's longing for Sien and her children. Each time he saw a cottage or hut— a fire glowing within—was painful. As he trudged along the muddy roads under wet skies, his dreams of home and hearth prompted spiritual yearnings. As happened so often at extreme moments in his life, his thoughts turned to God and the mysterious providence and circumstance He orchestrated. In this lonely ocean of plowed fields, Vincent sensed that he was part of an eternal plan, and as he says elsewhere, it was "more eternal than the ocean." At extreme moments, thoughts of God carried Vincent to his nativity, to the cradle, and an infant's secret knowledge—particularly of one who was unborn and resurrected before Vincent's own birth. It was the same for Dickens who, in describing a man on the way to his death, offered these thoughts writing of Sydney Carton, one of the characters in *A Tale Of Two Cities*, when contemplating his own death:

"'I am the Resurrection and the Life, saith the Lord: he that believeth in me, though he were dead, yet shall he live: and whosoever liveth and believeth in me shall never die.' Now that the streets were quiet and the night wore on, those words were in the echoes of his feet, and were in the air. Perfectly calm and steady, he sometimes repeated them to himself as he walked; but, he heard them always."

This journey into the wildness was another reprieve and, like illness, healing, and redemption were essential themes of Vincent's life and the ultimate meaning of his art. He was in a constant state of recovery from some kind of trouble or another. His immersion in the pastoral life of Drenthe was in many ways the most successful recovery he ever experienced. Nature spoke to him in the most consoling manner and provided him the nurturing that Sien never could.

Here in quiet Drenthe, where water washed the world clean, and trees, forests, and fields spoke the silent wisdom of infants fresh-born into the world, where water courses were ever flowing, perhaps here Vincent replaced and replenished the domestic dreams he had always cherished. Above all, his time there was a venture back to Brabant, to his own infancy and childhood dreams.

Vincent's letter from Drenthe ends with the question, "What does one bring home from such a day? Yet there is another thing one brings home—a calm ardor for work."

"But if one feels the need of something grand, something infinite, something that makes one feel aware of God, one need not go far to find it. I think I see something deeper, more infinite, more eternal than the ocean in the expression of the eyes of a little baby when it wakes in the morning, and coos or laughs because it sees the sun shining on its cradle. If there is a 'rayon d'en haut,' [a light on high] perhaps one can find it there."

And so it was that Vincent's time in Drenthe contained both the promise and fulfillment of a dream. Using this allusive metaphor, Millet stated that being a peasant painter was dreamily satisfying in ways that the flurry of city life could never be. Vincent, who had read and reread Millet's published writings, appears to have used Millet's dream motif in his own visionary letter in which he describes his epic journey into the pristine isolation of rural Zweelo, Holland. Two dreams coalesced—the fulfillment of the artists' domestication and birth as landscape painters.

The power of Millet words continue to resonate with us to this very day:

"There are people who say that I see no charms in the country. I see much more than charms there—infinite splendours. I see, as well as they do, the little flowers of which Christ said: 'I say unto you, that even Solomon in all his glory was not arrayed like one of these.'

"I see very well the aureoles of the dandelions and the sun spreading his glory in the clouds, over the distant worlds. But none the less I see down there in the plain the steaming horses leading the plough, and in a rocky corner a man quite worn-out, whose 'han' has been heard since morning, and who tries to straighten himself and take a breath for a moment. The drama is surrounded with splendour.

"It is not my invention, and this expression—'the cry of the ground'—was heard long ago. My critics are men of taste and instruction, I suppose, but I cannot put myself in their skin, and since I have never, in all my life, known anything but the fields, I try and say, as best I can, what I saw and felt when I worked there. Those who can do this better than I can are fortunate people."

—J. F. Millet

Opposite: "Farmhouse in Provence" by Vincent van Gogh, 1888. Oil on canvas.
In the collection of the National Gallery of Art, Washington, DC.

Episode Four

Vincent's Moral Heritage

Remembrance & Reconciliation
The Bishop's Doctrine & Starry Night

Remembrance & Reconciliation

"I won't hide from you that I don't dislike the country, as I have been brought up there—I am still charmed by the magic of hosts of memories of the past, of a longing for the infinite, of which the sower, the sheaf are the symbols—just as much as before. But when shall I paint my starry sky, that picture which preoccupies me continuously?...One must attack them nonetheless, however incompetent one may feel before the unspeakable perfection, the glorious splendors of nature."

—Vincent van Gogh

The much acclaimed Don Maclean song *Starry, Starry Night*, written in 1972, linked two of Vincent's most famous works, *The Starry Night* and *Portrait of a Peasant (Patience Escalier)*. The song portrays a star-crossed man who is repulsed in love and takes his life. It also is a story of child-like innocence shattered by an uncaring world. Here are some lines from the song:

> *"Starry, starry night.*
> *Flaming flowers that brightly blaze,*
> *Swirling clouds in violet haze,*
> *Reflect in Vincent's eyes of china blue.*
> *Colors changing hue, morning field of amber grain,*
> *Weathered faces lined in pain,*
> *Are soothed beneath the artist's loving hand.*
>
> *Starry, starry night.*
> *Portraits hung in empty halls,*
> *Frameless heads on nameless walls,*
> *With eyes that watch the world and can't forget.*
> *Like the strangers that you've met,*
> *The ragged men in ragged clothes,*
> *The silver thorn of bloody rose,*
> *Lie crushed and broken on the virgin snow.*

Now I understand what you tried to say to me,
How you suffered for your sanity,
How you tried to set them free.
They would not listen, they did not know how.
Perhaps they'll listen now."

The Starry Night and *Portrait of a Peasant (Patience Escalier)* had an even deeper connection than Don McLean intuited—one that has seemingly gone undetected by scholars and which, when fully examined, alters our understanding of these important works. The link between these paintings is supplied by Vincent's letters and literary preoccupation, especially his absorption in Hugo's popular novel *Les Misérables.*

We have noticed how paintings and literary influences constantly interacted with each other throughout Vincent's career. He found great inspiration in Hugo's epic *Les Miserables* with its huge cast of common people, noting how Hugo used the stars and luminous objects as symbols of enlightenment and moral transformation. During Vincent's confinement at San Remy, he needed to restore his spirituality and revitalize his father's moral and religious legacy. In active pursuit of this, he painted *The Starry Night.* While still in Arles, he had already painted *Portrait of a Peasant (Patience Escalier).* Then, drawing inspiration from the pages of the Gospel, he produced other significant works such as *The Good Samaritan, The Pieta,* and *The Raising of Lazarus.*

The circumstances surrounding these paintings coincided with Vincent's "terrible need" of religion. This "need" was provoked by his unresolved feelings about his father's death, as he was the primary representative of religion in Vincent's life. We recall from earlier chapters that a conflict separated Vincent and his father following Vincent's dismissal as a missionary in the Borinage mining camps. The tension between them still existed when his father passed away in 1885. Several years later, facing his own imminent death, Vincent felt the need to make peace with his father's memory and with the remaining members of his family.

"That does not prevent me from having a terrible need of—shall I say the word?—of religion. Then I go out at night to paint the stars, and I am always dreaming of a picture like this."

"Just as I'm writing to you, the poor peasant [Patience Escalier] who is like a caricature of Father happens to have come into the café. The resemblance is terrible, all the same. Especially the uncertainty and the weariness and the vagueness of the mouth. I still feel it is a pity that I have not been able to do it [to paint Escalier]."

Vincent had relocated to the small town of Arles in southern France following a tumultuous time in Paris between 1886-1887. As so often happened in Vincent's life, someone appeared at a crucial moment to play a decisive role. As he mentioned, the local peasant who entered the café Vincent frequented bore a startling resemblance to his deceased father. This chance meeting led to some of the most emotionally wrought portraits in the history of art—a father's posthumous portrait painted vicariously using the face of another. The result was several of Vincent's best known images, but the underlying meaning of these works has never been fully examined in any historical analysis.

His father's look-alike was Patience Escalier, an elderly field hand. Vincent persuaded him to pose and paid him for his time. One of the paintings that emerged from this unusual encounter was of a sun-darkened man, wearing a glowing yellow straw hat woven in heavily-pigmented strokes. A massive cerulean blue jacket with jade green accents cascaded over his sloping shoulders. The dividing line between his shoulders and the radiant orange background surrounding him was outlined in Prussian blue, which activated the colors. He wore a red scarf complemented by his orange-red sleeves. His stubby, leathered hands rested upon a cane. His face is bronzed, painted with sunset hues: yellow-orange, red-violet and gold-white. With his penetrating blood-shot eyes, weary red lips and chiseled jaw, he was totally vulnerable, yet venerable, and tenderly human. Translated as a peasant embodiment of the rural-residing Theodorus van Gogh, the portrait conveyed the father's love of nature, showing simple piety, unpretentiousness, and a rugged self-sacrificial aura. The surface of this work is resiliently tacky, the paint stuck on and still wet-looking after more than a hundred years. The glossy oil has the consistency of fruit juice hardened under a blazing sun. The pallette is hot and signals that Escalier had been sunburnt and exhausted by a hard life. It conveys a steady message of silent suffering. It is, in many ways, a portrait of death—the sunset of human life. In the most literal way it chronicles the daily sunset that ends Patience's working days.

Further insightful comments about this work entitled *The Old Peasant, Patience Escalier, 1888* (now in the Stavios Niarchos Collection in Athens), were made by art historian Judy Sund (2002):

"As Vincent observed to Wil [his younger sister], 'By intensifying all the colours, one arrives again at quietude and harmony...similar to what happens in Wagner's music, which, though played by a large orchestra, is nonetheless intimate.' The play of cool blues amid the heated hues of Escalier's 'sun-steeped' skin and against the vivid warmth of kerchief, cuffs and backdrop, makes for an uncannily calm effect. In this second image, Vincent traded the colouristic commotion of 'the height of harvest-time' for the 'sunset-radiance' of a palette that is heightened and allusive rather than 'locally true': the orange ground, he remarked, 'does not pretend to be the image of a red sunset', but 'may nonetheless suggest one.' In conjunction with explicit markers of age and fatigue (the model's bleary-eyed gaze beneath graying brows, and round-shouldered posture over his stick); this colouristic hint of day's end implies the closeness of death, even as the man's smock and hands bespeak his labouring life."

The similarities to Vincent's father are remarkable. Van Gogh was especially sensitive to names and word combinations. In this he was influenced by Charles Dickens, master of the double-name literary device. We recall Dickens's *David Copper-field* or *Stephan Black-pool* where the name combination gives the reader a clue into the identity of the character. In the portraits of the peasant, the French words *patience* and *escalier* carry an interesting literary connection with Vincent's father that has never been noted—*patience* meaning long-suffering, and *escalier* meaning stairs or a stairway. A simple combination of the names would be rendered "patient climbing" or even "steady progress." Considering that Pastor Theodorus was known for his long-suffering and moral perseverance, the name could not have been more appropriate. Vincent would not have missed the significance of the name and its connection with his deceased father.

The moral implication of the series is powerful, considering that Vincent always maintained that self-sacrificial love was the ultimate test of moral worth. What adds to our reading of the paintings is to learn that Vincent's father was in effect sacrificed as a result of Vincent's volatile behavior. The hands appear to be folded in prayerful resignation.

Vincent's unresolved feelings following his father's sudden death can be discerned in numerous letters and paintings made immediately after Theodorus's funeral in 1885. These included a still-life of his father's Bible, and another of his father's pipe and tobacco pouch. However, while these works feature still-life objects associated with his father's daily life, the Escalier portraits forced Vincent to literally face his father through the surrogate peasant and reckon with his guilt, working out his atonement through this series of works.

At roughly the same time in 1888, as he completed the Escalier portraits, he painted a series of portraits of his mother. This was the only time in his career he painted his parents (what has long been regarded as a profile of his father from the early 1880s is now believed to be his grandfather). When we bear in mind that Vincent's aesthetic projects were typically a means to work out real-life issues, the question would be what issues did these parental portraits portend? Unlike the Escalier painting, the *Portrait of the Artist's Mother* of 1888 (see Page 30) was celebratory rather than confessional. He had effectively reflected on both of his parents and their meaning to him during his mid-life.

Where the mournful mood of the Escalier painting troubles and provokes our solicitude, his mother's portrait comforts. Where the fatherly Escalier was solidly constructed and beautifully linear, she seems woven as much as painted with thick, decisive strokes. Contoured touches define cheeks, chin, and powerful forehead, and define amused lips and bright, alert eyes. Where Escalier blazes with a tender fire, Anna softly glows in strands of light-colored pigment set against a quiet green background. The overall soothing green is heightened with warm black, and brick-red drawing, with touches of lilac, soft brown, and cream white. The effect is life-giving in contrast to the death-torched expression of the Theodorus "stand-in." Her skin is smooth and healthy rather than parched and leathered. It has a lightness that suggests the healing cuisine of this gifted cook. The portrait is a tribute to a gifted knitter, water colorist, and indefatigable writer of comforting letters. The notion of a vitally alive, witty, and playful woman is broadcast in this image of Anna Cornelia Van Gogh. Vincent's artistic urges were encouraged and modeled by her, more than by his father, and her portrait seems to convey all of this.

Where his father's "double" is portrayed as powerfully vulnerable and dedicated, his mother is shown as resilient and lively. She did, in fact, outlive her husband (who died at sixty-three) by two and a half decades (and Vincent by 50 years), dying at the age of eighty-seven. She continued to write to Vincent until the end of his life. He was to send her one of his very last, most appreciative, and prophetic letters hinting at his own death. The letter resonated with the uncertainty of life and Vincent's hope of one day being reunited with those he loved, especially his parents. He quoted a key passage from St. Paul's famous Epistle on love which culminated in the unveiling of life's ultimate meaning: "For now we see in a mirror dimly, but then face to face" (1 Cor. 13:12 NASB).

The portraits of his parents allowed Vincent to resolve in some measure his conflicted feelings about them and his own sense of disappointment and regret at having caused them suffering. The portraits can also be understood to represent contrasting sides of Vincent's personality; one paternal and self-sacrificial to the point of self-immolation, the other maternal and healing. It was the powerful oscillations between these two poles that generated the moral tensions in his life. Consider, for instance, that in his final, most desperate days he wrote comforting letters to his next of kin, and painted a chain of consoling images based on re-generation and transcendent love. Then he shot himself in the most pragmatic fashion, denying himself all further consolation.

We can gain some perspective on the dynamics that influenced his actions by looking back over letters as early as 1882. There was a serious exchange in these letters, the first from Theo to Vincent:

"That you could not bear it there any longer is possible, and that you differ in opinion with people who lived all their lives in the country and have not come into contact with modern life is not unnatural; but confound it, what made you so childish and impudent as to embitter and spoil Father's and Mother's life in that way? It is not difficult to fight against someone who is already tired. When Father wrote me about it, I thought it might be a misunderstanding, but you yourself say in your letter: it will not be redressed so easily. Don't you know him then, and don't you feel that Father cannot live as long as there is a quarrel between you two?"

Vincent defensively fired back:

"Every time you say something to Father which he hasn't an answer for, he produces an expression of this kind; for instance, he will say, "You are murder-ing me," meanwhile reading the paper and smoking his pipe in complete tran-quility. So I take such expressions for what they really are...Father is excessively touchy and irritable and full of waywardness in his home life, and he thinks he is entitled to getting his own way...I told Father a good many things which his Honor saw fit to fling to the winds. So as to the things I said when I lost my temper, I think the same in a calmer mood...But when I flew into a rage, my diplomacy was swept away and, well, on this occasion I really let fly. I will not

apologize for this, and as long as Father and Mother persevere in this mood, I shall not take anything back...And further, as to such expressions as "I cannot bear it," "I am being murdered," "My life is embittered," I do not attach importance to them any more, for they are only a manner of speaking."

Theo seemed to have had a deeper understanding of his father's vulnerability than did Vincent: "Don't you know him then, and don't you feel that Father cannot live as long as there is a quarrel between you two?" The suggestion that unresolved conflict might actually kill their father was made by someone who knew him well. Yet Vincent ignored Theo's pleas. It was also around this time (1882) that his parents seriously considered committing Vincent to a mental institution.

Two years later in 1884, following his breakup with Sien, Vincent returned in a final homecoming, but from the start it was overshadowed by tragedy. Within a month of his arrival, Vincent's elderly mother fell while boarding a train and fractured her right thighbone. The leg was set in a full-leg cast which forced her to remain bed-ridden for several months. As a result of her lengthy convalescence, she developed bed sores and complications which slowed her recovery. Vincent wrote to his friend Rappard:

"Now I am glad I am here, as my sisters are physically weak too, and I can easily find something useful to do...My mother will require a lot of nursing— the doctor assures us that she can recover completely—but under the most favorable circumstances it will take at least half a year before she can walk again and even then that leg will be shorter than the other one."

And then:

"My mother is recovering steadily; the fracture is healed now, and the plaster cast has been taken off. But she will still have to keep her leg in a horizontal position for about six weeks. Yesterday, however, we carried her to the living room

on a kind of litter as a trial, and later on we shall be able to carry her into the open air too once in a while."

As her nurse and companion, Vincent's skills were praised by both his mother and the attending doctor, and it was acknowledged that Vincent played a crucial role in Anna's recovery and morale. This care helped to soothe the troubled waters he had left in his wake two years earlier. During Anna's recovery, she was visited almost daily by her next door neighbor, the auburn-haired Margot Begemann.

While caring for his mother, Vincent began a series of paintings of weavers (local male craftsmen who operated the large looms of the region). The weavers were sullen, silent men who worked against the tide of history, their livelihood already undermined by industrial weaving factories. Vincent saw them as long-suffering victims, much like his father, put out to pasture with dwindling reward.

Vincent purchased a spinning wheel (seemingly inspired by the mysterious old spinning woman whom he featured in his letter from Drenthe) and made numerous drawings of it. Male weavers and female spinners, maternal and paternal images overlapped and later, after his father's death, they intensified. "I can assure you those compositions with the figures are no joke, and I am deep in my work. It is like weaving— one needs all one's attention to keep the threads apart—one must manage to keep an eye on several things at once."

His bedridden mother spent her time quietly knitting. It was evident from his letters that Anna's healing and hobbies sparked a flow of domestic ideas and visual corollaries for Vincent. They centered on the persona of his mother. The healing of art and the art of healing were actualized in her convalescence. She knitted as her bones knit back together, and all the while her son wove paint into the brooding images of the weavers. Weaving, spinning, and knitting, as Judy Sund and other scholars have noted, are related to cyclical themes and seasonal cycles, time and duration, as in the weaving of fate, the web of destiny, and the thread of life.

Now, his mother's mortality allowed Vincent to conjoin these layered meanings into a sacred whole, and Vincent was celebrated in the role of her nurse. Through this healing role we discern important things about the purpose and appeal of his art. He had begun to practice art seriously as a form of therapy following his mining experiences, and then took up art as a profession in the context of his family studio while living with Sien. In that little apartment, Vincent was actively involved in Sien's recovery, as he was now with his mother.

Art was a healing activity for Vincent, a way to stanch the suffering of humanity and bind him more totally to the world he inhabited. We see this clearly in his use of domestic media in an aesthetically-medicinal way. This is in part the great appeal of his work—it brings us into the real world in the most concrete of ways, and then transports us.

Vincent's art would fulfill what we read of the beneficent Bishop from Hugo's *Les Miserables*, a book that had a profound impact on Van Gogh's moral outlook.

"He inclined towards the distressed and the repentant. The universe appeared to him like a vast disease; he perceived fever everywhere, he auscultated suffering everywhere, and, without essaying to solve the enigma, he endeavored to staunch the wound." —Victor Hugo

Of this book Vincent wrote to Theo:

"I wish you had read Les Misérables—then it would be easier for me to speak to you about it, for you might be struck by the same things that are continually coming back to my mind—this would not surprise me. I already knew the book, but since I've reread it, many things in it keep returning to my thoughts again and again."

The next passage featured his parents, winders of yarn, a weaver, and an infant, all shaded by contrasting destinies. Life and death seemed to tug at each other in this letter, as they always did in Vincent's mind, one extreme prompting another, the extremes of youth and age begging reflection about the meaning of life:

"Taking her difficult situation into consideration, I am glad to say Mother's spirits are very even and bright. And she is amused by trifles. The other day I painted for her the little church with the hedge and the trees (like this).

You will easily understand that I love the scenery here. When you come, I shall take you into the cottages of the weavers. The figures of the weavers, and the women who wind the yarn, will certainly strike you.

The last study I made is the figure of a man sitting at the loom, the figure apart, the bust and hands. I am painting a loom of old, greenish, browned oak, in which the date 1730 is cut. Near that loom, in front of a little window which looks out on a green plot, there is a baby chair, and a baby sits in it, looking for hours at the shuttle flying to and fro. I have painted that thing exactly as it was in reality, the loom with the little weaver, the little window and the baby chair in the miserable little room with the loam floor...
...Love from all, Write to Mother a little more often, letters are such a distraction."

Months later, when his mother was on her feet again, and just as the family had breathed a collective sigh of relief, Vincent shocked everyone when it was discovered that he was involved emotionally with the passionate Margot Begemann. The repercussions were devastating. Margot was impressed by Vincent's assured healing ways as she visited Vincent's recuperating mother, and she fell in love with him. Margot's family attempted to break up the relationship—reminiscent of the previous affair with Kee. In desperation she swallowed poison. In a dramatic, last-minute intervention, Vincent saved her life by carrying her to a local doctor who pumped her stomach.

The rippling news of Margot's suicide attempt spread throughout the tiny village. Approaching the Begemann family as a peace maker, Vincent's father was rebuffed, and his reputation as a village pastor tarnished. As if this scandal were not enough, a peasant girl who had been modeling for Vincent became pregnant, and Vincent was rumored to be the father.

"He vowed to remain in Brabant, and his work continued apace until Gordina de Groot, an unmarried Catholic working woman who sometimes modelled for Vincent, became visibly pregnant. The Protestant artist—a bourgeois interloper in peasant garb—was rumored to be the father (unjustly, he insisted)..."
—Sund 2002

The shock of Anna's fall, the suicide attempt of a neighbor, repeated scandals, and years of Vincent's unceasing assaults against corruption in the clergy, were all more than his father could take. Theodorus had a sudden stroke, as he had predicted he would, and died. Vincent was surely haunted by his father's prophetic words: "I am being murdered."

Following his father's death, as if hounded, Vincent embarked on a three-year drinking binge in Paris. This was the most destructive period of his life. Even so, he continued to produce some remarkable work inspired by the Impressionists who exhibited in the great city. As he gradually regained his equilibrium, he began to think of the damage he had done, recalling something he had often said in his younger days:

"It always strikes me, and it is very peculiar, that whenever we see the image of indescribable and unutterable desolation of loneliness, poverty and misery, the end or extreme of all things, the thought of God comes into our minds"

Before his descent into an alcoholic haze, and after his father's funeral in 1885, his sister, Anna, drove him out of their house. Vincent moved temporarily to Montmartre where he moved in with Theo, putting such a strain on him that Theo's health also was to suffer badly.

A. Bonger, Theo's future brother-in-law, wrote:

"Did I tell you that Vincent has moved to Montmartre? Theo is still looking frightfully ill; he literally has no face at all. That poor fellow has many cares. Moreover, his brother is making life rather a burden for him, and reproaches him with all kinds of things of which he is quite innocent."

Vincent's life in Paris was largely unrecorded as he was now living with Theo. During this rather domesticated time, he produced an astonishing number of flower paintings. We learn from later letters that it was a period of building friendships with Impressionist painters, of experimentation and the brightening of his pallette. But his primary experimentation seemed to have been with absinthe, the immensely popular, unstable liquor made from unrefined wormwood alcohol, and known to cause nerve damage, blindness, and insanity.

On Christmas Eve of 1888, after drinking a large quantity of absinthe, Vincent slashed off a portion of his ear. There are conflicting accounts of the damage. From this point, he suffered chronic bouts of epilepsy and insanity which contributed to his eventual suicide.

Absinthe was distilled (in those days very crudely) from the very ordinary-looking wormwood plant. It apparently held a secret: its aromatic leaves and flowers were naturally rich in *terpene thujone*, an aromatic, bitter substance believed to induce an inexplicable clarity of thought, an increased sense of perception, and enhanced creativity, inspiration and the ability to "see beyond"—at least according to all the absinthe-drinking nineteenth-century poets, writers, and painters.

As Trachtman reported (2005):

"*Absinthe was finally outlawed by French authorities in 1915. But while Vincent lived in Paris, the formidable green liquid, sweetened by pouring it over sugar, ran freely in the bars frequented by artists such as Manet, Degas and Lautrec. Lautrec was one of Vincent's closest companions during that time, and together they haunted the same establishments, and partnered in the same debauchery, for the most part in the working-class district of Montmarte, notorious for thieves and brothels, as well as its hangouts for the Bohemian element of avant-garde artists and literary anarchists.*

Radicals had been attacking official French culture ever since poet Charles Baudelaire urged painters to depict modern life, and the painter Gustave Courbet declared that "art must be dragged through the gutter." Lautrec's teacher, Cormon, painted large tableaux of the Stone Age, but he knew his students were drawn to the street life beyond his atelier, and he tolerated their forays into the "gutter." . . .

Lautrec, however, seemed driven to squander his glory by drinking himself into an early grave. At the height of his success, there were nights when he would completely disappear, eventually dragging himself from the gutter as if taking Courbet's prescription quite literally. Towards the end, hallucinations and paranoia, induced by alcoholism and syphilis, would overwhelm him. On one occasion, when visiting friends in the country, a shot was heard from his room. He was found sitting on his bed brandishing a pistol against "attacking" spiders. Eventually, he was locked up in an asylum where, like his friend Vincent, he continued to work. In a burst of artistic energy, he produced a brilliant series of circus drawings from memory to convince his doctor he was sane.

Eleven weeks later, he was released, but he was soon drinking again. He spent his last days in his mother's garden, where he often painted her, and died in her arms in 1901, shortly before his 37th birthday."

The parallels between Lautrec and Van Gogh are striking: they both died at around thirty-seven years of age, suffering from alcoholism, venereal disease, and insanity. Vincent later commented on this time in his life:

"Some days ago I was reading in the Figaro the story of a Russian writer [Dostoevsky?] who suffered all his life from a nervous disease which he finally died of, and which brought on terrible attacks from time to time. And what's to be done? There is no cure, or if there is one, it is working zealously. I dwell on this more than I should. And altogether I would rather have a downright illness like this than be the way I was in Paris while this was brewing. And you can see this when you put the portrait with the light background that I have just finished next to the self-portraits in Paris, and that I look saner now than I did then, even much more so."

Vincent's large consumption of absinthe combined with the syphilis he had contracted years earlier provoked strange behavior during this period. He suffered from blackouts and bizarre mental behavior and mood swings. He claimed that when he finally left Paris during the spring of 1888, he was on the verge of a stroke, the very thing that had killed his father. And he was haunted by guilt, and the idea that he did not deserve his brother Theo's kindness. He also felt he had caused Theo's descent into ill health. Realizing he had to make changes, he fled to rural Arles in Provence, and swore he would never live in a large city again. He remained true to his word.

In Arles, Vincent reported that his health had greatly improved as a result of the fresh air and hearty food. The countryside reminded him of rural Holland, Drenthe, his childhood, and of his parents. It was during this time of recovery that he painted the portraits of Escalier and his mother. And in some ways, the tie between his parents' moral values and his noticeably improved health became apparent to Vincent. His licentious life in Paris, and his bouts of self-destruction, now stood in sharp contrast to the simpler ambience of rural Provence. His art and letters became a continual discourse on existential issues, spiritual yearning, moral themes, sincere regrets, and thoughts about the after-life. His "terrible" need for religion was to intensify.

In early 1889, after his first self-committed stay at the San Remy Asylum, he was able for the first time in his life to admit his shortcomings:

"I often feel much self-reproach about the things in the past, my illness being more or less my own fault, in any case I doubt if I can make up for faults in any way"

Vincent's thoughts moved back and forth— from past regrets to eternal hope. These tugging and "terrible" urges received embodiment in one of his most thematically rich works, *The Starry Night of 1889*. His life-long preoccupation with bodily resurrection reappeared. He wanted to discuss Christ with artists such as Emile Bernard whom he met in Paris. In a letter to Bernard, he likened Christ to a divine artist whose ultimate work was the transformation of life and death into resurrected glory and eternal life:

"Christ alone—of all the philosophers, Magi, etc.—has affirmed, as a principal certainty, eternal life, the infinity of time, the nothingness of death, the necessity and the raison d'etre of serenity and devotion. He lived serenely, as a greater artist than all other artists, despising marble and clay as well as color, working in living flesh. That is to say, this matchless artist, hardly to be conceived of by the obtuse instrument of our modern, nervous, stupefied brains, made neither statues nor pictures nor books; he loudly proclaimed that he made...living men, immortals.

This is serious, especially because it is the truth...And who would dare tell us that he [Jesus] lied on that day when, scornfully foretelling the collapse of the Roman edifice, he declared, Heaven and earth shall pass away, but my words shall not pass away...
...But seeing that nothing opposes it—supposing that there are also lines and forms as well as colors on the other innumerable planets and suns—it would

remain praiseworthy of us to maintain a certain serenity with regard to the pos-
sibilities of painting under superior and changed conditions of existence, an ex-
istence changed by a phenomenon no queerer and no more surprising than the
transformation of the caterpillar into a butterfly, or the white grub into the
cockchafer.

The existence of painter-butterfly would have for its field of action one of the
innumerable heavenly bodies, which would perhaps be no more inaccessible to
us, after death, than the black dots which symbolize towns and villages on ge-
ographical maps are in our terrestrial existence."

As his health started to decline as rapidly as it had seemed to improve, he visualized hope now in an eternal abode, seeing a place where the healing concerns of his mother and spiritual legacy of his father were ultimately translated into the moral beauty of Christ transfigured into His Resurrection. *The Starry Night* was the embodiment of these concerns; it was a work that expressed his deepest spiritual aspirations in an image of transcendent beauty understood as the resurrection of humankind and of the universe, as described so powerfully in the Book of Revelation and so poetically in the Book of Romans in the New Testament. Its diverse themes include transformation, transportation, redemption, fulfillment, and deliverance from the cycles of death and suffering into eternal life.

"Then I saw a new heaven and a new earth; for the first heaven and the first
earth passed away, and there is no longer any sea. And I saw the holy city, new
Jerusalem, coming down out of heaven from God, made ready as a bride adorned
for her husband." (Revelation 21:1-2, NASB)

In his movement toward eternal light, Vincent had to pass beyond darkness and despair—a darkness that involved terrible bouts of epilepsy, some of which lasted weeks at a time, profound hyper-anxiety, and hyper-sensitivity to sounds and voices. For Vincent, this dark period had to be worked through visually. He regarded insanity as obscuring light, or as some strangely distorted perspective that made what was near appear far away. Yet he would ultimately find a way out of the darkness through his strong belief in God.

Opposite: "Bedroom in Arles" by Vincent van Gogh, 1889. Oil on canvas.
In the collection of the Musee d'Orsay, Paris.

THE BISHOP'S DOCTRINE

*"I won't hide from you that I don't dislike the country, as I have been
brought up there—I am still charmed by the magic of hosts of memories of
the past, of a longing for the infinite, of which the sower, the sheaf are the symbols—
just as much as before. But when shall I paint my starry sky,
that picture which preoccupies me continuously?
...One must attack them nonetheless, however incompetent one may feel
before the unspeakable perfection, the glorious splendors of nature."*

—Vincent van Gogh

Vincent's favorite motif was as we recall that of a shining star, or blazing sun or moon, shining into the darkness inviting comfort. The theme had first appeared in his letters written during those dark days in the Borinage as he literally descended and ascended the mineshafts in rattling elevator cages. The motif of light out of darkness was also the central motif of *Les Misérables*, the literary source that now came to dominate his thoughts. "All lava begins at midnight. The catacombs, where the first mass was said, were not merely the cave of Rome; they were the cavern of the world."—Victor Hugo.

One of the main characters in *Les Misérables* was a father-figure in the most literal sense, a priest named Father Bienvenu, also referred to by Hugo and Van Gogh as "the Benedictine Father," "Monseigneur," "the Bishop," or "M. Myriel". Vincent described the Bishop as "sublime," a word he rarely used, and only in reference to one other being—Jesus Christ.

'It is very beautiful, that figure of Monseigneur Myriel or Beinvenu I think sublime...It is good to read such a book again, I think, just to keep some feelings alive. Especially love for humanity, and the faith in, and consciousness of, something higher, in short, quelque chose la haut [that which is on high]."

Hugo presents us with the creed of Bishop Bienvenu:

"Love one another; he declared that to be complete; he desired nothing more, and it was his whole doctrine. One day, this man, who counted himself 'a philosopher,' this senator before mentioned, said to the bishop: 'See now, what the world shows; each fighting against all others; the strongest man is the best man. Your love one another is a stupidity.' ' replied Monseigneur Bienvenu, without discussion, 'if it be a stupidity, the soul ought to shut itself up in it, like the pearl in the oyster.' And he shut himself up in it, he lived in it, he was satisfied absolutely with it, laying aside the mysterious questions which attract and which dishearten, the unfathomable depths of abstraction, the precipices of metaphysics."

Vincent found the doctrine of the Bishop deeply consoling, and must have noted that the name Bienvenu, like Patience Escalier, also had a rich double meaning in French; in addition to its common meaning of "welcome," when broken into its parts, bien means good and venu means timing, or "glad tidings." Hugo, who like Dickens invented names that revealed underlying personal characteristics, equated the Bishop to the Gospel's angelic heralding of Christ's birth (glad tidings of comfort and joy). Hugo intended that the Bishop be perceived as a Christ-figure. Creating characters that were "morally beautiful" and Christ-like was a goal for a number of important nineteenth-century writers, including Hugo, Dickens, and Dostoevsky. Vincent had a strong interest in all of these writers and their views, including Dostoevsky's:

"Dostoevsky had, of course, proclaimed as early as 1854 that 'there is nothing more beautiful [prekrasnee]...than Christ', but it was only after these reflections of 1864 that he repeatedly classified, not only the supreme moral state that Christ uniquely possessed, but good moral states, acts, and agents generally under the rubric 'beautiful', in both his fiction and nonfiction. Perhaps the best-known instance is his remarks to correspondents about his work on The Idiot. To his friend Maykov, he wrote at the end of 1867 that the novel's idea was 'to depict a thoroughly beautiful person'. In a letter of early 1868 to his beloved

niece Sofya, he expanded on this notion, turning once again to the model of Christ: The chief idea of the novel is to depict a positively beautiful person. Nothing in the world is more difficult, especially now." —Scanlan, 2002

Vincent's attraction to Hugo's work concerned the issue of moral beauty. Vincent struggled all his life to live by the doctrine of loving one another, thus abiding by strict moral imperatives. Hugo's character was based on an actual French bishop who had lived in a small village, this being another parallel for Vincent with his father. At the time of Theodorus's death in 1885, an ancient Romanesque church tower near Nuenen that Vincent greatly admired was demolished by local developers. Vincent painted the tower and its surrounding graves many times. It was an image like those found in Hugo. The demise of this ancient symbol along with the death of his pastor father (and incidentally of Victor Hugo) all in the same year, reminded Vincent of the central theme of *Les Misérables*—the permanence of God and the moral beauty of Christ, in the face of institutional decay and the death of its ministers.

After his father's funeral, Vincent cited the following:

"And now those ruins tell me how a faith and a religion moldered away— strongly founded though they were—but how the life and the death of the peasants remain forever the same, budding and withering regularly, like the grass and the flowers growing there in that churchyard. "Les religions passent, Dieu demeure" [Religions pass away, God remains], is a saying of Victor Hugo's whom they also brought to rest recently."

Father Bienvenu knew full well that the dark night of the soul is a universal experience for every believer. The Bishop's pragmatism imaginatively helped Vincent to set aside his long-standing hatred of the religious administrators who had fired him years earlier in Belgium. This in turn helped him make peace with his father's memory as a religious representative. This chain of moral reflections circled back again to the Bishop who offered Vincent the form, theme, and spiritual motivation to commence painting his long desired *Starry Night*.

Many scholars of art have wondered about the source of *The Starry Night*, arguably Vincent's best-known painting. They all feel that the title is important and likely stems from a literary source or idea. However, to date no absolute identification has ever been found that would satisfy many of the uncertainties about this work. However, in this writer's estimation, there is conclusive proof of the title and content of this work. But before offering this proof, it is important to first analyze one of the most widely accepted opinions on its origin.

The most authoritative interpretation of the origins of *The Starry Night* was based on a reading of Van Gogh's letters, and provided by the late, great art historian, Meyer Schapiro. He suggested (in the following quote) that *Les Misérables* and Vincent's *Starry Night* have profound connections:

"His sincerity, requiring always faithfulness to direct experience, kept him from inventing religious pictures. When inspired by the vision of The Starry Night, he put into his painting of the sky the exaltation of his desire for a mystical union and release, but no theology, no allegories of the divine...There is, however, in the coiling nebula and in the strangely luminous crescent—an anomalous complex of moon and sun and earth/shadow, locked in an eclipse—a possible unconscious reminiscence of the apocalyptic theme of the woman in pain of birth, girded with the sun and moon and crowned with the stars, whose newborn child is threatened by the dragon (Revelation 12, I ff.). When he returns to his theme at Saint Remy, after a period of crisis and religious hallucinations, the pressure of feeling, with its hidden tendencies and content, forces the bounds of the visible and determines the fantastic projections, the great coiling spiral nebula, the eleven magnified stars, and the incredible orange moon, with the light between its horns—a confused memory, perhaps, of an eclipse (he quoted Hugo: "God is a lighthouse in eclipse"), or an attempt to unite sun and moon into one figure; the tremendous flame/formed cypresses, the dark earthly, vertical counterpart of the dragon nebula, may also be an invention here, transferred from other landscapes, as a vague symbol of a human striving.

The whole owes its immediacy and power to the impulsive, torrential flow of brush/strokes, the release of feeling along great paths..."

Schapiro's comment that there are "no allegories of the divine" in *The Starry Night* was correct. Vincent did not allegorize; he visualized from experiences in daily life or envisioned from what he read. Following Schapiro's analysis of the painting, he quoted a letter in which Vincent had Hugo say: "God is a lighthouse in eclipse." Shapiro cited from Vincent's letter but slightly misquoted Vincent who actually says: "God is an occulting lighthouse (in French it would even more accurately translate as an eclipsing lighthouse)."

Schapiro has for some reason not used Vincent's actual wording. The lighthouse imagery in this passage is important for it provides a clue into what I believe is its intended meaning and provides insight into the likely source of Vincent's painting. The passage in Vincent that Schapiro cites regarding the lighthouse seems to be a paraphrase by Vincent of something the bishop says in the novel.

Hugo's view of the lighthouse is quite different from an eclipse and the related ominous death of stars that one finds in the first chapters of the book of Revelation and which Schapiro believed Vincent was recalling. In Hugo's view, the oscillating, flashing, signal of a lighthouse as a beacon of light is stressed. All the same Vincent used the phrase but not in the negative way Shapiro would prefer.

Schapiro's claim that the work had "apocalyptic" meanings but "no theology" is an apparent contradiction, for the book of Revelation is a truly theological work. But it is not to St. John's vision which included destruction and wrath leading to the transformation of the universe that we need to look, for apocalyptic signs such as the moon darkening or turning to blood, or stars falling, are completely absent from the Van Gogh painting.

The desire to give Vincent's work a torrential and tormented meaning, apocalyptic or otherwise, was common earlier in the twentieth century. Critic after critic beginning in the 1950s insisted on expressive and hyper-symbolic meanings closer to abstract expressionist angst and cold-war perplexity than to the realistic, saturated world that Vincent inhabited. However, it is not necessary to quote art historians on the meaning of this work as Vincent himself gave us all of the information we need.

Meyer Schapiro was wise to read Vincent's letters, for Shapiro came the closest to discovering the source of the work in *Les Miserables* following the lead Vincent gave him. But Schapiro did not look far enough into the massive novel. If he had, he would not have been content with lighthouses and eclipsing moons alone however relevant these symbols seem; he would have sought the entire starry sky. To find this and the exact title Vincent used for *The Starry Night* he needed to read the Bishop's prayer, a passage Vincent clearly loved. The meaning is as naturally supernatural as the resurrection of the dead, where the body is given new flesh and bone and made eternal for an endless existence. Let us examine the actual passage in Vincent's letters that Schapiro referenced, and see what Vincent's underlying concerns may in fact have been:

"Enclosed a little sketch of a square size 30 canvas, the starry sky actually painted at night under a gas jet. The sky is greenish-blue, the water royal blue, the round mauve. The town is blue and violet, the gas is yellow and the reflections are russet-gold down to greenish-bronze. On the blue-green expanse of sky the Great Bear sparkles green and pink, its discreet pallor contrasts with the harsh gold of the gas.

Two colorful little figures of lovers in the foreground. . . .
. . . And it does me good to do difficult things. That does not prevent me from having a terrible need of—shall I say the word?—of religion. Then I go out at night to paint the stars, and I am always dreaming of a picture like this with a group of living figures of our comrades. . . .

That Benedictine Father [Bishop Bienvenu] must have been very interesting. What would the religion of the future be according to him? He will probably say, Always the same as that of the past. Victor Hugo says, God is an occulting lighthouse [the French call it an eclipsing lighthouse], and if this should be the case we are passing through the eclipse now...

...I should not be surprised if you liked the "Starry Night" and the "Plowed Fields," there is a greater quiet about them than in the other canvases...As for the "Starry Sky", I'd still like very much to paint it, and perhaps one of these nights I shall be in the same plowed field if the sky is sparkling.

Tolstoy's book My Religion was published in French as early as 1885, but I have never seen it in any catalogue. He does not seem to believe much in the resurrection of the body or the soul. Above all he seems not to believe much in heaven—he reasons so like a nihilist—but—and here he parts company with them—he attaches great importance to doing what you are doing well, since it is probably all you have.

But he does not believe in the resurrection, he seems to believe in the equiva-lent—the continuance of life—the progress of humanity—the man and his work almost infallibly continued by humanity in the next generation, so the solution he gives is ephemeral."

Note to begin with that Vincent used lower case letters the first time he mentioned the starry sky, and upper case the second time he referenced it. I believe this emphasis is explained by his reference to "That Benedictine Father" (the Bishop) which is included in the same pas-sage; Vincent was implying that he planned to later paint the Bishop's celebratory *Starry Night* in contrast to the earlier, more earthly (1888) version of *Starry Sky* which featured the Rhone River and a prosaic gas-lit view of Arles with lovers.

The second version of 1889 had obviously not yet been painted (the letter was written in 1888). Plans for the later version appeared in context with Tolstoy and include speculation about eternal life. Clearly, the second version was tied to theological concepts, specifically the res-urrection as Vincent indicated clearly.

We recall how important reading was for Vincent following his severe exhaustion in the Borinage and how reassuring stories encouraged him. Dickens, Stowe, and Hugo all played a major role in his effort to stabilize his life. In his final years, Vincent also derived a sense of familial cohesion by recalling family circumstances and events associated with certain novels. Novels, in addition to their implicit messages, offered Vincent a sense of continuity which was especially important as he struggled to recover his memory after each attack of insanity. Note how he relates *Les Misérables* and *A Tale of Two Cities* to memories of his grandfather:

"Dickens, who usually wrote about his own time, could not resist writing the Tale of Two Cities, and every now and then we see descriptions of the old days inserted in his work—a description of the London streets before there were street lamps, for instance...In Les Misérables, although it treats of a later era, I find what I have been looking for—aspects of the past that induce me to remember how everything looked in my great-grandfather's day, or even no longer ago than my grandfather's time."

Vincent made extensive comments about *Les Misérables* and its link to generalized paternal figures and to Holland's past. Hegel's *Aesthetics* celebrated their paternal and fraternal piety, Dutch home life, and related activities such as weaving and farming; all of these things had their parallels in French history and in *Les Misérables*.

"I am reading Les Misérables by Victor Hugo. A book which I remember of old, but I had a great longing to read it again, just as one can have a great longing to see a certain picture again. It is very beautiful, that figure of Monseigneur Myriel or Beinvenu I think sublime...It is good to read such a book again, I think, just to keep some feelings alive. Especially love for humanity, and the faith in, and consciousness of, something higher, in short, quelque chose la-haut [that which is on high].

I was absorbed in it for hours this afternoon, and then came into the studio about the time the sun was setting. From the window I looked down on a wide dark foreground—dug-up gardens and fields of warm black earth of a very deep tone. Diagonally across it runs a little path of yellowish sand, bordered with green grass and slender young poplars. The background was formed by a gray silhouette of the city, with the round roof of the railway station, and spires, and chimneys. And moreover, backs of houses everywhere; but at that time of evening, everything is blended by the tone. So viewed in a large way, the whole thing is simply a foreground of black dug-up earth, a path across it, horizon, the red sun. It was exactly like a page from Hugo, and I am sure that you would have been struck by it".

A short time after sending this letter, he cites Hugo again:

"I am reading the last part of Les Misérables; the figure of Fantine, a prostitute made a deep impression on me—oh, I know just as well as everybody else that one will not find an exact Fantine in reality, but this character of Hugo's is true—as indeed, are all his characters, being the essence of what one sees in reality."

We already can sense the evolution of Vincent's thought regarding *The Starry Night*. Vincent had begun to envision it and its grounding in *Les Misérables* as early as 1883, as indicated in the above letters.

"The background was formed by a gray silhouette...So viewed in a large way, the whole thing is simply a foreground of black dug-up earth, a path across it, horizon, the red sun. It was exactly like a page from Hugo, and I am sure that you would have been struck by it."

We recall what Vincent had said about the landscape of the Borinage—"it was like a page of the Gospel". Now the landscape was like a page out of Hugo—we see him uniting themes of comfort, the natural landscape, and healing with the beauty of the Gospel and its moral call: "The faith in, and consciousness of, something higher...that which is on high."

The tall slender trees, the distant village, the spire of a church, the plowed earth, and the general mood in the landscape Vincent saw through the window can all be found in *The Starry Night*. The visual memory of this "page from Hugo" had been married to the Bishop's night prayer from the same novel. Vincent had literally taken these pages from Hugo and specifically *Les Misérables*, and had merged them with his memories of Holland and the general view from his window at the hospital in St. Remy. We know that there was no village to be seen from his window there, no church spire, or plowed field—he had lifted these from Hugo and blended them "by the tone."

In the last years of his life, *Les Misérables* was especially comforting to Vincent because it offered him a composite range of Gospel themes and images. Consolation and forgiveness had profound meanings to a son wrestling with regret at his father's suffering and death. This passage from Hugo, in which the Bishop accompanied a condemned man to his death, must have spoken deeply to Vincent as he neared the end of his life:

"On the morrow when they came for the poor man, the bishop was with him. He followed him, and showed himself to the eyes of the crowd in his violet camail, with his bishop's cross about his neck, side by side with the miserable being, who was bound with cords.

He mounted the cart with him, he ascended the scaffold with him. The sufferer, so gloomy and so horror-stricken in the evening, was now radiant with hope. He felt that his soul was reconciled, and he trusted in God. The bishop embraced him, and at the moment when the axe was about to fall, he said to him, 'whom man kills, him God restoreth to life, whom his brethren put away, he findeth the Father. Pray, believe, enter into life! The Father is there.' When he descended from the scaffold, something in his look made the people fall back. It would be hard to say which was the most wonderful, his paleness or his serenity...

...As the most sublime things are often least comprehended, there were those in the city who said, in commenting upon the bishop's conduct that it was affectation, but such ideas were confined to the upper classes. The people, who do

not look for unworthy motives in holy works, admired and were softened."

Vincent wrote:

"I discovered that in Paris, how much more Theo did his best to help Father practically than I, so that his own interests were often neglected. Therefore I am so thankful now that Theo has got a wife and is expecting his baby. Well, Theo had more self-sacrifice than I, and that is deeply rooted in his character."

Vincent's later confinement with pathologically distressed inmates at St. Remy allowed him to see at first hand unprovoked outbursts and self-inflicted violence, witnessing similar behavior to that he had inflicted upon his father and Theo. He felt great remorse and guilt over the way he had treated his parents, realizing that they had in fact been justified in their disapproval of his frantic pursuit of his cousin Kee, and also his attitude towards the missionary society in the Borinage for his dismissal. He even admitted that his parents had good cause in attempting to send him to a mental institution. Vincent emerged from his illness with a candid self-appraisal and a late-found maturity.

From 1889 to the end of his life, there was no longer any trace of the anger and readiness to blame others that had characterized his earlier life. He had found humility. Vincent's final letters expressed compassion, identification with the suffering of others, and courage in the face of life's difficulties. The last letters to his elderly mother, sister, and Johanna were especially touching. He mused with them over his rural childhood, and expressed an abiding love and respect for his parents. He asked his mother to confirm certain details and memories from which they might derive mutual comfort. But above all, he wanted her to know how much he had appreciated the steady devotion she, his father, and Theo had shown him.

"I feel deeply...that other people, seeing symptoms of mental derangement, have naturally had apprehensions better founded than my unfounded certainty that

I was thinking normally, which was not the case. So that has much softened many of the judgments I have too often passed with more or less presumption on people who nevertheless were wishing me well. Anyhow, it is certainly a pity that with me these reflections reach the stage of feeling rather late. And that I can alter nothing in the past, of course."

"Dear Mother,

Toward the end of the year I came once more to say good day to you—you will say that I have forgotten that several times. It is a year since I fell ill, and it is difficult for me to say how far I have or have not recovered. I often feel much self-reproach about the things in the past, my illness being more or less my own fault, in any case I doubt if I can make up for faults in any way.

But reasoning and thinking about these things is sometimes so difficult, and sometimes my feelings overwhelm me more than before. And then I think so much of you and of the past. You and Father have been, if possible, even more to me than to the others, so much, so very much, and I do not seem to have had a happy character. I discovered that in Paris, how much more Theo did his best to help Father practically than I, so that his own interests were often neglected. Therefore I am so thankful now that Theo has got a wife and is expecting his baby. Well, Theo had more self sacrifice than I, and that is deeply rooted in his character. And after Father was no more and I came to Theo in Paris, then he became so attached to me that I understood how much he had loved Father. And now I am saying this to you, and not to him—it is a good thing that I did not stay in Paris, for we, he and I, would have become too interested in each other.

And life does not exist for this, I cannot tell you how much better I think it is for him this way than in the past, and he had too many tiresome business worries, and his health suffered from it."

Vincent had come to recognize his part in provoking family tensions: "You and Father have been, if possible, even more to me than to the others, so much, so very much, and I do not seem to have had a happy character." The "others" are his brothers and sisters. The main point is that Vincent now sees that he was given preferential treatment over his siblings and, in spite of this, he caused his parents the greatest grief. He believed the damage was too great to undo. In addition to his past disregard towards them, now his skill as an artist had been undermined along with his nerves.

His last drawings from Auvers supported this appraisal. They are inchoate and disorganized. His once powerful rendering ability was now reduced to twisted scrawling. Convinced he was beyond healing, he determined to end his life.

What is remarkable is that even with suicide in mind, he continued reaching out and encouraging others. We recall in earlier chapters the letter Jo (Johanna) sent to Vincent on the evening of her labor. Vincent responded to Theo:

"Today I received your good news that you are at last a father, that the most critical time is over for Jo, and finally that the little boy is well. That has done me more good and given me more pleasure than I can put into words. Bravo— and how pleased Mother is going to be. The day before yesterday I received a fairly long and very contented letter from her too. Anyhow, here it is, the thing I have so much desired for such a long time. No need to tell you that I have often thought of you these days, and it touched me very much that Jo had the kindness to write to me the very night before. She was so brave and calm in her danger, it moved me deeply. Well, it contributes a great deal to helping me forget the last days when I was ill; at such times I don't know where I am and my mind wanders."

Not only did he write comforting letters in his final days, but he honored women in a series of maternal paintings. They featured a mother comforting a child in a berceuse—a rocker. He was recalling his mother.

"And I must tell you—and you will see it in "La Berceuse," however much of a failure and however feeble that attempt may be—if I had had the strength to

continue, I should have made portraits of saints and holy women from life who would have seemed to belong to another age, and they would be middle-class women of the present day, and yet they would have had something in common with the very primitive Christians."

Debora Silverman enlarges on this unity of maternal and celestial themes in Vincent's work. This synthesis of the maternal and eternal should come as no surprise— we have seen it repeatedly in Van Gogh's art and life. Vincent saw infinity in a crib and especially in an infant's eyes: "I think I see something deeper, more infinite, more eternal than the ocean in the expression of the eyes of a little baby". Sailors, Vincent believed, rocking in their hammocks at sea, found similar maternal and eternal comfort as they navigated by the stars of the sea.

"When Vincent lived in Antwerp in 1885-1886, he walked the city and discovered the Andrieskerk, the Church of Saint Andrew, in the poor fishermen's quarter. Here a large-scale 'Maris Stella' stained glass window impressed him deeply, one of the rare instances in which the interior of a church sanctuary engaged his attention. Vincent described the window panels in detail in a letter to Theo. The sixteenth-century window presents the Virgin Mary as Maris Stella (Latin for 'Star of the Sea'), 'protectress of mariners in distress'...The Maris Stella window has never been mentioned in relation to La Berceuse or to Vincent's planned triptych project. Yet it made a deep impression on him when he saw it in 1886 and it bears some interesting affinities to the later ensemble as a visual and sacred precedent. —Debora Silverman, 2000.

The 1889 *La Berceuse* project was one of the most extensive in Vincent's career and consisted of several panels. The paint handling and attitude of the central figure recalled Vincent's portraits of his mother. There is also a strong formal connection in *La Berceuse* between the nimbus-like floral movement in its background and the caressing cloud forms and radiating stars of *The Starry Night*.

Celestial objects, flowers, maternal and paternal figures and nativity themes all held a lifelong interest for Vincent. For instance, we can recall how he placed a vase of flowers in the window for Sien and her newborn child. Or how he brought an iron crib into his studio and tacked a Rembrandt etching of the Nativity over it. We also recall how as a young man Vincent walked on a starry night to the bedside of a dying friend to offer final comfort.

The parental portraits, the *La Berceuse* series, and *The Starry Night* all celebrate parental nurturing, spiritual cultivation, and resurrection. This vision of resurrected resolution is the ultimate message of Vincent's art and life. It was already envisioned years earlier when he journeyed to the graveside of his still-born brother and waited for the sunrise:

"The sky was overcast, but the evening star was shining through the clouds, and now and then more stars appeared. It was very early when I arrived at the churchyard in Zundert; everything was so quiet. I went over all the dear old spots, and the little paths, and waited for the sunrise there. You know the story of the Resurrection—everything reminded me of it that morning in the quiet graveyard."

And it resonated on a starry night years later as he dreamt of an eternal embrace:

"The moon will shine like the sun, and the sunlight will be seven times brighter, like the light of seven full days, when the Lord binds up the bruises of his people and heals the wounds he inflicted. (Isaiah 30: 26-27, NIV)

Victor Hugo's *Les Misérables* was most certainly the origin of Vincent's painting, *Etoile Nuit (Starry Night)*. Vincent himself first established the relationship between the novel and his tribute to it. We know that Vincent was inspired by literature throughout his career and had aspired to be an illustrator, ultimately becoming both illustrator and fine artist.

He would create some of his last great works in homage to Hugo's astonishing *Les Misérables*, the words of which gave him enormous hope for humankind. It was a novel with the theme of human redemption at its core, and it appealed to Vincent since he was utterly repentant at the very end of his life. *Les Misérables* is a massive tome, exceeding 1,000 pages, yet it utterly absorbed Vincent.

Establishing the true origin of *The Starry Night* is extremely important because its literary source helps to reveal the painting's underlying meaning—something that has baffled art historians for over a century. Yet if we look carefully at Vincent's work, and then compare it with its source in Hugo's *Les Misérables,* we find some fascinating revelations.

The most noticeable feature of *The Starry Night* is the sapphire blue sky which is intensified by accents of ultramarine and violet. The contrasting colors create an atmosphere that seems both radiant and alive. The cold blue complements the warmer colors and allows the yellow orange stars and clouds to shimmer in the night sky. The stars themselves are unique, resembling flowers with expanding centers and flame-like petals springing forth from their cores. They seem to breathe as much as shine. The clouds also are strange and, rather than cluster and pile up as one would expect, they seem to gather into spirals and in the center into what appears to be an infant-like form. On the far right is a dazzling moon closing in on itself and generating a brilliant light in the night sky, pulsating outward like a celestial lighthouse. There is no hint of darkness in this glorious, transcendant orb. Lying below is what appears to be the profile of a reclining man configured by the far reaching cobalt mountains. The man seems covered under a yellow haze of light which lifts his shroud-spirit into the cosmic spectacle, wheeling and spinning his vital force up into the heavenly realms.

In the lower section of the painting lies the silent earth, green yet somber, undulating, a scintillating sea of verdant vegetation. A small Dutch village appears at center stage huddled around a sharp-spired rustic church. The church is similar to the one in which Vincent's father had ministered. On the left of the painting is a towering evergreen tree that writhes finger-like boughs into the radiating sky, human-like and adoring before the sublime spectacle. And as if humbled, the lower earth loops and crochets itself, while the sky glimmers with hundreds of converging brush strokes that breathe and exhale star pollen into a blue ocean of sky. Together they suggest a heaven and earth unity. The whole work exudes a vast mystery, an ocean of stars and a nurturing-adoring earth.

Then, we read in Hugo's *Les Misérables* of the saintly Bishop who inspired Van Gogh's prayerful nocturnal painting:

"Monseigneur Bienvenu had been formerly, according to the accounts of his youth and (even of this) early manhood, a passionate, perhaps a violent, man. His universal tenderness was less an instinct of nature than the result of a strong conviction filtered through life into his heart, slowly dropping in upon him, thought by thought; for a character, as well as a rock, may be worn into by drops of water. Such marks are ineffaceable; such formations are indestructible....

...As we have seen, prayer, celebration of the religious offices, alms, consoling the afflicted, the cultivation of a little piece of ground, fraternity, frugality, self-sacrifice, confidence, study, and work, filled up each day of his life. Filled up is exactly the word; and in fact, the bishop's day was full to the brim with good thoughts, good words, and good actions. Nevertheless it was not complete if cold or rainy weather prevented his passing an hour or two in the evening, when the two women had retired, in his garden before going to sleep. It seemed as if it were a sort of rite with him, to prepare himself for sleep by meditating in the presence of the great spectacle of the starry firmament. Sometimes at a late hour of the night, if the two women were awake, they would hear him slowly promenading the walks. He was there alone with himself, collected, tranquil, adoring, comparing the serenity of his own heart with the serenity of the skies, moved in the darkness by the visible splendours of the constellations, and the invisible splendour of God, opening his soul to the thoughts which fall from the Unknown. In such moments offering up his heart at the hour when the flowers of night inhale their perfume, lighted like a lamp in the centre of The Starry Night, expanding his soul in ecstasy in the midst of the universal radiance of creation, he could not himself perhaps have told what was passing in his own mind; he felt something depart from him, and something descend upon him; mysterious interchanges of the depths of the soul with the depths of the universe.

*He contemplated the grandeur, and the presence of God; the eternity of the fu-
ture, strange mystery; the eternity of the past, mystery yet more strange; all
the infinites deep-hidden in every direction about him....*

*He did not study God; he was dazzled by the thought. He reflected upon
these magnificent unions of atoms, which give visible forms to Nature, revealing
forces in establishing them, creating individualities in unity, proportions in ex-
tension, the innumerable in the infinite, and through light producing beauty.
These unions are forming and dissolving continually, thence life and death.*

*He would sit upon a wooden bench leaning against a broken trellis
and look at the stars through the irregular outlines of his fruit trees. This quarter
of an acre of ground, so poorly cultivated, so cumbered with shed and ruins,
was dear to him, and satisfied him.*

*What was more needed by this old man who divided the leisure hours
of his life, where he had so little leisure, between gardening in the day time, and
contemplation at night? Was not this narrow enclosure, with the sky for a
background, enough to enable him to adore God in his most beautiful as well as
in his most sublime works? Indeed, is not that all, and what more can be desired? A little garden to walk, and immensity to reflect upon. At his feet something to cultivate and gather; above his head something to study and meditate
upon; a few flowers on the earth, and all the stars in the sky."*

Victor Hugo's magisterial novel and Vincent van Gogh's life are
profoundly connected. The prayer of the Bishop included flowers that
exude perfume at night. We see flower-like stars in *Starry Night* in which
Vincent combined flower petals and star effusions in depicting the celestial orbs. The Bishop talked of descending love from God falling
silently into a sleeping, suffering world; and Vincent showed us descending radiating clouds that blanket the sky and touch the earth. The Bishop
spoke of the need to listen silently to God; and Vincent told us how he
needed to feel the presence of God as something on high. The Bishop
spoke of innumerable stars and constellations that make up the heavenly sights; and Vincent pictured and painted them. The theme of the
work was one of adoration and supplication—exactly what the Bishop
demonstrated. The mood of the Bishop's words is heartbreakingly
poignant, the romance of man and God wrapped in a lover's ecstatic
outpouring.

There are also the motives and external circumstances that surround both works. The parallels are obvious. In particular, the mood of repose at the end of day, or the end of life. Like the Bishop who, in the cool comfort of his garden at night with the vast heavens above, sought solace from the heat and labor of a long day, Vincent too sought peace at the end of a tumultuous life. The symbolism of the garden as a place of birth and regeneration is timeless, beginning with the Garden of Eden to the Garden of Gethsemane, and on to the garden in which Christ appeared resurrected. The garden is a symbol for nature itself and the origins of things. But its sacred meanings are many, including prayer (as in Gethsemane), re-creation (as in the account of the Resurrection), as well as birth (as in Eden). Hugo seemed to have all of these ideas in mind with Bishop Bienvenu.

The garden theme had been central in Vincent's body of work —he painted numerous gardens. By the time he painted *The Starry Night*, he had spent much of his time painting in the enclosed cloistered inner gardens of the St. Remy asylum, just as he had previously painted in the public gardens in Arles, and before that in his parent's vicarage garden. And one of his earliest childhood memories was of his father's garden in their first home in Brabant.

At the end of his life, Vincent contemplated these things in his portraits of Patience Escalier. The Bishop resided in the same general area near Arles where Escalier lived and worked. And, interestingly, Arles was specifically named in Hugo's novel as one of the towns over which the Bishop had jurisdiction. The Bishop worked in a garden just outside his house, and there were similar gardens both at St. Remy and Arles that Vincent could see from his window.

The Bishop's appearance and moral character is reminiscent of Vincent's deceased father (as is Patience Escalier), and the Bishop's one-time violent nature was, like Vincent's, transformed by the signaling of his moral conscience. The Bishop and Vincent's father shared an extraordinary range of similarities. Hugo described the Bishop as having "a fine head", and was described as handsome by his parishioners. He traveled long distances to comfort the sick and the poor. In similar fashion,

Theodorus Van Gogh was, according to Johanna van Gogh-Bonger,

"a man of prepossessing appearance (called by some "the handsome dominie"), with a loving nature and fine spiritual qualities; but he was not a gifted preacher, and for twenty years he lived forgotten in the little village of Zundert ere being called to other places, even then only to small villages like Etten, Helvoirt, and Nuenen. But in his small circle he was warmly loved and respected, and his children idolized him."

The Bishop resided in a small village rather than a major bishopric, like Vincent's father. They both shared a home (or rectory) with two women—in the Bishop's case, with his sister and housekeeper—and in Theodorus's case with his wife and daughter. In addition, they both possessed a compassion that transcended denominational boundaries.

Both Vincent's father and Hugo's Bishop crossed religious barriers and demonstrated the idea that denominational differences dissolve but God remains. Vincent, as we noted earlier, came from a long line of missionaries who crossed boundaries to aid others whether Protestant, Catholic, or unbeliever. In his youth, on a given Sunday he often attended three or more services each at a different denomination. He said he found God in all of them. Much like his father, Theo van Gogh inherited and retained a mediatory outlook throughout his life, and assisted many people including his brother Vincent who also had strong mediatory impulses as in his care for Sien and the miners in the Borinage. Now, at the end of his life, he needed mediators himself. He needed Patience Escalier and Bishop Bienvenu to help him work through the moral gap that separated him from his father's spiritual legacy and his quest for salvation.

The Bishop had offered a benediction over life and death leading to eternal rest, equating in his blessing moral beauty with light: "the innumerable in the infinite, and through light producing beauty. These unions are forming and dissolving continually, thence life and death." He saw light as a symbol for the stirring of conscience and a vehicle illuminating all things in the universe. This preoccupation with light as a redemptive symbol was, as we have seen, a lifelong concern for Vincent van Gogh.

In this starry prayer, there was a literary resurrection of Vincent's father through the mediation of the Bishop just as there had been through the "terrible" Patience Escalier. Vincent's implicit need for moral guidance and reorientation can be surmised in the light-giving title. Starlight implies in Vincent's view that the darkness of sin, guilt, and death are overcome by divinely mediated grace. Divine forgiveness is symbolized by light, and light reveals in this sense the moral beauty Dostoyevsky spoke of regarding Christ.

Father Bienvenu's starry vision coincided therefore with Vincent's need for divine reconciliation and assurance in the face of his own suffering and sense of imminent death. Elsewhere in *Les Misérables*, Hugo equated the flashing of the stars with the prompting of conscience which was consistent with a need to reform and seek repentance:

"The Unknown is an ocean. What is conscience? It is a compass of the Unknown. Thought, meditation, prayer, these are the great, mysterious pointings of the needle. Let us respect them. Whither tend these majestic irradiations of the soul? Into the shadow, that is, towards the light."

The conscience beckons a return to God, but humankind "occults" or obscures God's offer to find forgiveness. The lighthouse can be best understood as it applied to Vincent's thought at the time of his writing the letter and producing *Starry Night*. The moral signaling of the lighthouse is present but humankind can absent itself from its call. God symbolically is like the pointing needle on a compass, or flashing light from a lighthouse. It is a sacred call—for Vincent, a moral reckoning that must be answered involving his unresolved guilt concerning his father's death, compounded now with his own impending passing. Hugo's Bishop, the title of the painting itself, Vincent's letters, paintings and drawings made in response to Hugo's grand novel, all offer important insights into Vincent's mind and beliefs during these last years of his life. The word serenity appears often in *Les Misérables*, prominently in the passage above comparing the serenity of his own heart with the serenity of the skies. Vincent used the word serenity constantly in his letters; peace and serenity were things he desperately sought. Serenity is in fact the primary theme of *The Starry Night*—it is the state of the heart, and the emotion that follows sincere repentance.

As a work of sacred art, *The Starry Night* is the embodiment of light-saturated moral beauty transformed into radiant glory. It is a gathering together of diverse themes which weave and spin, like the clouds in Vincent's celestial masterpiece. These themes conjoin the moral beauty of Christ, the spiritual legacy of Van Gogh's father, the cultivated sentiment and healing consolation of his mother, and Vincent's love of nature found in both heaven and earth. Not just a work of art, it is resurrected matter and rekindled conscience in the form of a final eulogy. In his own words, Vincent had attempted to express "the unspeakable perfection, the glorious splendors of nature" with a "host of memories of the past, of a longing for the infinite." These "terrible" longings were the pointing of the compass, the call of the conscience expressed in one of his most glorious, radiant and prayerful paintings.

Opposite: Vincent's House in Arles, 1888. Oil on canvas.
Van Gogh Museum, Amsterdam, The Netherlands.

EPISODE FIVE

A STARRY LEGACY

GAUGUIN'S ABSOLUTION
VINCENT'S ENDURING BEQUEST

ORANA MARIA

Gauguin's Absolution

But if one analyzes from up close, one sees that the greatest and most energetic people of the century have always worked against the grain, and they have always worked out of personal initiative. Both in painting and in literature. (I do not know anything about music, but I suppose it has been the same there.) To begin on a small scale, to persevere quand même, to produce much with small capital, to have character instead of money, more audacity than credit, like Millet and Sensier, Balzac, Zola, de Goncourt, Delacroix.
—Vincent van Gogh.

In telling the story of Gauguin's relationship with Vincent, one is at a great disadvantage. Compared to the spare and honest words of Van Gogh, we find the opposite in a man intent on obfuscation and eclipsing a clear view of himself. Where Vincent excelled in natural unaffected eloquence, Gauguin practiced a seasoned form of verbal slight of hand. Vincent said that he instinctively did not trust Gauguin because he soon saw that Gauguin spoke untrue words to a man who could only deal with the truth. The conniving and manipulative nature of Gauguin (Vincent called him a "schemer") would provide art's history with a stunning lesson: when words and works of art have veiled meanings, trust is compromised, as it was when Vincent admitted Gauguin into his studio at the "Yellow House" in Arles. Within a short time Vincent felt ill at ease; he was unnerved by the changing moods and obsured messages being conveyed. Much like an eclipsing moon it wrapped its light in darkness.

It was unsettling. That an ominous dialogue should occur be-

Opposite: "Ia Orana Maria" (Hail Mary) by Paul Gauguin, 1891. Oil on canvas.
In the collection of the Metropolitan Museum of Art, New York

tween two of art's deepest thinkers was fascinating, but what it revealed was that art itself cannot flourish in such circumstances, any more than Gauguin could continue to live as a divided self in constant dread that he would have to someday give an account of his most sordid actions as they were revealed in his aging body plagued by overindulgence.

This plague of spiritual and mortal disease was in many ways the antithesis of Vincent's own demise. His erosion was the result of overwork and profound guilt compounded by his father's death and his part in provoking it. Vincent's death was premeditated in a way that Gauguin's raging revolt against life could never match. Gauguin's scheming eventually entrapped his legacy.

It was Gauguin's good fortune to have known Vincent even short as this was. Evidence is abundant that their sharing the Yellow House in Arles left a permanent spiritual mark on Gauguin's conscience. As Bishop Bienvenu said through the shining words of Victor Hugo—the conscience is a compass that ever points to the true North. When it draws one in the direction of its forceful power, lives change. Unheeding lives perish.

Gauguin did feel a strong stirring of his conscience, and proof of this can be found not in his misleading words but in the deeds of his art. Art is not designed to tell lies; it is at its best the outpouring of conscience softened by the senses and stimulated by ideas of beauty—even tragic beauty. In seeking the real Gauguin, one needs to look intently into his art as a silent but truthful revelation. Two contrasting works of art created a year apart demonstrate far better than any word the state of his spirit.

The first work is his Self Portrait, *Les Misérables* of 1888 while the second work is *Self Portrait with Yellow Christ* of 1889 (see Page 216). They seem to have been created to be inspected perhaps by Gauguin in order to see things in himself he would rather hide or deny. Whatever he may have intended in his obscure ways, the message in these works is extremely clear. As the saying goes, a picture can say a thousand words.

In the 1888 portrait, we are confounded by a glowering demonic face leaning and lurching forward as if drawn into some vortex of sin and destruction as the side of the cheek glows with a malevolent blue cast. The staring wolf-like sharp eyes seem to cut as they splinter into the viewer. This face is one capable of crime perhaps lusting for whatever evil thing it can light its darkness upon. It is sinister and chilling in its power and frightening in its utter intensity. This frightful evocation was sent to Vincent prior to Gauguin's actual arrival.

What then did it portend? It portended disillusion and abandoment to the simple uneffected Vincent who was no match for the calculated hatred of which Gauguin was more than capable. Gauguin once said that he found it interesting that four men he had been close to had become insane. This candid and self-amusing comment was stated as if in surprise, and as if he had nothing to do with the collapse of these men. But he knew inwardly that he was responsible.

In the second (1889) portrait, the mood is radically different. We now see a normally lit face, the goatee beard is gone along with its satanic satyr-like look. Now the face is clear and strongly lit, not at all blue and portentious in any way. Gauguin looks younger and more innocent as he peers outward with blue eyes and dark eyebrows and hair. The most obvious feature of this work is the overarching arm of Jesus on his cross as it halos over Paul's head. It is as if the redeeming sacrifice is disarming the criminal who had earlier proudly paraded his vile nature.

Instead, we find a startling admission that his criminal mask was a distortion. Mirroring deep guilt and self-loathing, it was in that sense an accurate reflection of an evil reality. But it was not his true self. This was revealed in the *Yellow Christ* portrait. The solidity and physical power of the man who looks outward from this work is healthy and ruddy. He broadcasts a sense of moral unrest and seems drawn to the arched arm of Christ. The radiant yellow background behind Gauguin's head seems to draw him sideways toward the source of that light. It is Christ, the Light of the World, in his most self-giving gesture of utter sacrifice for the sins of the man portrayed herein.

215

top: Paul Gauguin, "Self-Portrait Les Miserable", 1888. Oil on canvas; Van Gogh Museum, Amsterdam.
Bottom: Paul Gauguin, "Self-Portrait with the Yellow Christ", 1889. Oil on canvas; Private collection.

Gauguin had a full understanding of the implication of the sacrificial and atoning death of the God/man and was drawn to the redeeming embrace. This portrait is confessional, somber and unambiguous in its message. To the right of Paul one sees a mask-like idol, most likely a deity of some ancient tribe or place. Gauguin had shown a fascination with exotic religious practices and spirits of the dead. Now, he draws his head away from the disturbing presence which is shrouded in ominous browns and blacks. The distorted head of the god unsettling, while the patient and loving visage of the *Yellow Christ* beckons and reassures.

Gauguin had begun to return to his religious heritage and away from much of his subversive chatter. It would not produce an overnight change in the man as the facts of his life in Tahiti proved. All the same, the troubling change of conscience would bring him eventually right to the foot of Golgotha in a convincing and summary portrait—the single greatest portrait of his life (see Page 235). He stands before a dark hill fixed with crosses. They seem to be absent of victims. It is as if he were facing some silent tomb where the body of Christ now lay in repose waiting for an Easter Morning to arise. The man we see here seems reborn in a white linen garment. He appears as if he had himself arisen Lazarus-like from a tomb. This work more than any Gauguin ever produced of himself is the most to be trusted. It is free of guile and arcane symbolism, and comes very close to the rigorous simplicity of Vincent's portraits following his confinement at St. Remy. There is a sense of the fatigue that follows a hard won battle. And this sense could not be more apt, for Gauguin's life was if anything a relentless war with and against the world. Unlike Vincent, he had never developed the sensitivity to feel with another and offer true compassion. He was far too self-deceived for that. Now near the end of his journey, Gauguin had found himself in the shadow of Golgotha—a place Vincent only too well.

Like Dickens's character Blackpool, Gauguin had fallen into a dark place of the soul and suddenly saw a flash of starlight. It was not the radiant sky of Vincent's *Starry Night* but rather the still, strong, pulsating beam of a lighthouse or a compass. He tells us in his very attitude that his life is at an end and there is no escape. Golgotha is the place of everyman's no-return; the hill of death is one from which there is no escape. For Gauguin, the final decision is not etched in stone as on a tablet taken from a blazing mountain. But it is promising all the same. Light shines in the darkness and the light of a distant star reassures. Vincent understood this earlier in life as he journeyed by night to the side of a dying friend, and then to the tomb of his dead brother. He waited for the sun to rise and make of that small cemetery an Easter sunrise—the Easter sun he described to his parents in his early letter of departure.

Gauguin's Golgotha is supremely powerful in showing that for once in his life he revealed his true self with nothing to hide and everything to gain. He stood now near the little cemetery near Calvary quite near the gravesite of Vincent himself. What silent confession did Gauguin make that night?

A letter from Paul-Louis Vernier on March 8, 1904, to Jean de Rotonchamp on Gauguin's life and death in Atuona is very revealing:

"I would be happy to give you a few details on the last period of M. Paul Gauguin's life and of his death, all the more since it was I who cared for him until the morning of his death, which came unexpectedly on 8 May 1903, a Friday, at about eleven o'clock in the morning. And if I was not his friend— really knowing him very little, since Gauguin was unsociable—I was at least his neighbor and, consequently, fairly up-to-date on his life. Several times he came to see me; three times he called me to come to him for a consultation, since I am something of a doctor.

"I always knew M. Paul Gauguin to be ill and almost crippled. He rarely left his house, and the few times when one would run into him in he valley of Atuona he cut a pathetic figure, dragging himself along with difficulty, his legs wrapped in strips of cloth and dressed, moreover, in the very original costume of the Maori: the colored loincloth and the Tahitian blouse, barefoot, almost always wearing a green beret with a silver buckle on the side. A very likable man, perfectly sweet and natural with the Marquesans. They were cer-

tainly that way with him. And when your friend died, I can remember hearing several of the natives cry something like: 'Ua mate Gauguin, ua pete enata!'— Gauguin is dead, we are lost!' alluding to the help Gauguin had often given them, delivering them from the hands of the police, who were often hard and unjust where the natives were concerned. Gauguin, who was very generous and chivalrous, defended the natives. There are numerous examples of his goodness and his consideration.

"He had very little rapport with the Europeans in Atuona. I believe he cordially detested them, with a few rare exceptions. He was, above all, horrified by the gendarme and by the constabulary in general. He had resounding quarrels with them. One day, about three months before his death, he was sentenced to fifteen days in jail and fined 500 francs for supposedly insulting the police. But Gauguin was sure he would be acquitted on appeal. He was, in fact, preparing to go to Tahiti when death surprised him. Gauguin appeared to be in the right and to have justice on his side, but in truth, he was above all that.

"As for the country, he had the highest ideals, a true worship for this nature, so beautiful in itself and so savage, where his soul naturally found its niche. He could immediately discover the special poetry of this region that is bathed in sunlight and still untainted in places. You must have perceived this in the paintings he sent you from down there. The Maori soul no longer held any mystery for him. Meanwhile, Gauguin found that our islands lost some of their originality every day."

He then later wrote:

"One morning near the beginning of April 1903, I received the following note from Gauguin:

'Dear Monsieur Vernier,
May I be so bold as to ask you for a consultation, since my powers have become wholly insufficient? I am very sick. I can no longer walk.

P.G.'

"I went immediately to the artist's home. He suffered horribly in his legs, which were red and swollen and covered with eczema. I recommended the proper medication, offering to rub it on for him if he wished. He thanked me very kindly, saying he could do it himself. We talked. Forgetting his pain, he spoke to me of his art in very admirable terms, portraying himself as an undiscovered genius. He made a few allusions to his troubles with the police, named a few of his friends, although, to tell the truth, I do not remember hearing your name; he loaned me several of Dolent's and Aurier's books and L'Apres-midi d'une faune, which he had from Mallarme himself. He gave me a sketch of the latter, with the following words: To Monsieur Vernier, a piece of art. P.G.

"I left him and did not see him for ten days. Old Tioka, a friend of Gauguin's, said to me, 'You know, things are not well at the white man's, he is very sick!' I went back to your friend's house and found him, very low indeed, in bed and moaning. Once again, he forgot his illness when speaking of art. I admired his obsession.

"The morning of 8 May, he had this same Tioka call me. I went. Gauguin, still in bed, complained of sharp pains in his body. He asked me if it was morning or evening, day or night. He told me that he had had two fainting fits and he worried about them. He spoke to me of Salammbo. I left him on his back, calm and resting, after this short conversation. Around eleven o'clock that same morning, the young Ka Hui, a servant (unfortunately too irregular, in the sense that he often deserted his master's house during his illness) came and called me with all haste: 'Come quick, the white man is dead!'

"I flew. I found Gauguin lifeless, one leg hanging out of the bed, but still warm. Tioka was there, he was beside himself: he said to me: 'I came to see how he was, I called him from below, Ko Ke (the native name for Gauguin). Not hearing anything, I came up to see. Aie! Aie! Gauguin did not stir. He was dead.' And, having said this, he began to chew hard on his friend's scalp, a particularly Marquesan way of bringing someone back to life. I myself tried rhythmic pulling of the tongue and artificial respiration, but nothing would work. Paul Gauguin really was dead, and everything leads to the conclusion that he died of a sudden heart attack.

"I am the only European to have seen Gauguin before he died. I must say, he never spoke to me of his family in Europe, nor did he make any suggestions or express any last wishes. Did he leave a will? I do not think so. The authorities went through all his papers, and I do not believe anything was found.

The word was that he had a family in Europe, a wife and five children. There was a photograph of a family group that, people said, was them. I saw that photograph. Moreover, people said a lot of things. We did not know what to believe. Naturally, I never asked Gauguin anything about that subject. Now I must tell you several things of the circumstances of his burial and the circumstances in which these were produced.

"When I arrived a Gauguin's hut on the famous Friday when I was told of his death, I found that the Catholic bishop and several brothers of the Christian faith were already there. I was immensely surprised to see them. Everyone knew what Gaugjin's sentiments toward these gentlemen were, and these gentlemen knew them as well. My astonishment turned to indignation when I saw that the bishop decided to bury Gauguin with a full Catholic ceremony, which is what was done on Saturday, 9 May. The corpse was to be moved at two o'clock. I wanted at least to assist at the removal of the body, and to that end I went to Gauguin's residence at the appointed hour. His body had been transported to the church by one-thirty! A real sleight-of-hand trick, as you can well see. And Gauguin now rests in the Catholic Calvary, sacred ground par excellence! In my opinion, Gauguin should have had a civil burial.

"Some of the things that were left by Gauguin were sold at two auctions. The first sale, at Atuona, took care of the things that the natives and the few local Europeans would buy; his clothes, his trunks, his carpentry and woodworking tools, his kitchen utensils, his saddle, his horse, his preserves, his wine, his house and his land (all in one lot), assessed by an American at 1,050 francs, I think. The green beret went to Tioka, who wears it day and night; and that was given him by the auctioneer. Poor Gauguin!

"The second sale took place in Tahiti and dealt only with the valuable things, the paintings in particular, and the rare objects. Doctor Segalen told you everything on that subject...."

Paul Gauguin, "Christmas Night" by Paul Gauguin, 1896. Oil on canvas.
In the collection of the Indianapolis Museum of Art.

Looking at the evolution of Vincent's artistic reputation, a disconcerting sequence of events occurred after he and Gauguin decided to exchange self-portraits. The exchange took place a few months prior to their sharing Vincent's studio known as "The Yellow House" in Arles in 1888. Upon receiving Gauguin's self-portrait, Vincent wrote:

"I have just received the portrait of Gauguin by himself and the portrait of Bernard by Bernard...The Gauguin is more studied, carried further. That, along with what he says in his letter, gave me absolutely the impression of its representing a prisoner. Not a shadow of gaiety. Absolutely nothing of the flesh, but one can confidently put that down to his determination to make a melancholy effect, the flesh in the shadows has gone a dismal blue. So now at last I have a chance to compare my painting with what the comrades are doing. My portrait, which I am sending to Gauguin in exchange, holds its own, I am sure of that. I have written to Gauguin in reply to his letter that if I might be allowed to stress my own personality in a portrait, I had done so in trying to convey in

my portrait not only myself but an impressionist in general...And when I put Gauguin's conception and mine own side by side, mine is as grave, but less despairing. What Gauguin's portrait says to me before all is that he must not go on like this..."

Gauguin had offered this explanation of his self-portrait:

"I have done a self-portrait for Van Gogh who asked me for it. I believe it is one of my best efforts: absolutely incomprehensible (upon my word) so abstract is it. First the head of a brigand, a Jean Valjean (Les Misérables), likewise personifying a disreputable impressionist painter burdened for ever with a chain for the world. The drawing is altogether peculiar, being complete abstraction. The eyes, the mouth, the nose, are like the flowers of a Persian carpet, thus personifying the symbolical side. The colour is a colour remote from nature; imagine a confused collection of pottery all twisted by the furnace! All the reds and violets streaked by flames, like a furnace burning fiercely, the seat of the painter's mental struggles. The whole on a chrome background sprinkled with childish nosegays. Chamber of a pure young girl..."

Note that Vincent gave Gauguin's painting equal weight with Gauguin's own written comments. He took him at his word: "what he says in his letter, gave me absolutely the impression of its representing a prisoner. Not a shadow of gaiety. Absolutely nothing of the flesh..." Vincent criticized what Gauguin said, finding it confusing. Gauguin used the language of a Symbolist—vague and indeterminate. One is never sure how to take it. Vincent did not play at words. He knew how to get to the essence of things. With words or paint, Vincent remained unswervingly committed to reality in contrast to the obscurity of the Symbolists. By comparison, Gauguin's Symbolist language was exaggerated, ambiguous, and strange where Vincent's letters were clear, concise and descriptive. Debora Silverman explained the difference between Van Gogh and Gauguin in this way:

"The conception of art as a lesson, earnestly considered by Vincent in the simplicity of Millet's labor types and their emulators, was vehemently rejected by Gauguin; Gauguin's deliberately ambiguous symbolism made his work an art for the initiated only. Its meaning might be suggested only if the hermetic code of the artist's vision was cracked by the words of the creator himself."
—Debora Silverman, 2000

In his self-portrait, Gauguin imagines himself—some might say in a sinister way—to be in the bedroom of a "pure young girl". His painting and supporting letter projects guilt and self-loathing. When Vincent wrote, "What Gauguin's portrait says to me before all is that he must not go on like this." he meant quite simply that Gauguin was charting a dangerous path, deliberately advertising moral depravity as a sign of genius. This contrivance of Gauguin was later emulated by many avant garde artists for whom despair and moral depravity were to become proof of genius, and by association set progressive art outside the realm of morality and humane values.

In 1897, Gauguin wrote:

"Ever since my infancy misfortune has pursued me. Never any luck, never any joy. Everyone always against me, and I exclaim: God Almighty, if You exist, I charge You with injustice and spitefulness...What use are virtue, work, courage, intelligence? Crime alone is logical and rational."

Despair was something Vincent tried to stave off for it had incapacitated him following his Borinage dismissal. But with Gauguin, anguish, spitefulness, and rebellion were an indication that his flesh could hardly contain the powerful flowing lava of his fevered imagination. Eventually, these ideas were canonized as the myth of the suffering artist. After the nineteenth century, one artist after another would be eager to wallow in Gauguin's wake as proof of their own genius. But Vincent fought against the despair that Gauguin celebrated. When we see Vincent's later self-portraits—with his bandaged ear, for instance—it is sobering, and certainly not ambiguous or confounding as was Gauguin's portrayal. The injured ear, like Vincent's supporting letters, was a reminder that he had again ignored his health and paid a tragic price.

Vincent wanted others to learn from his suffering and how to avoid it. His late letters are filled with regret over the ruination of his own health, and he hoped there would one day be a generation of artists with good health. Vincent clearly saw tragedy, but instead of spitefully celebrating it in cryptic fashion as Gauguin did, he saw the light beyond leading to divine hope and escape. His view of art was not a hermetic code to be cracked by a cryptic colleague but rather a covenant pledged to life—a commitment based on a promise to redeem not only his life but the lives of others. He said:

"It always strikes me, and it is very peculiar, that whenever we see the image of indescribable and unutterable desolation of loneliness, poverty and misery, the end or extreme of all things, the thought of God comes into our minds".

Gauguin was a self-proclaimed egotist who rejected his own family in the name of his genius—something that Vincent would never have done. We recall, for example, how Vincent tried to persuade Sien to accompany him to Drenthe. But Gauguin left his wife and family behind, and would take several child mistresses. For Gauguin, art was a private drive that made personal mythologizing part of a ritual of artistic exhibitionism, whereas for Vincent, art was tied to action taken on behalf of others in order to fulfill a moral calling. The disreputable side of Gauguin was something that Vincent sensed even before sharing his studio with him in 1888: "I feel instinctively that Gauguin is a schemer..."

Gauguin's estranged wife Mette was all too familiar with this side of her husband:

"Ah! If I did not have such devoted friends, what would become of me! God in heaven! But my heart is filled with bitterness at the thought that Paul could be so criminally egoistic, and never have I heard or seen such a thing. No, Schuff, from him nothing can be expected! He never thinks of anything but himself and

his welfare; he prostrates himself in complete admiration before his own magnificence. That his children have to be fed through his wife's friends is a matter of perfect indifference to him, he does not want to be told of it!"

As their letters now reveal, Gauguin not only abandoned his wife and family, he ignored Vincent's pathetic cries for help following his ear-slitting episode. Instead of staying to help his so-called friend and benefactor, he precipitously boarded a train for Paris. Later, Gauguin said he hadn't wanted to awaken Vincent who rebutted this claim. Vincent told how, instead of being asleep, he had strenuously begged Gauguin to stay and help but to no avail.

Vincent paralleled the Russian writer Dostoevsky in his moral and spiritual stance, opposing the cult of artistic egoism that Gauguin embraced and embodied. Dostoevsky had toured Europe in 1862 and was alarmed by the growing spread of egotism. Vincent offered the same indictment of Gauguin, and the hubris so prevalent in Paris and elsewhere at that time.

. . . "the personal principle, the principle of isolation, of intense self-preservation, of self-solicitousness, of the self-determination of one's own ego, of opposing this ego to all of nature and all other people as a separate, autonomous principle completely equal and equivalent to everything outside itself. And just as such self-absorption was a cardinal moral failing, so the selfless love of others—to the point of self-sacrifice, if need be—was the height of moral nobility." —Scanlan 2002

Counter to the veiled meanings of Gauguin's portrait, in his own self-portrait Vincent presented himself as a clearly-lit artist who retained his ties to the natural order of things. And contrary to Gauguin's misuse of *Les Misérables* and identification with the criminal element, Vincent instead extolled its moral meanings and themes. Hugo's message was not used cryptically by Vincent, but it was Gauguin who ignored the moral transformation of the novel's character Valjean from convict to saint. Moral transformation and love of others to the point of self-sacrifice was the central theme of *Les Misérables*. Vincent was drawn to the saintly Bishop Bienvenu, and embraced the story's redemptive message. The Bishop had reflected that an aesthetic was consoling, not confounding, vague, or abstract as in Gauguin's interpretation.

"Vincent believed in miracles, in maternity. The mad man (decidedly he was mad) kept watch for forty days at the bedside of the dying man; he prevented the air from ruthlessly penetrating into his wounds and paid for medications. He spoke as a consoling priest (decidedly he was mad). The work of this madman had revived a Christian from the dead. When the wounded man, finally saved, descended into the mine again to resume his work, you could have seen, said Vincent, the head of Jesus the martyr, carrying on his forehead the halo and the jagged crown of thorns..." Paul Gauguin, 1894. (Written four years after Vincent's death as a tribute to Van Gogh's compassionate example).

In surprising contrast to Gauguin's portrait with his self-projection as a loathing menace, he had a soft underbelly that occasionally revealed itself in spite of his desire to hide it. When he did allow these moments of tenderness to arise, he was able to produce works of the highest magnitude and spiritual depth. Perhaps because these mellow moods were so seldom visited in his daily life, when they did surface they came on with unrelenting power and held him in a heart-bending grip; the stinging pangs of depravity stirred by his troubled conscience.

So it was with Gauguin, as his friends and enemies reported. But as bad as he wanted to seem, he was no Marquis de Sade. Religious art still moved him and he found himself transfixed by Romanesque crucifixes and Pilgrimage shrines and markers. He was drawn to it so much that he began to use it in his art (though he tried to maintain it was simply the style he liked so much not the content). He moved to Brittany and immersed himself in the colorful local processionals, religious festivals and pious myths. He claimed it was like the hermetic Symbolist poetry, and absinthe-induced visions promoted by the head shops and arcane practices of the Paris art underworld. Gauguin loved to be noticed in such places especially when there was an attractive young woman to meet.

Debora Silverman, in her groundbreaking study of the religious roots of Van Gogh and Gauguin, suggests that Gauguin, like Van Gogh, made a return to his Christian moral foundation but only in his last days. Vincent never really abandoned his as his letters and story show. In support of the view that there was a return to religion, there is an extensive manuscript presently in the Getty archive in Los Angeles. Debora Silverman has noted this in the Appendix of her book, *Van Gogh and Gauguin: The Search For Sacred Art.* Silverman writes:

"Further evidence of Gauguin's religious concerns, textural methods, and range of knowledge is apparent in another set of writings that have never been published or discussed by scholars. These suggest again the long-term hold of his seminary formation. The Getty Research Institute Collections have a series of handwritten manuscript pages by Gauguin in which he presents discussions of the split between 'matter and spirit'; 'the mystery of the immaterial'; and the status of Christ as a 'supernatural force.' These pages include interpretations and quotations from St. Matthew, St. Paul, and St. Luke. The Getty manuscript papers are archived as 'Paul Gauguin, Letters and Writings.'

Such papers have been dated to around 1897—the year in which he suffered a heart attack. It is believed that he was preparing a book or series of articles for publication in newspapers or he had a book on religious questions in mind. These were well-formulated questions concerning free will and revelation. Questions on institutionalized religious control that minimized private insight and personal access to sacred experience. His focus was in many ways Protestant in that he believed that all scripture provided direct access into the Mind of the Spirit.

Additional more extensive writings have recently been found that offer a conceptual frame of reference for the ideas expressed in his most ambitious work. The brooding religiously inspired monumental canvas *D'ou Venons-nous? Que Sommes-Nous? Ou Allons-Nous ?* (Where Do We Come From? What Are We? Where Are We Going?). Silverman wrote the following about this fascinating canvas:

"Gauguin's immense, frieze-like painting depicted thirteen figures along a riverbank on a canvas four and a half feet high and twelve fee long. Gauguin himself provided extensive commentary in his letters on the circumstances and meaning of the canvas, which offered is some ways a visual parallel to the themes and questions of his wide-ranging religious writings of 1887. In one summary of the painting, for example, Gauguin described how he had completed 'a philosophical work on a theme comparable to the Gospels.'"

We recall that Van Gogh remained lifelong an advocate of the simple messages of the Gospel with their practical parables and appeal to every man, woman and child. The idea that the Kingdom of God was available and accessible to the child above all was because of the direct and uncomplicated way a child reasoned. Gospel themes permeate the monumental work and some surprising previously unacknowledged details have been noted by Silverman, namely, a preliminary drawing for this work which reveals its underlying Christ centric scheme and its personal value to Gauguin. We return to Silverman again:

"Just above the drawing he listed the three questions the canvas addressed, each on a separate line but joined by a curling bracket. To the left side of the three linked questions, Gauguin placed a cross. A second cross appeared in the upper left corner of the ink drawing, while the upper right corner showed a fish, sign of Jesus Christ, and, under it, Gauguin's signature."

The latter personal appeal to Christ is unmistakable. Silverman enlarges vastly on the sophisticated philosophical and religious foundation of the painting, and additionally devotes an important chapter in her book on Gauguin's extensive education in a seminary school in Orleans. This preparatory school was, according to Silverman, ahead of its time in its tutorial methods. The school was founded by Felix-Antoine-Philibert Dupanloup (1802-1878), a leading French Bishop and cutting-edge educator. Bishop Dupanloup wrote and published two sets of widely-known books on educational theory, *De L'education en General* and *De la Haute Education Intellectuelle*, each in six volumes which appeared between 1850 and 1863.

Gauguin had been given sophisticated courses in theological and philosophical thought by the Bishop himself who took a personal interest in Gauguin as he did with each of his students. Dupaniloup made it his mission to devote private time outside the classroom getting to know his students. He took them on walks in the seminary garden and encouraged spontaneous exchanges. He believed that the imagination should be used and stimulated rather than relying on dry reason alone. His approach was very close to the Montessori School Method in current practice in the 21st century where children are encouraged to be actively involved in imaginative decision making and creative problem solving.

Gauguin's ability to think abstractly as an advanced artist of his time was due in no small part to his training in systematic thought. He had polished writing skills which were developed at the same time and made evident in his numerous letters and autobiographical writings. In summary, his background in religious thought, while not as extensive as Van Gogh's (who went on to the University of Amsterdam to study theology and prepare for the ministry) was still impressive enough to dazzle Vincent who wrote admiringly of Gauguin's intelligence and range of knowledge.

We know that religious debates and discussions were part of the evening fare following one of Gauguin's well-cooked meals. Vincent had no cooking skills whatsoever so he was amazed that Gauguin was able to transform a ham flank into a delicious stew. Vincent noted that Gauguin "cooked marvelously" and how convenient it was to be able to eat well using fresh produce purchased in the open market instead of eating in a cafe. There were in fact many things about Gauguin that he admired in spite of his awareness that Gauguin was an opportunist not given to loyalty. Having sacrificed his wife and five children, he had to be a practiced survivor. He had hardened himself as a result with some strange consequences. He claimed a good row sustained him.

Gauguin once wrote that he knew he was alive when he either took a fist to the face or administered one to an opponent. But in an artistically aesthetic vein, he rhapsodized over the dull, muffled sound that his wooden shoes made on flint pathways, and sought to bring a somber gravity into his paintings.

Gauguin's aesthetic preferences were made up of a complex composite of unlikely sources and forms. His privileged education in an elite boys seminary school and its mystical visual culture, its High Masses and stained glass light, had steeped him in spiritual beauty. Then, in stark contrast to this sublime foundation, he went to sea as a merchant mariner and was exposed to the native arts of South America and the brilliant patterns and shapes of tropical cultures. He hired onto the construction of the Panama Canal in 1887 and worked as a laborer under harsh and excessive conditions where malaria was rampant. He learned how to cook on the high seas and in labor camps. He was a quick student, and made economical use of everything that could sustain him. Then, as if transformed, he married into a Danish upper class family, became a successful merchant, and eventually a highly successful stockbroker with a strong preference for fine clothes and cuisine. His cooking skills improved all the more as his fortune improved.

Then, the great bank failure of the late nineteenth century in France decimated his savings. He took up painting, took private lessons and made rapid progress. Art quickly became an obsession and he never looked back. Knowing the methods of the market place allowed him to sustain his insatiable art habit, he promoted and exhibited his work finding clever ways to make a sale. He was a natural promoter. Butt he was undeniably a great artist. His aesthetic senses were highly developed and he had a knack for finding fresh ways of saying things. He soon took up with the leading Impressionists, meeting them in bars and cafes. He studied with Pissarro, and was soon on speaking terms with Rodin, Degas, Manet and Monet.

Before long, Gauguin was showing with the elite of the Paris art world and came to the attention of Theo Van Gogh, a highly respected advocate of progressive painting. And he met Vincent through Theo.

Gauguin was offered free housing and a guaranteed income from Theo who now was providing for two people in addition to his little family and his retired parents.

Arles seemed to reignite Gauguin's religious feelings as the local population held colorful feast-day celebrations and processions. He found similar themes in *Les Misérables* and wrote of it and titled works of art after it. Like Van Gogh he was touched by Bishop Bienvenu and Valjean. Hugo's saintly Bishop touched Gauguin in a very personal way. It brought back the memory of Bishop Dupanloup and the unique bond he had with this remarkable man. He was also strangely touched by the honesty and courage of little Vincent who by all reports was on the short side and in almost comical contrast to the taciturn and tall Gauguin who was as strong as an ox. Gauguin reported that he once carried Vincent home under his arm following a night of absinthe consumption. But occasionally the pious moods seem to gather around Vincent whose nature tended toward exaltation and pious thoughts.

Proof of Gauguin's pious leanings, sporadic as they may have been, can be seen in several deeply felt works that seem refreshingly free of the unsettling characteristics of his art he tended most often to promote. It is almost as if taking on the role of a hardened egotist he was embarrassed to admit to having moments of vulnerability and tugs of compassion. But we see flashes of compassion in the tribute he wrote about Vincent and his role as a missionary artist descending into the mines. Gauguin used madness as a poetic way of saying that Vincent displayed a profound selflessness in treating miners suffering from firedamp burns—"yes, he was decidedly mad." This tribute was not purely altruistic but the strong sentiment for Vincent as a suffering fellow artist is evident all the same.

Examining the art of Gauguin offers more evidence of a well-formed Christian belief system—a system of thought that he did not attempt to live out but which, like a well-loved pious melody, moved him all the same. We have a series of radiant Madonna's in Tahitian garb perhaps inspired by Puvis de Chavannes who created similar religious works and whose clear outlines and strong areas of flat design Gauguin admired. We can easily move into the mood of these ethereally beautiful works that glisten in with radiant hues drawn as much from the pallet of the tropical forests and flowers as from a Persian carpet, and designed to display the piety of a medieval believer. We know that Gauguin had in mind actually painting a religious fresco in a church in Brittany. But the offer was rejected by the officiating priest when he caught wind of Gauguin's reputation as a womanizer and carouser. All the same the primitive piety of a Brittan peasant appealed to the self-proclaimed primitive of art and stuck some ancient cord in his religious memory.

Hegel reminds us that spiritual ideals do not die an easy death in art or in life. The Gospel themes that haunted Gauguin and compelled him to produce what he believed was his artistic credo and last will was cut from the same cloth as Van Gogh's desire to paint the pages of the Gospel written in the snow-blanketed landscape of the forsaken Borinage mining region.

It was that very descent into darkness that Gauguin eulogized in his tribute to Van Gogh who helped save the wretchedly wounded. Wounded himself and dying from heart failure, skin disease and massive swelling of his ankles due to poor blood circulation and fluid retention, Gauguin could now fully identify with the victims Van Gogh had saved. Yet in his eulogy to Vincent, it was more than a nurse that he celebrated in his memory. In paying Vincent homage, he likened Van Gogh to Christ—a suffering servant sent to offer light in the darkness.

Seven years after Vincent's death we find a similar theme in Gauguin's life and work. At the very center of Gauguin's vast composition we see the main subject, a golden skin man likely in a tropical Adam in a Tahitian Garden of Eden reaching upward as if to receive a miraculous gift. With a radiantly red fruit in his grasp he looks heavenward in rapt adoration to something above him and just beyond view. It is as if he is seeing something or someone who is redeeming him and transforming his corruptible body into immortality. We see the Resurrection itself, the lifelong aesthetic preoccupation of Van Gogh to which his entire body of work was devoted and most notably his *Starry Night* and *Resurrection of Lazarus*. Placed side by side, these two works tell the same simple Gospel story they heard first as children that the Kingdom of God belongs to children reborn and washed clean as the sincere in heart. But heavenly kingdoms are not taken by storm; they are entered by the repentant.

In devoting himself to paying final tribute to Vincent in his eulogy, and in painting his extended series of religiously inspired works, Gauguin was clearly performing acts of atonement. Like Vincent, who sought forgiveness with his father though his penitent portraits of Patience Escalier, so Gauguin used his sacred works similarly to make peace with Van Gogh's memory, and that of his family and country.

Above: "Self-Portrait Near Golgotha" by Paul Gauguin, 1896. Oil on canvas.
In the collection of the Sao Paolo Museum de Arte.

Vincent's Enduring Bequest

"They spent most of their time together [in the last months of Vincent's life and became great friends—a friendship not ended by death, for Dr. Gachet and his children continued to honor Vincent's memory with rare piety, which became a form of worship, touching in its simplicity and sincerity. "The more I think of it, the more I think Vincent was a giant. Not a day passes that I do not look at his pictures. I always find there a new idea, something different each day...I think again of the painter and I find him a colossus. Besides, he was a philosopher...", Gachet wrote to Theo shortly after Vincent's death. Speaking of the latter's love for art, he said, "Love of art is not exact; one must call it faith—a faith that maketh martyrs!" None of his contemporaries had understood him better."

— *Johanna van Gogh-Bonger*

Ezra Pound proposed in his ABC of Reading (1934) that the great writer manifests certain characteristics. He then produced a controversial six-tiered chart of literary greatness which applied to all of the arts. At the top of Pound's chart he placed inventiveness and mastery. These were set above mere imitation and art lacking salient, or enduring qualities. At the bottom of his chart he placed "starters of new crazes." Crazes are expedient, generally generated by less than laudable intentions, and are for the most part short-lived and emotionally shallow. The essential Van Gogh story is, accordingly, not the tale of a man and a fad but of one who stood against moral decay and compromise. To borrow the metaphor of the star—Vincent's star rose slowly over a bedrock of study, application, audacity and courage. Furthermore, this courage was demonstrated in holding to the values of the past while he took readily from the future. He was both innovator and conservator, inventor and pioneer, progressive and conservative, all at once. To this balance of opposites was the most important quality of all—Vincent's ardent decision to produce works of art that could speak universal truths in a common language to a vast majority of viewers across time.

Opposite:"Portrait of Doctor Gachet" by Vincent van Gogh, 1890. Oil on canvas. Private collection

In this spiritual sense he was very much akin to Charles Dickens whose populist writing merged and married the timeless and contemporary into a time-tested modernity. In America, in the 21st century, Bob Dylan comes closest to embodying these characteristics. He too has creatively merged the moods and methods of the past with an ear for the present-day, and in so doing provides a sense of stability in the face of constant change. In the visual arts, Chuck Close now offers a similar fusion and the late American painter, Andrew Wyeth, even more so.

Van Gogh is great, according to Ezra Pound, because his work is inventive and ingenious. But, like Dickens, he was also audacious in creating a body of morally uplifting work when he could easily have done otherwise. Simply put, his creativity was used to create images of awe-inspiring beauty and transcendent logic. Vincent's worldview, while cast in suffering, resonated with redemption. Furthermore, the art is honest. What we admire in his painting we find in his life and letters, again a daring commitment to eternal values in the face of their erosion and steady decline—beliefs evident in his devotion to by-gone artistic mentors and literary heroes, many of whom were viewed as passe. Gauguin, for example, dismissed many of his artistic predecessors over minor stylistic matters. Vincent on the other hand, rather than dismiss them, tended to revere painters like Delacroix and Millet. He defended a host of artists who were sadly considered to be well out of fashion—Rembrandt, Millet, Breton, Daumier. Also on the list of dismissed talents were hundreds of illustrators, relegated to the dustbin of the obsolete, according to the rather misguided theories of advanced European art of the time.

Vincent, in true Dickensian manner, defended these artists for their honesty and strength of expression, and for their narrative skill and social conscience. He believed that those strong, virile characteristics would outlive the vague, trendy, and style-for-style-sake art that was current in the social circles of his time. Having said that, it is important to reassert what Ezra Pound proposed about greatness, namely that such work should be highly inventive and original. Such qualities do apply in great measure to Vincent's work but in a surprising way. His innovations in color, expressive brushwork and radical design were married to traditional components. Vincent exploited plunging perspective when perspective was being rejected by advanced painters of the time. Vincent resurrected many practices from history that had been ignored, minimalized, and relegated to the past. We see this in his use of kitchen cuisine and antique lead to bolster the physical elements of his art. He was innovative in very complicated ways. To this diet of the past he added modern color theory, Japanese design, flattening of form alongside strong shapes, and powerful swirling calligraphy. His methods created a bridge to the past and a bridge to the future. Much like Dickens, he stood solidly on tradition in the most progressive of ways.

Viewed within the perspective of the history of art, what strikes us about Vincent was his wise appraisal of values in art. Ezra Pound helped us see just what those values were. Instead of glamor, fads and crazes, we were presented with sackcloth and coal dust, blanketing a world shining under starlight, and guided by spiritual yearnings. We saw a man weak and broken at times but who told his story true to life. In all his undertakings, in his art and in his letters, his allegiance was to reality.

The honest testimony of his life gives us grace, and shows the value of honesty even when it is not expedient or faddish. In our contemporary world of overtly explicit media, Vincent's art and his life resonate with grit and courage. Even his peccadillos are there for us to learn from, as we can from the imperfections and corrections in his art. This sort of transparency is seldom promulgated as an artistic value; yet they are all the more potent because they are so authentic.

More than anything, what made Vincent great, in addition to his creativity and endless inventiveness, was his endurance, an endurance rooted in the universal truisms of faith, hope and love. This covenant of human and divine ways of thinking, transfigure and redeem life. Great art offers a window or, as Vincent repeatedly said, a Gospel page in which we more clearly see the glorious potential life has to offer. Art is a covenant—an agreement—because it unites by sacred bond the extremes of life, death, time and history. It offers people hope that life is meaningful, and that miracles are as common as the next staggering sunrise or sunset. The miracle is the foundation of such art for it requires faith to believe it can be created, and faith to believe its ardent message. It is a miracle that such things are preserved and passed on to posterity, a common message rescued from the violence of wars or ethnic strife. Vincent's rising star was not suddenly seen. His credibility was challenged, and his genius not only questioned but vehemently denied by some.

By what means, therefore, did he triumph, and at what cost? Vincent, in life and death, provoked strong reactions. There were those, like Dr. Gachet and Emile Bernard, who revered Vincent, and wrote his eulogy. Bernard wrote:

"On the walls of the room where the body reposed, all his last canvases were nailed, making a kind of halo around him and, because of the lustre of genius that emanated from them, rendering this death even more painful for us artists. On the coffin, a simple white drapery and masses of flowers, the sunflowers that he so loved, yellow dahlias, yellow flowers everywhere. It was his favorite color, if you remember, symbol of the light that he dreamed of finding in hearts as in artworks. Also nearby, his easel, his folding stool, and his brushes had been placed on the floor in front of the casket. Many people arrived, mostly artists, among whom I recognized Lucien Pissarro and Lauzel, the others unknown to me; there were, as well people from the area who had known him a little, seen him once or twice, and who loved him, for he was so good, so human."

In contrast, another account of his death was penned by the Dutch artist, Anton "Tommy" Hirschig who, upon his arrival in Auvers on June 16, 1890, had taken the room adjacent to Vincent's at the same inn. Hirschig wrote:

"I still see before me all that work, which is now preserved [in museums], as if it were sacred, with the greatest care, jumbled together in the dirtiest sty imaginable, a sort of hovel in a backyard barn where goats were penned up. It was dark there, the brick walls were unplastered and full of straw. At the end there were steps. There was hung the work of Vincent, and everyday he brought in new pieces. They lay on the ground and hung on the walls, and no one cared for them. There was The Town Hall of Auvers on Bastille Day with flags, a portrait of the daughter of the wine merchant where we lived, and so many others. I still see him sitting on the bench in front of the window of the little café, with his cut-off ear and bewildered eyes in which there was something insane and into which I dared not look...When he was dead, he was terrible to behold, more terrible than when he was alive. From his coffin, which was badly made, there escaped a stinking liquid: everything was terrible about this man..."

What can we learn from these contrasting accounts of Vincent's last days, one made immediately after Vincent's death by Bernard and the other by Hirshig from memory forty-four years later in 1934? It could be argued that they are simply personal narratives, each revealing some important truth or mischaracterization. It might be argued that the two contrasting narratives serve to cancel each other out and simply demonstrate that there is no singular, simple truth to be gleaned from Vincent's life and art. Some say that truth is purely relative. In Hirschig's portrayal of Vincent, his flesh, art and existence are seen as horrible, even too terrible to look at. Many of the apocryphal stories surrounding Vincent's suicide, insanity, severed ear, and so forth indicate that his art was contaminated and diseased—the outpouring of a degenerate mind, a stammering robotic corpse, determined to fail by virtue of bad genetics. In the very decade of the 1930's, when Hirschig made his damning assessment of Van Gogh, the notion of genetic degeneracy was widespread, endorsed for example by Hitler who put the genetic fallacy to devastating effect in the Holocaust.

Note how such views have come full circle, how closely Tommy's depiction of Van Gogh matches some current postmodern views of humankind:

"We—Postmodernist humanity—are what is left over after the end. And what is left over is precisely that vacated self, lying like flotsam on the beach of eternity...There can be no meaningful action from this robotic corpse, which acts only from its conditioning. As Alexandre Kojeve wrote, "the end of human Time, or History—that is, the definitive annihilation of Man properly speaking, or of the free and historical Individual—means quite simply the cessation of action [emphasis mine] in the full sense of the term." —McEvilley, 1997

Like many current day deterministically based views of mankind, Hirschig suggests that genius is non-existent. He finds it absurd that people would regard Vincent's work as having any intrinsic value. Vincent is nothing more than a list of negatives. The facts Hirschig offers are based almost entirely on Vincent's physical appearance. We find no reference to anything other than the immediate and observable, no mention of his letters which Hirschig had decades to read had he so chosen.

Bernard's contrasting report contains the very things missing in Hirschig's report, namely spiritual resonance and acceptance. "On the walls of the room where the body reposed, all his last canvases were nailed, making a kind of halo around him and, because of the lustre of genius that emanated from them, rendering this death even more painful for us artists...". Bernard and Hirschig had both seen Vincent when he was suffering the most. In fact, Bernard was far more familiar with Van Gogh's illness having known him over a much longer period of time than had Hirschig. Yet Bernard arrived at a completely sympathetic view of Vincent.

When put alongside many other similar accounts of those who knew him best and over a long period of time a clear picture emerges. It is the picture of an honest man guided by spiritual yearnings who left an enduring and undeniable legacy. The adulation of his admirers was sincere given by some of the most talented young artists of the era: Bernard, Pissaro, Monet and even (begrudgingly) Gauguin. They all noted his greatness enlarging on Vincent's bequest to humankind. Vincent himself said, especially using the example of his own life:

"But if one analyzes from up close, one sees that the greatest and most energetic people of the century have always worked against the grain, and they have always worked out of personal initiative. Both in painting and in literature. (I do not know anything about music, but I suppose it has been the same there.) To begin on a small scale, to persevere quand même, to produce much with small capital, to have character instead of money, more audacity than credit, like Millet and Sensier, Balzac, Zola, de Goncourt, Delacroix."

Audacity was one of Vincent's favorite words; it implies boldness, fearlessness, heroism, strength of spirit. Equally for him, it is backed by wisdom which is perceptive, insightful, astute, judicious, and sound. These attributes guided his artistic techniques and dictated the themes or content of his art. Content has to do with the contribution or critique a work of art offers the world. For Vincent, content was identical with universal values such as appreciation of nature, love, kindness and compassion. In advocating such values he went against the grain of his time for these were the immortal virtues of a by-gone era, that of Dickens and Millet.

Vincent van Gogh remains a great artist because his work continues to communicate timeless truths from one generation to the next. Even his mistakes and missteps are there for us to learn from, just as his art contains imperfections and corrections left for us to see and ponder. This sort of transparency is not often seen as an artistic or moral value but they are values because they are true. The Gospel pages that Van Gogh saw written in coal fields extended to his surrounding world and it is a vision much needed in our era.

Debora Silverman put it this way:

"The conception of art as a lesson, earnestly considered by Vincent in the simplicity of Millet's labor types and their emulators, was vehemently rejected by Gauguin; Gauguin's deliberately ambiguous symbolism made his work an art for the initiated only. Its meaning might be suggested only if the hermetic code of the artist's vision was cracked by the words of the creator himself."

More than anything else, what makes Vincent important is not that he was totally authentic or supremely inventive although he was undoubted both of these things to an usually high degree. Van Gogh's very endurance provides us with proof that the universals of faith, hope and love are real and when they chart and guide art and life they ennoble. It might even be said that these human and divine ways of thinking, transfigure and resurrect life.

Great art like Vincent's offers a window or a Gospel page in which we more clearly see the glorious potentiality of life. Hegel, like Van Gogh demonstrated that the rational unity we can see everywhere in nature is found even more so in the deepest levels of human consciousness. In order for rational unity and meaning to be seen art must embody it.

In a real sense, a redemptive work of art is a concrete covenant made to make peace between the mind and body and the internal and external world. Its power is in its implicit unity and finite reality. This covenant concept is found in the Dutch art of the seventeenth century. Rembrandt, for instance, expressed the supernatural by representing sublime aspects of nature rather than depicting mystical religious subjects such as swooning saints. Rembrandt made the spiritual real and the finite, spirit-filled. His was a covenant form because it bound together the world of God and mankind. That is what covenants—do they are binding agreements. They are the marriage vows taken to stay together till death. Above all, it was a sacred agreement between God and his chosen people. The Dutch of the seventeenth century saw themselves as chosen as well, and their art reflected this in ways that Van Gogh fully understood.

The Gospel is echoed in all of Van Gogh's art and writings as Mark Roskill so eloquently explains:

"He was not averse to provisional experiment, but in the long run he always fell back on to fundamentals; the content of the Bible, for example, was as much of a fundamental to him at the end of his life as it had been in his youth, even though specific reference to it came to play a much smaller part in his letters than it had in the years when religion had offered him a practical goal...The solidity of Van Gogh's thought has a further and broader aspect. In terms of the cultural predicament of his time, this took the form of a passion for wholeness to set against the fragmentation of artistic sensibility that had increasingly characterized the nineteenth century...As he [Van Gogh] saw it, men were the poorer in that art was no longer something one felt called to, in the way he did, as a way of transmitting the basic common truths of love and faith and suffering. Instead, the subjects of art had split apart from one another and so had its technical means... It was above all necessary that art absorb back into its bloodstream the universals of human existence...It had to command the presence of values, now lost, in works of art and literature transmitted from the past...and it needed also a wholesome and Godly soundness of its own."

In the end, Vincent's art was the finite expression of a covenant made between Vincent and life itself. Through the mediatory power of art, Vincent returned to the rainbow and the sacred origins of life. Art was a covenant that helped promote peace between Vincent and his own divided nature. This covenant was extended through the mediation of Bernard and his final account of Vincent's last moments and now, at this moment, in our reflecting upon it. Art's future can be shaped by the wisdom revealed in Vincent's art and life.

What we can glean from Vincent's legacy is as star-studded as his "Starry Night" leading to art's starry dawn. Art is part of a mysterious covenant that is dateless .It is as awe-inspiring as a wing or a flame and beckons like a rainbow overarching the crisp horizon of cloud-banked Brabant...like the pages out of the Gospel and the resurrection promise that Van Gogh and Dickens could never let go. Without it their art and lives were stripped of moral grandeur and value.

The Vincent we most admire was described by Dr. Paul Ferdinand Gachet, who, as a medical practitioner, was well aware of Vincent's brokenness. In fact, he was the attending physician at Vincent's death. Yet, according to Gachet, illness, weakness, and corrupting flesh did not describe Vincent any more than they epitomize Abraham Lincoln. Rather than Vincent's insanity, it was a cluster of other strengths that characterized him. It was the heroic way he dealt with his illness and made practical plans to prepare for it by admitting himself to the St. Remy asylum. Vincent's art embodies a unity of the virtues that made his character something to admire.

The following is a reminder of the qualities Gachet came to admire in Vincent—his clear mindedness and willingness to stare down the vague, purely theoretical, or the inartistic:

"I saw Mesdag's 'Panorama'. I was there with the painter De Bock, who collaborated on it, and he told me of an incident that happened after the Panorama was finished and that I thought was quite funny. Perhaps you know the painter Destrée. Between you and me and the lamppost: the incarnation of mealymouthed arrogance. Well, one day this gentleman came up to De Bock and said to him, very haughtily, very blandly, very condescendingly, 'De Bock, I was invited to paint that Panorama too, but because it was so inartistic, I refused.' To which De Bock answered, 'Mr. Destrée, what is easier, to paint a Panorama or to refuse to paint a Panorama? What is more artistic, to do a thing or not to do it?' I thought this answer very much to the point....the positive consciousness of the fact that art is something greater and higher than our own adroitness and accomplishments or knowledge; that art is something which, although produced by human hands, is not created by these hands alone, but something which wells up from a deeper source in our souls; and that with regard to adroitness and technical skill in art I see something that reminds me of what in reli-

gion may be called self-righteousness. My sympathies in the literary as well as in the artistic fields are strongly attracted to those artists in whom I see the working of the soul predominating."

What we admire in his painting we find in his life and letters, namely an audacious commitment to human and divine values in the face of their erosion and decline. Beliefs shown in his devotion to bygone artistic mentors and literary heroes. For instance, where Gauguin disdained earlier artists over minor technical matters, Vincent saw beyond his personal preferences to bigger issues.

Van Gogh always revered Rembrandt, Millet, Breton, and Daumier for the spiritual radiance of their work, in spite of the fact that stylistically they were out of fashion in nineteenth century Parisian circles. Like his dismissal of Rembrandt, Gauguin also broke promises, marriage vows and art partnerships for expedience and personal aggrandizement.

As one considers Van Gogh within the broad perspective of the history of art, one comes to admire his steady, reliable, even predictably strong values. With Vincent, instead of obscurity and irony, we get honesty. Instead of glamor and crazes, we get sackcloth and coal dust blanketing a world illuminated by starlight, and guided by spiritual yearnings. We see a man weak and broken at times but who ultimately makes his story true to life. The honest testimony of his life gives us grace to keep the faith and tell the truth even when it is not expedient, or especially when it is not fashionable or politically correct.

In the final poignant scene in Hugo's *Les Misérables,* we are given the last words and covenant of Jean Valjean. His adopted daughter Cossette and her husband Marius are at his side. The scene is like the one Vincent once disclosed when he journeyed on foot to the bedside of a dying family friend and then waited for the dawn to invade the simple cemetery where his brother was buried. Valjean promises with a binding covenant blessing that God will protect them.

To make real his words, he lays his hands on the heads of the

Cosette and Marius.

The covenant is a physically administered act like a marriage ceremony given publicly that God will never desert them as long as they ardently seek Him. This promise was given in the most profound covenant agreement ever enacted according to the Gospel namely the Incarnation and Sacrifice of the God/Man. The theological meaning of this act is understood as a cosmic expression of unutterable love who become fully human and dies on mankind's behalf and to offer absolution to appease a previously broken covenant made at Sinai and confirmed by Moses.

This awesome binding written in blood was well understood by both Vincent and Gauguin. They were willing to covenant with the divine in order to make real and evident tangible works of art as a minor form of resurrection. A final eulogy is closely related to a covenant for in the eulogy one binds oneself to the memory of a departed loved one and agree to live for that person. This solemn act resurrects the departed in memory and walks bound forever with the meaning of that life. So too works of sacred art fully covenantal in ways that can never be fully explained. We meet this mystery in *Les Misérables*. Now we know why in his twilight hours Vincent resurrected this cosmically themed book and pledged his life to God. Now perhaps we better understand Bishop Bienvenu's mysterious dialogue with the ineffable starlit presence of God in the dark confines of his garden.

Without his art to work as a healing mode he felt uprooted, and disconnected from the world on which he had lavished his eye, mind and spirit with ecstatic embrace. It was as if the Bishop's starry prayer was suddenly interrupted, or his sacred garden destroyed.

Vincent had made a covenant with himself to work faithfully on behalf of the forsaken and to produce works of art that would deeply move, comfort and assure others. When he no longer had the means to sustain this profound dialogue with nature, he felt banished from life. It was as if the binding agreement he had made to use art to grow, to share, and to heal had been broken by an outside force.

Vincent knew that he was responsible for abusing absinthe and alcohol. He admitted this to his mother in one of his last letters to her in which he sought her forgiveness. But he also said that in some important ways it was too late to remedy his ruined health. He was convinced that it was irredeemable. True, his moral redemption should have included forgiving himself for even the long-term destruction of his body, but we must recall that Vincent was passionately self-sacrificial to begin with and had little fear of death. We recall that he began his life closely bound to his stillborn brother and namesake. In the most mortal sense, part of his being resided in a grave that bore his first, middle and last name. We know he had an extremely strong sense of belonging with his deceased brother—the unknown Vincent—and one can only imagine how it would feel to stand next to a grave stone with one's own identity etched upon it. Vincent had a powerful desire to die, and when his reason for living was gone, it was hardly surprising that he chose to end it all.

When most of the known pieces are assembled, Vincent's suicide, as tragic and sudden as it may seem, could be predicted. He was uprooted from his life-giving therapeutic art, and he was a steady emotional and psychological strain on his closest loved ones, namely Theo and Johanna. Vincent's end was the result of the same resolute pragmatism that had allowed him to accomplish so much in his short life. He had conducted his painting campaigns with the utmost care and precision counting the cost at every step. He had made a covenant to live for others though his art, and when this covenant was shattered by a collapsing body his purpose was gone.

The fact that his art provides so many viewers so much sustenance is living proof that Vincent had achieved his stated purposes. That many are moved and changed by his passionate example of self-expending love as evidenced in his letters is even further proof. His legacy is powerful because it contains lessons about the preciousness of life. A glorious life made all the stronger in stark contrast against the shadowed thrust of death.

Victor Hugo's inspired words offer a blessed eulogy for Vincent:

"Such are the distributions of God. He is on high, he sees us all, and he knows what he does in the midst of his great stars. So I am going away, my children. Love each other dearly always. There is scarcely anything else in the world but that: to love one another. You will think sometimes of the poor old man who died here. Oh my Cosette! It is not my fault, indeed, if I have not seen you all this time, it broke my heart; I went as far as the corner of the street, I must have seemed strange to the people who saw me pass, I looked like a crazy man, once I went out with no hat. My children, I do not see very clearly now, I had some more things to say, but it makes no difference. Think of me a little. You are blessed creatures. I do not know what is the matter with me, I see a light. Come nearer. I die happy. Let me put my hands upon your dear beloved heads...Cosette and Marius fell on their knees, overwhelmed, choked with tears, each grasping one of Jean Valjean's hands. Those august hands moved no more. He had fallen backward, the light from the candlesticks fell upon him; his white face looked up toward heaven, he let Cosette and Marius cover his hands with kisses; he was dead. The night was starless and very dark. Without doubt, in the gloom some mighty angel was standing, with outstretched wings, awaiting the soul."

Opposite: Cypresses with Two Female Figures, 1889. Oil on canvas.
In the collection of the Kröller-Müller Museum, Otterlo, The Netherlands.

APPENDICES

Please note: The Van Gogh Museum in Amsterdam has created an excellent
online resource for Vincent van Gogh's letters, paintings, drawings, and
sketches. This may be accessed at www.VanGoghMuseum.com.

The sizes of Van Gogh's paintings remained within a modest range (24" x 32")
generally. Vincent was limited to smaller canvases due to the fact that he
was shipping his work as railway cargo to Theo, and he would have paid
a premium for exceeding specified size requirements.

A Literary Review

The two most extensive, long-term studies of Van Gogh were based upon his letters following their publication in 1914: Marc Edo Tralbaut's (1969) monumental biography, *Van Gogh*, and *Van Gogh: A Documentary Biography* by A.M. and Renilde Hammacher (1982). Remarkably, both Tralbaut and A. M. Hammacher began their research in 1917! And both studies, took over fifty years to complete! They were written by Dutch scholars who were friends of the Van Gogh family. Tralbaut's biography included interviews with remaining Van Gogh family members, including Vincent's sisters, sister-in-law Johanna van Gogh-Bonger, and her son Vincent. The Hammacher's documentary biography shares important similarities with the Tralbaut study in its dependence on private documents, including Vincent's personal collection of prints, books, and studio items. However the Hammachers traced Vincent's travels, reading habits, and other activities, shedding light on his psychological and creative processes where Tralbaut stresses the more historic and tangible side of Van Gogh. Taken together along with Johanna's personal reflections these studies provided a solid foundation for later Van Gogh research.

Many present-day scholars of the nineteenth century history have mined the private letters of artists, poets, and social commentators. They discovered a virtually unknown nineteenth century; one that is more complex in ethical and religious questions and contradictory than historians realized. By turning to personal letters and historical documents, they began to reappraise longstanding or canonized views not only of Van Gogh but also of his era. A few selected examples of this research include: *Van Gogh* by Judy Sund (2004), *Van Gogh and Gauguin: The Search for Sacred Art* by Debora Silverman (2000), *Romanticism and Its Discontents* by Anita Brookner (2000), Differencing the Canon: Feminist Desire and the Writing of Art's Histories by Griselda Pollock (1999), At Eternity's Gate: The Spiritual Vision of Vincent van Gogh by Kathleen Powers Erickson (1998), Van Gogh's Progress: Utopia, Modernity, and LateNineteenth-Century Art by Carol Zemel (1997), The Glory of van Gogh: An Anthropology of Admiration by Natalie Heinich (1996), The Letters of Vincent Van Gogh selected and edited by Ronald de Leeuw (1996), The Copy Turns Original: Vincent Van Gogh and a New Approach to Traditional Art Practice by Cornelia Homburg (1996), True to Temperament: Van Gogh and French Naturalist Literature by Judy Sund (1992), The Letters of Vincent Van Gogh edited and introduced by Mark Roskill (1991), The Genesis of Modernism: Seurat, Gauguin, Van Gogh, & French Symbolism in the 1880's by Sven Loevgren (1971), and Realism by Linda Nochlin (1971).

I will begin by discussing Linda Nochlin's (1971) Realism, a milestone work that indirectly influenced many scholarly studies that followed. Nochlin describes how nature and the external world were rejected as subjects in art by advanced painters of the nineteenth century in favor of privatized formal experimentation. This change of attitude was the outgrowth of an "art for the sake of art alone" mentality. Within this context Nochlin showed how Van Gogh and a few others were able to resist the tendency to turn from traditional moral values in art while remaining open to aspects of technical experimentation, optical research and personal experience. The previously mentioned scholars made extensive use of nineteenth-century documents and data to reconstruct the spiritual disquietude of Van Gogh's time. Subsequently, they were able to shed new light on lesser known concerns. In particular, private religious experience in an era previously thought of as deeply secular. These findings were underscored by Erickson (1998) and Silverman (2000), from whom we learn that Van Gogh's and Gauguin's religious preoccupations, while extremely different from each other, were not as rare in European nineteenth-century cultural and artistic life as previously believed. We learn from Pollock (1999) that canons of taste affected the content and practice of art and in particular how women were seen exploited, trivialized and marginalized. These attitudes appear in many guises in the painting and popular novels of the era and Van Gogh and Gauguin for example were not immune to some of the gender bias reflected in public media.

Erickson (1998), Silverman (2000), and Zemel (1997) enlarge on the religious implications of Van Gogh's sympathy with the nineteenth-century English Art and Craft Movement of the 1840s and 50s. The title of Zemel's work, Van Gogh's Progress: Utopia, Modernity, and Late-NineteenthCentury Art, makes reference to Bunyan's religious allegory, Pilgrim's Progress, one of Vincent's favorite devotionals. Expanding on these themes, Judy Sund—in her 2004 study, Van Gogh, and her earlier 1992 work, True to Temperament: Van Gogh and French Naturalist Literature, demonstrates how rooted in realist literature and social awareness Van Gogh was in contrast to the majority of nineteenth-century artists. This perception is supported by Deborah Silverman (1992) in Pilgrim's Progress and Vincent van Gogh's Metier. Here we discover his involvement in illustration as an art form with ties to populist literature. All of these Van Gogh scholars enlarge on his identification with the alienated lower classes, their symbolic appearance as Christ-like, despised servants or pilgrims and their connection with rural life and humble occupations such as weaving, farming, mining, blacksmithing, etc. Within the city, the theme of the alien, outsider, or underground man, factory worker, menial office employee, servant and hired man became a favored subject for writers such as Hugo, Dickens and Dostoevsky. Van Gogh also saw coal weavers, miners, labors, exploited children, prostitutes and marginalized women as part of this broad cast of unfortunate people.

Natalie Heinich (1996) examines major aspects of the Van Gogh myth. She shows how Van Gogh became the subject of adulation as a "genius/martyr" within the fabric of nineteenth-century artistic life. She explains how his association with the lower classes acquired for him a romantic status as an artistic rebel freed from the excesses and social distortions taking place in European society. Heinich's (1996) research like that of Carol Zemel (1997) demonstrates that the rural craft practices that Vincent identified with were of a grass-roots origin. This connection between modernism and the common man has been downplayed by critical art historians Nochlin (1971), Kathleen Powers Erickson (1998), and others show how Van Gogh resisted the trend away from redemptive themes in art. These scholars began to recognize that Vincent had a profound understanding of his artistic enterprise than was previously known. Researchers such as Mark Roskill (1991) came to see that Van Gogh had the literary skill and philosophical insight to describe philosophical issues and ability to chronicle the finite realities of studio life and to record unapologetically his personal failures and artistic shortcomings.

Debora Silverman (2000), in contrast to Heinich's focus on urban intellectual developments, reconstructs the rural religious roots and educational background of Van Gogh and the traditional Catholic upbringing of Gauguin. She relates these religious roots to specific paintings Gauguin and Van Gogh created together at Arles in 1889. Her research makes it clear that these modernist artists were profoundly involved with religious ideas, even though they often criticized some traditional religious practices such as the worship of saints, relics, Mariology etc., they continued to have distinctly spiritual views of art and life. Her discoveries, along with those of Anita Brookner's, are forcing a reappraisal of modernist art history, reversing the long-held theory that modern art is essentially a secular, anti-religious, anti-traditional movement. A strong indication of this renewal can be seen in the overtly religious paintings of Van Gogh and Gauguin that were shown together for the very first time in a major exhibition at the Chicago Institute of Art (2000). Since 2000, other important exhibitions of religious art can be cited; for instance, El Greco at the Metropolitan Museum in New York in 2003-2004 and Rembrandt's Late Religious Portraits at the Getty Museum in Los Angeles in 2005 and Holy Image, Hallowed Ground Icons from Sinai in 2006-2007. Such exhibitions within the United States alone indicate that there is a strong interest in religious experience within art historical and studio practice. This interest in religious experience is part of a much wider return to religion taking place in America and throughout the world at the present time. Heinich (1996) considers the paradox of the skyrocketing prices ($83 million, for example) for a Van Gogh in light of the fact that Vincent sold virtually nothing during his lifetime. She suggests that the staggering prices of Vincent's work may be a form of cultural expiation, a way to relieve accumulated guilt for his neglect and social ostracism by a culture now profiting from his actual suffering (1996, 101-103).

The secular sanctification of Van Gogh is, like Critical art historical theory, a way of thinking that makes Vincent the real person secondary to an abstract process in the grip of a deterministic force. The image of the mythical-martyr is not something Vincent wanted to promote. He hoped to be remembered for his unremitting personal honesty and dedication to gospel values. He wanted to leave written "epistles" (and often used this New Testament word) concerning what art can be as a form of communication having a public impact and redemptive role to play.

According to Erickson, leaving specific examples of Van Gogh's religious work in basement storage vaults is not an isolated thing. What she noted clearly was part of a long tradition of ignoring art based on moral or religious themes within nineteenth and twentieth century art. In effect, ignoring religious art meant leaving not only certain paintings in basements, but also ignoring sacred themes and uplifting spiritual moments in art generally:

Some art historians have openly lamented van Gogh's religious paintings, claiming, "The return of so many of his earlier ideas was unhappily flawed by a reemergence of religious hysteria" [Chetham, 1976]. This view reveals both disgust with the deepening of van Gogh's faith at St. Remy and the view that van Gogh's former pursuit of a clerical vocation was a kind of fanatical hysteria. (154)

Erickson's comments regarding the rejection of sacred themes in Van Gogh's art—and more generally within nineteenth and twentieth century art history—can be substantiated easily by examining any standard college modern art textbook. Few, if any of them, contain sacred images, even though a great number of important paintings based on sacred themes were created by major artists during this period. Erickson's account reveals yet another tendency within art historical practice: namely, to ignore artists' personal commentaries on their art when they differ from historians personal bias and agendas. This is demonstrated by the fact that Van Gogh made numerous suggestions regarding the installation of a number of his works (1978/1889, 3:171). He diagrammed several sets of paintings, including his well known and frequently reproduced Sunflowers series, and suggested that they be arranged as triptychs (sets of three) and by this configuration make reference to traditional three-part altarpieces. As of the twenty-first century, the Sunflowers remain separated in various museums and denied their meaning as a sacred still-life triptych. The Sunflowers are not a simple, isolated installation problem. They underscore the fact that many of his paintings were intended as triptychs with formal references made between specific works. The disregard of Vincent's instructions and diagrams has resulted in installation practices which suppress aspects of his intended moral meanings and sacred vision.

This disregard offers a graphic demonstration of what also has happened to a balanced and complete account of his art/life. Erickson's reference to sacred themes and the neglect or dismissal of artists' letters is more significant than it might appear, for it raises an important issue regarding art historical practices. The issue is to what extent an artist's written statements regarding works of art, especially ones reflecting sacred themes, should be taken into consideration in historical analysis, reproductions in publications, and exhibitions of art. Another way of putting it is to what degree should so-called secondary documents, such as private letters, manifestos, and first-person statements, be used to interpret primary aesthetic objects, such as finite 3-D works of art, religious or otherwise when they are presented publicly?

In The Letters of Vincent Van Gogh, Ronald de Leeuw (1997) has selected a thoughtful overview of Van Gogh's letters along with a critical commentary and introduction. Since he is the director of the Van Gogh Museum in Amsterdam, he has personal access to the actual letters and other materials in the museum archives. In his book he has included never before published letters that shed light on the complex situation brought about by Vincent's father's attempt to have him committed to a mental institution. In True to Temperament: Van Gogh and French Naturalist Literature, Judy Sund (1992) has produced one of the most important studies of the literary dimensions of Van Gogh. She takes us into the heart of European reading habits from the middle of the nineteenth century to the beginning of the twentieth. She tracks Vincent's tendency to read particular books to provide him entrance into the thoughts or attitudes of a region or cultural context. I

In The Copy Turns Original: Vincent Van Gogh and a New Approach to Traditional Art Practice, Cornelia Homburg (1996) similarly demonstrates how Van Gogh could adapt another artist's work into his personal vision by translating, expressively transforming, or rearranging it. He would take a black and white print, for instance, and render it in vibrant colors or ratchet up a low-impact color scheme. Homburg underscores what Judy Sund had noted in her literary study, that Van Gogh was unusually adept at reinterpreting a theme, subject, or concept from a literary or visual source.

The Letters of Vincent Van Gogh, edited and introduced by Mark Roskill (1991), offers a selection of letters that complement Ronald de Leeuw's compilation, since the two authors do not always select the same letters to discuss. Roskill weaves a dense, deeply reflective commentary into the body of his personal letters and enlarges and contextualizes their broader cultural meanings. What is most remarkable about Roskill's work is his introduction where he offers profound insights into Van Gogh's moral views of art and life and describes his unique cluster of operational skills, perceptive powers, and unitary vision. I am heavily indebted to Roskill for his philosophical views and I have endeavored to flesh out and follow several his thoughtful leads while adding a number of my own to the list. Sven Loevgren's (1971) The Genesis of Modernism: Seurat, Gauguin, Van Gogh, & French Symbolism in the 1880's is essential reading. His study probes the way in which neurotic attitudes and narcotics were features of much late nineteenth century Symbolist thought. The Symbolists can be linked in a number of important ways to the early twentieth century Dada movement and in turn to the Beatniks and Hippies. The dark side of the arts of this period and their destructive tendencies are evident in Sven Loevgren's work. Van Gogh's rejection of the Symbolist ideology and exiting Paris where such practices were common was as much a quest for personal health and stability as it was an artistic difference of opinion.

Literary & Other Sources: Episode One

LITERARY & OTHER SOURCES: EPISODE TWO

Page 87   end of quote, Victor Hugo (BIB 47)

Page 88   end of top paragraph, ...prior to that time. (BIB 50) [giving credit for historical source]

Page 90   bottom of page, end of quote by Pierard (BIB 64)

Page 92   end of quote, "October 1, 1879." (BIB 34)

Page 102   end of Dickens quote (BIB 22)

Page 104   at top, end of Dickens quote (BIB 22)

Page 104   first paragraph, Levin (BIB 53)

Page 108   top, end of Ackroyd quote (BIB 01)

Page 108   end of Hammacher quote at bottom of page, (BIB 39)

Page 109   end of Dickens quote (BIB 19)

Page 110   Chekhov quote (BIB 13)

Page 110   end of next quote, which is Dickens's (BIB 19)

Page 111   top, end of Dickens quote (BIB 19)

Page 111   end of Dickens quote (BIB 19)

Page 114   end of Merleau-Ponty quote in first paragraph and then at end of long quote (BIB 58)

Page 114   end of Roskill quote (BIB 70)

Page 114   end of Erickson quote (BIB 26)

Page 117   end of Gauguin quote (BIB 30)

Page 121   top, end of Victor Hugo quote (BIB 47)

Page 114   end of Roskill quote (BIB 70)

Page 114   end of Erickson quote (BIB 26)

Page 117   end of Gauguin quote (BIB 30)

Page 121   top, end of Victor Hugo quote (BIB 47)

LITERARY & OTHER SOURCES: EPISODE THREE

LITERARY & OTHER SOURCES: EPISODE FOUR

Literary & Other Sources: Episode Five

IMAGE SOURCES & CITATIONS

Page 10 *The Sheaf Binder [After Millet]*, 1889. Oil on canvas.
Van Gogh Museum, Amsterdam, The Netherlands.

Page 12 Peasant Mowing. Charcoal with black crayon.
Van Gogh Museum, Amsterdam, The Netherlands.

Page 13 Change title to Peasant Mowing, 1885. Black crayon.
Van Gogh Museum, Amsterdam, The Netherlands.

Page 18 Women Miners Carrying Coal, 1882. Watercolor on paper heightened
with white pigment.
Kröller-Müller Museum, Otterlo, The Netherlands.

Page 19 (As for Page 18)

Page 20 Self-Portrait at the Easel, 1888. Oil on canvas.
Van Gogh Museum, Amsterdam, The Netherlands.

Page 22 Photograph of Joanna Bonger with Vincent Willem Van Gogh, 1890.

Page 26 Woman Sewing with a Girl, 1883. Chalk, pen, ink, and watercolor.
Van Gogh Museum, Amsterdam, The Netherlands.

Page 29 Vincent van Gogh, Theo van Gogh, and Johanna van Gogh-Bonger.
Images in the Public Domain.

Page 30 Portrait of the Artist's Mother, 1888. Oil on canvas.
Norton Simon Museum, Pasadena, California.

Page 32 Van Gogh Family Coat of Arms.
Image in the Public Domain.

Page 34 Source Unknown.
Image in the Public Domain.

Page 43 Portrait of a Peasant (Patience Escalier), 1888. Oil on canvas.
Private Collection.

Page 44 Source Unknown.
Image in the Public Domain.

Page 47 Bottom image: The State Lottery Office, 1882. Watercolor.
Van Gogh Museum, Amsterdam, The Netherlands.

Page 48 Source Unknown.
Image in the Public Domain.

Page 49 Van Gogh's Chair with Pipe [detail], 1888. Oil on canvas.
Van Gogh Museum, Amsterdam, The Netherlands.

Image Sources & Citations

Page 55 Charles Dickens.
Image in the Public Domain.

Page 56 Self-Portrait at the Easel (detail), 1888. Oil on canvas.
Van Gogh Museum, Amsterdam, The Netherlands.

Page 59 Van Gogh's Chair with Pipe, 1888. Oil on canvas.
Van Gogh Museum, Amsterdam, The Netherlands.

Page 61 Jacob van Ruisdael, View of Haarlem, 1670. Oil on canvas
Rijksmuseum, Amsterdam, The Netherlands.

Page 71 William Powell Frith, Ramsgate Sands: 'Life at the Seaside', 1852-54.
Oil on canvas.
Royal Collection, London

Page 77 The Raising of Lazarus [After Rembrandt], 1890. Oil on paper.
Van Gogh Museum, Amsterdam, The Netherlands.

Page 78 Jacob van Ruisdael, The Jewish Cemetery, 1657. Oil on canvas
Detroit Institute of Art, Detroit, USA.

Page 79 Mining Town in the Borinage, 1882. Watercolor on paper.
Whereabouts unknown.

Page 81 Le Moulin de la Galette, Montmarte, 1886. Oil on canvas.
Glasgow Museum, Glasgow, Scotland.

Page 87 Peasant Burning Weeds, 1883. Oil on panel.
Private collection.

Page 88 The Miners Return, post-1881. Pencil, pen, and brush.
Kröller-Müller Museum, Otterlo, The Netherlands.

Page 91 A Pair of Shoes, 1886. Oil on canvas.
Van Gogh Museum, Amsterdam, The Netherlands.

Page 97 The Iron Mill in the Hague, 1882. Gouache, watercolor, wash, pen,
India ink, and pencil on paper.
Christie's

Page 99 Backyards of Old House in Antwerp in the Snow, 1885. Oil on canvas.
Van Gogh Museum, Amsterdam, The Netherlands.

Page 113 Snowy Landscape with Arles in the Background, 1888. Oil on canvas.
Private collection.

IMAGE SOURCES & CITATIONS

Page 118 Portrait de l'artiste (Self Portrait), Paul Gauguin, 1893-94.
   Oil on canvas.
   Musee d'Orsay, Paris, France.

Page 122 Still Life with Bible, 1885. Oil on canvas.
   Van Gogh Museum, Amsterdam, The Netherlands.

Page 124 View of Paris from Montmarte, 1886. Oil on canvas.
   Offentlische Kunstsammalung, Kuntsmuseum, Basel, Switzerland

Page 125 (Same as Page 124)

Page 129 Bowl with Peonies and Roses, 1886. Oil on canvas.
   Kröller-Müller Museum, Otterlo, The Netherlands.

Page 143 House in Auvers, 1890. Oil on canvas.
   Museum of Fine Arts, Boston, USA.

Page 144 The Man is at Sea [after Demont-Breton], 1889. Oil on canvas.
   Private collectio.

Page 153 Girl Kneeling by a Cradle, 1883. Pencil and charcoal, heightened
   with white.
   Van Gogh Museum, Amsterdam, The Netherlands.

Page 159 Farmhouse in Provence, 1888. Oil on canvas.
   National Gallery of Art, Washington, D.C., USA.

Page 160 Still Life: Drawing Board, Pipe, Onions, and Sealing-Wax, 1889.
   Oil on canvas.
   Kröller-Müller Museum, Otterlo, The Netherlands.

Page 161 (Same as Page 160)

Page 162 The Good Samaritan (After Delacroix), 1890. Oil on canvas.
   Kröller-Müller Museum, Otterlo, The Netherlands.

Page 164 Starry Night Over the Rhone, 1888. Oil on canvas.
   Musee d'Orsay, Paris, France.

Page 183 Bedroom in Arles, 1888. Oil on canvas.
   Musee d'Orsay, Paris, France.

Page 184 A Lane in the Public Garden at Arles, 1888. Oil on canvas.
   Kröller-Müller Museum, Otterlo, The Netherlands.

Page 207 Vincent's House in Arles, 1888. Oil on canvas.
   Van Gogh Museum, Amsterdam, The Netherlands.

Image Sources & Citations

Page 208 The Starry Night, 1889. Oil on canvas.
Museum of Modern Art, New York

Page 209 (Same as Page 208)
Page 210 Self-Portrait, 1889. Oil on canvas.
Musee d'Orsay, Paris

Page 212 Ia Orana Maria (Hail Mary), 1891. Paul Gauguin. Oil on canvas.
Metropolitan Museum of Art, New York

Page 216 Top: Paul Gauguin, Self-Portrait Les Miserables, 1888. Oil on canvas.
Van Gogh Museum, Amsterdam, The Netherlands.

Page 216 Bottom: Paul Gauguin, Self-Portrait with the Yellow Christ, 1889.
Oil on canvas. Private collection.

Page 221 [photograph of Gauguin]

Page 222 Paul Gauguin, Christmas Night, 1896. Oil on canvas.
Indianapolis Museum of Art, Indianapolis, USA.

Page 235 Paul Gauguin, Self-Portrait Near Golgotha, 1896. Oil on canvas.
Sao Paolo Museum de Arte.

Page 236 Portrait of Doctor Gachet, 1890. Oil on canvas.
Private collection.

Page 251 Cypresses with Two Female Figures, 1889. Oil on canvas.
Kröller-Müller Museum, Otterlo, The Netherlands.

Page 252 Reaper with Cap Mving to the Right, 1885. Charcoal with light
lithographic crayon.
Van Gogh Museum, Amsterdam, The Netherlands.

Page 253 (Same as Page 252)

BIBLIOGRAPHY

1   Ackroyd, P. 1990. Dickens. New York: HarperCollins Publishers.

2   Bacharach, S. 2005. Toward a metaphysical historicism. The Journal of Aesthetics and Art Criticism 63 (Spring): 165-173.

3   Bedarida, F. 1970. Cities: Population and the urban explosion. In the nineteenth century: The contradictions of progress, ed. A. Briggs, 99-130. New York: McGraw-Hill.

4   Bernard, E. 1986. Letter from Emile Bernard to G.-Albert Aurier: On Vincent's burial, 1 August 1890. In Van Gogh: A retrospective, ed. S. A. Stein, 219-222. New York: Park Lane.

5   Biro, M. 1998. Anselm Kiefer and the philosophy of Martin Heidegger. Cambridge: Cambridge University Press.

6   Blocker, H. G. and J. M. Jeffers, 1998. Introduction in Contextualizing aesthetics: From Plato to Lyotard. Edited by H. G. Blocker and J. M. Jeffers. Belmont, CA: Wadsworth Publishing Company.

7   Bonger, A. 1978. Excerpt in The complete letters of Vincent van Gogh. 2d ed. 3 vols., trans. J. van Gogh-Bonger and C. de Dood. Boston: New York Graphic Society. Original work published 1914.

8   Briggs, A. 1970. The shape of the century: Man at the crossroads of history. In The nineteenth century: The contradictions of progress, ed. A. Briggs, 11-38. New York: McGraw-Hill.

9   Brookner, A. 2000. Romanticism and its discontents. New York: Farrar, Strauss and Giroux.

10 Carroll, N. 2002. The wheel of virtue: Art, literature, and moral knowledge. The Journal of Aesthetics and Art Criticism 60 (Winter): 3-26.

11 Carlyle, T. 1927. Letter to the author. In The life of Charles Dickens, Vol. 1, by J. Forster, Dedication (n.p.). New York: E. P. Dutton & Co., Inc. Original work published 1874.

12 Cartwright, J. 1902. Jean Francois Millet: His life and letters. New York: The MacMillan Co.

13 Chekhov, A. 1947. A day in the country. In A treasury of short stories, ed. B. Kielty. New York: Simon & Schuster.

14 Costa, M. B. 1978. Personal Memories of Vincent van Gogh During His Stay at Amsterdam. In The complete letters of Vincent van Gogh, 2d ed. 3 vols., trans. J. van Gogh-Bonger and C. de Dood. Boston: New York Graphic Society.

Bibliography

15 Daum, M. (2005). B-List TV: Just 15 minutes more.
    Los Angeles Times (June 26): E1 & E27).

16 de Leeuw, R. 1997. Introduction. In The letters of Vincent van Gogh,
    ed. R. de Leeuw, trans. A. Pomerans, ix-xxvi. London: Penguin Books.

17 Devereaux, M. 2004. Moral judgments and works of art:
    The case of narrative literature. The Journal of Aesthetics and
    Art Criticism 62 (Winter): 3-11.

18 Dickens, C. 1946. A Christmas carol. In Christmas Stories, 13-110.
    Cleveland: The World Publishing Company. Original work published 1843.

19 1961. Hard times. New York: The New American Library.
    Original work published 1854.

20 1983. A tale of two cities. London: Dent. Original work published 1859.

21 1985. American notes. New York: St. Martin's Press, Inc.
    Original work published 1842.

22 1998. The Old Curiosity Shop: With the original illustrations. Edited and with
    an introduction by Elizabeth M. Brennan. Original work published 1841.

23 Dostoevsky, F. 1960. Notes from underground and the grand inquisitor.
    Translated by R. E. Matlaw. New York: E. P. Dutton. Original work
    published 1864.

24 Elkins, J. 1999. What painting is. New York: Routledge.

25 Ellison, R. 1972. The invisible man. New York: Vintage Books.
    Original work published 1947.

26 Erickson, K. 1998. At eternity's gate: The spiritual vision of Vincent van
    Gogh. Grand Rapids, MI: William B. Eerdmans.

27 Feagin, S. L. and P. Maynard. 1997. Introduction. In Aesthetics,
    ed. S. Feagin and P. Maynard, 3-10. Oxford: Oxford University Press.

28 Forster, J. 1927. The life of Charles Dickens. 2 vols.
    New York: E. P. Dutton & Co., Inc. Original work published 1874.

29 Gauguin, M. 2003. Letter from Mette Gauguin to Emile Schuffenecker.
    In Letters to his wife and friends. Edited by M. Malingue. Translated
    by H. J. Stenning. Boston: MFA Publications. Original work published 1949.

30 Gauguin, P. 1986. Essais d'art libre: "Still Lifes."
    In Van Gogh: A retrospective, ed. S. A. Stein, 121-122. New York: Park Lane.

BIBLIOGRAPHY

31 2003. Letters to his wife and friends. Edited by M. Malingue. Translated by H. J. Stenning. Boston: MFA Publications. Original work published 1949.

32 Gilson, E. 1952. Being and some philosophers. 2d ed. Toronto: Pontifical Institute of Mediaeval Studies.

33 Gogh, V. 1955. Verzamelde brieven van Vincent van Gogh. 2 vols. Amsterdam: Wereld-Bibliotheek.

34 1978. The complete letters of Vincent van Gogh. 2d ed. 3 vols. Translated by J. van Gogh-Bonger and C. de Dood. Boston: New York Graphic Society. Original work published 1914.

35 1982. The reaper with cap, moving to the right. Drawing, August 1885. As reproduced in A. M. Hammacher and R. Hammacher, Van Gogh, a documentary biography, plate 84. New York: MacMillan Publishing Co., Inc.

36 Gogh-Bonger, J. 1978. Memoir in The complete letters of Vincent van Gogh. 2d ed. 3 vols., trans. J. van Gogh-Bonger and C. de Dood. Boston: New York Graphic Society. Original work published 1914.

37 Grun, B. 1982. The timetables of history: A horizontal linkage of people and events. New York: Simon and Schuster.

38 Guass, C. E. 1949. The aesthetic theories of French artists: 1855 to the present. Baltimore, MD: John Hopkins Press.

39 Hammacher, A. M. and R. Hammacher, 1982. Van Gogh, a documentary biography. New York: MacMillan Publishing Co., Inc.

40 Hegel, G. W. F. 1977. Phenomenology of spirit. Translated by A. V. Miller. Oxford, UK: Oxford University Press. Original work published 1807.

41 1988. Lectures on the philosophy of religion. Edited by P. C. Hodgson. Translated by R. F. Brown & J. M. Stewart. Berkeley, CA: University of California Press. Original work published 1827.

42 1998. Aesthetics: Lectures on fine art. 2 vols. Translated by T. M. Knox. Oxford: Clarendon Press. Original edition, Oxford: Oxford University Press, 1975. Original work published 1835.

43 Heinich, N. 1996. The glory of van Gogh: An anthropology of admiration. Translated by P. L. Browne. Princeton, NJ: Princeton University Press.

44 Hilburn, R. (2005). With Live 8, rock changes the way it calls for change. Los Angeles Times (July 3): A13.

Bibliography

45 Hirschig, A.. 1986. Letter from Anton Hirschig to Dr. A. Bredius: Oud-Holland: Recollections of Vincent van Gogh, 1934. In Van Gogh: A retrospective, ed. S. A. Stein, 210-211. New York: Park Lane.

46 Homburg, C. 1996. The copy turns original: Vincent van Gogh and a new approach to traditional art practice.
Amsterdam: John Benjamins Publishing Co.

47 Hugo, V. 1997. Les Miserables. Translated by C. E. Wilbour. New York: Alfred A. Knopf. Original work published 1862.

48 Huizinga, J. H. 1968. Dutch civilisation in the seventeenth century, and other essays. Translated by A. J. Pomerans. London: Collins.

49 Ives, C. 2005. Out of line: How Van Gogh made his mark. In Vincent Van Gogh: The drawings, by C. Ives, S. A. Stein, S. van Heugten, & M. Vellekoop, 3-20. New York: The Metropolitan Museum of Art.

50 Joll, J. 1970. Authority and protest: Patterns of change from 1848-1900. In the nineteenth century: The contradictions of progress, ed. A. Briggs, 71-98. New York: McGraw-Hill.

51 Kodera, T. 1990. Vincent van Gogh: Christianity versus nature. Amsterdam: John Benjamins Publishing Co.

52 Lambert, J. C. 1984. Cobra. New York: Abbeville Press.

53 Levin, D. M. 1999. The philosopher's gaze: Modernity in the shadows of enlightenment. Berkeley, CA: University of California Press.

54 Levinson, J. 2004. Intrinsic value and the notion of a life. The Journal of Aesthetics and Art Criticism 62 (Fall): 319-329.

55 Lewis, R. and V. Bennett. 2005. Start to make it better, Live 8 urges. Los Angeles Times (July 3): A1, A12.

56 Loevgren, S. 1971. The genesis of modernism: Seurat, Gauguin, Van Gogh, & French symbolism in the 1880's. Bloomington, IN: Indiana University Press.

57 McEvilley, T. (1997). The millennial body: The art of the figure at the end of humanity. Sculpture Magazine: 10-12.

58 Merleau-Ponty, M. 1968. The visible and the invisible: Followed by working notes. Edited by Claude Lefort. Translated by Alphonso Lingis. Evanston, IL: Northwestern University Press. Original work published Hamburg, Classen & Goverts, 1948.

Bibliography

59 Millet, J. F. 1902. Letter. In Jean Francois Millet: His life and letters, by Julia Cartwright. New York: The MacMillan Co. Original letters 1850-1865.

60 Moltmann, J. 1993. God in creation: A new theology of creation and the Spirit of God. Minneapolis: Fortress Press. Original work published Munich, Christian Kaiser Verlag, 1985.

61 Mullin, A. 2004. Moral defects, aesthetic defects, and the imagination. The Journal of Aesthetics and Art Criticism 62 (Summer): 249-261.

62 Nochlin, L. 1990. Realism. New York: Penguin Books. Original edition, New York: Pelican Books, 1971.

63 Obama, B. 2005. What I see in Lincoln's eyes. Time (July 4): 74.

64 Piérard, L. 1978. La vie tragique de Vincent van Gogh. In The complete letters of Vincent van Gogh. 2d ed. 3 vols., translated by J. van Gogh-Bonger and C. de Dood, 222-230. Boston: New York Graphic Society. Original work published 1914.

65 Podro, M. 1982. The critical historians of art. New Haven, CT: Yale University Press.

66 Pohl, F. K. 2002. Framing America: A social history of American art. New York: Thames & Hudson.

67 Pollock, G. 1999. Differencing the canon: Feminist desire and the writing of art's histories. London: Routledge.

68 Pound, E. 1934. ABC of reading. New York: New Directions Paperbook, 1960.

69 Rosenberg, J., S. Slive, and E. H. ter Kuile 1972. Dutch Art and Architecture: 1600 to 1800. Rev. ed. Harmondsworth, Middlesex: Penguin Books Ltd.

70 Roskill, M. 1991. Introduction. In The letters of Vincent van Gogh, ed. M. Roskill, 1131. New York: Atheneum Publishers. Original edition, London: William Collins Sons & Co., Ltd., 1963.

71 Roth, J. 1976. American dreams: Meditations on life in the United States. San Francisco: Chandler & Sharp Publishers, Inc.

72 1997. Private needs, public selves: Talk about religion in America. Urbana and Chicago, IL: University of Illinois Press.

73 Scanlan, J. P. 2002. Dostoevsky the thinker. New York: Cornell University Press.

74 Schama, S. 1999. Rembrandt's eyes. New York: Alfred A. Knopf.

Bibliography

75 Schapiro, M. 1978. Modern art, 19th & 20th centuries: Selected papers. New York: George Braziller.

76 Scigliano, E. 2005. Michelangelo's mountain: The quest for perfection in the marble quarries of Carrara. New York: Free Press.

77 Silverman, D. 1992. Pilgrim's Progress and Vincent van Gogh's Metier. In Van Gogh in England: Portrait of the artist as a young man, ed. M. Bailey, 95-113. London: Barbican Gallery.

78 2000. Van Gogh and Gauguin: The search for sacred art. New York: Farrar, Straus and Giroux.

79 Solomon-Godeau, A. 1994. Going native: Paul Gauguin and the invention of Primitivist Modernism. In Modern art and society: An anthology of social and multicultural readings, ed. M. Berger, 73-94. New York: HarperCollins.

80 Spurling, H. 1998. The unknown Matisse: A life of Henri Matisse: The early years, 1869-1908. New York: Alfred A. Knopf.

81 Stetson, B. 2005. Disagreeing isn't intolerant: Tolerance has been redefined to require approval of the nontraditional. The Orange County Register (August 28): Commentary 2.

82 Stevens, M. and A. Swan. 2004. de Kooning: An American master. New York: Alfred A. Knopf.

83 Stokvis, B. J. 1978. Investigations about Vincent van Gogh in Brabant. In The complete letters of Vincent van Gogh. 2d ed. 3 vols. Trans. J. van Gogh-Bonger and C. de Dood. Boston: New York Graphic Society. Original work published 1926.

84 Sund, J. 1992. True to temperament: Van Gogh and French naturalist literature. Cambridge: University of Cambridge.

85 2002. Van Gogh. London: Phaidon Press Limited.

86 Ten Boom, C. 1974. The hiding place. Toronto: Bantam Books.

87 Trachtman, P. 2005. Toulouse-Lautrec. Smithsonian 36 (May): 84-90.

88 Tralbaut, M. E. 1969. Vincent van Gogh. New York: The Viking Press, Inc.

89 Tyrangiel, J. 2002. Bruce rising: An intimate look at how Springsteen turned 9/11 into a message of hope. Time (August 5): 52-59.

90 Van Crimpen, H. 1987. The Van Gogh family in Brabant. In Van Gogh in Brabant: Paintings and drawings from Etten and Nuenen, trans. P. Wardle, 72-91. Zwolle, Netherlands: Waanders.

Bibliography

91 Van de Wetering, E. 1997. Rembrandt: The painter at work. Amsterdam: Amsterdam University Press.

92 Vernier, P. 1987. Letter from Paul-Louis Vernier to Jean de Rotonchamp. In Gauguin: A retrospective, ed. M. Prather and C. F. Stuckey, 336-338. New York: Park Lane. Original work 1904.

93 Washington, P. 2002. Introduction. In Dostoevsky the thinker, trans. C. E. Wilbour, ix-xxii. New York: Cornell University Press.

94 Wolin, R. 2005. Jürgen Habermas and post-secular societies. The Chronicle of Higher Education (September 23): B16-B17.

95 Wolfe, T. 1976. The painted word. New York: Bantam Books.

96 Worth, S. E. 2004. The ethics of exhibitions: On the presentation of religious art. The Journal of Aesthetics and Art Criticism 62 (Summer): 277-284.

97 Zemel, C. 1997. Van Gogh's progress: Utopia, modernity, and late-nineteenth-century art. Berkeley, CA: University of California Press.

OBSERVATIONS & REFLECTIONS:
VAN GOGH & MODERNIST THEORY

OBSERVATIONS & REFLECTIONS

Van Gogh's literary passions ran counter to the early doctrines of modernism that minimized literacy and the use of literary content in art. By contrast, for Van Gogh the literary and visual arts were inseparable because they gave form to primary human experience. One of the most remarkable things about Van Gogh is that he challenged the very idea of aesthetic dualism—for instance, the modernist idea that the visual arts are merely retinal and the literary arts essentially linguistic or that the human universals which bond private and public life can be easily severed.

Van Gogh's holistic aesthetic approach challenges the modernist tendency to see each of the arts as representative of an independent sense perception or a hyper-private experience—movement for dance, audio perception for music, touch for sculpture, sight for painting, verbal language for literature—and that which is derived from these separate sources having no meaning beyond itself. This splintered view of the senses led away from "common sense" or the shared import of the senses together (i.e., common sense) to uncommon isolated sense experience or "non sense."

This in turn produced artistic theories and practices that removed art from the reality of public life and its problems, claiming art had no other purpose than to provide isolated, private aesthetic sensation which by definition (according to Kant) was non-utilitarian. The inevitable result was an "art for art's sake alone," mentality with art disconnected from a sense of public vocation, cultural meaning, purpose and tradition. As the history of art demonstrates, the result of all this was to remove content—literary, spiritual, moral, and otherwise—from the arts and replace them with private, isolated experience, ambiguity, and confusion.

The Impressionists, in spite of their progressive ideals, provided the motivation for the modernist tendency of looking out at the world—or even away from it altogether—with dispassionate eyes and elevating purely private visual "sensation" above all of the troubling things of life in the real world. Van Gogh, on the other hand, made it clear that for him personal vision and the broader themes of life must be intimately connected. There was no fundamental separation between public and private worlds in his artistic conception.

Vincent made reading, painting, and writing a social activity, not a purely private passivity. For him art was tied to action, taken to fulfill moral and ethical needs, not simply retinal sensation or isolated optical research devoid of social meaning. Van Gogh wanted to engage others in his letters and art; he did not keep an exclusively private diary or make art for himself alone. His letters, even when written about himself, are directed outward, toward others. This is why his letters are important: they contain the objective and subjective poles essential to cultural reflection; in other words, they offer a dialogue between his private and public experience. They include personal analysis and broad cultural reflection, symbolic subjective discourse, and analytical objective evaluation set within a real life. The letters provide both a deconstruction and a reconstruction of art and its meaning as it pertains to his actual life. They also include a critique of art itself within this life.

In a real sense, the letters provide us with the components needed to consider art as a central part of life experience, not divorced from its social roles as in much modernist thought. What will surprise those who have not studied Vincent's letters is that he had a real understanding of the philosophical issues of art, including the processes of historical reconstruction.

The more one studies Van Gogh the more it becomes evident that he believed that the arts constituted what can be called experiential knowledge or embodied truth. Further, he believed that these experiential truths could be consulted and acted upon, provided they were accurate reflections of human nature in dialogue with the real world. For instance, he believed that a novel or painting had a collective cultural value because it offered greater reflective depth than private experience alone.

Van Gogh believed, like the philosopher Hegel, that good art gathers up, or Begreifen [grips together], accumulative cultural content and by its very nature unifies private and public experiences, thereby bridging cultural divides. This is all the more potent because Vincent actually began to rely on such literature and art to navigate through life, not always knowing where his explorations would lead but always wanting to leave a record of his experiences in his letters so others after him could learn from his successes and failures.

Within a shifting cultural context, Van Gogh and a few others were able to resist the tendency to turn away from traditional and moral values in art while at the same time remaining open to aspects of technical experimentation, optical research and personal experience.

However, Van Gogh's adherence to people, places, and subjects drawn literally from life is contrasted by Nochlin (1971) with trends toward exclusively personal abstract experimentation with form and the increasing rejection of cultural content and subject matter in art in 1880's Paris. To demonstrate this change of focus, Nochlin comments on a letter Van Gogh sent the young modernist painter, Emile Bernard:

How severely Van Gogh criticizes Emile Bernard in 1888 for too great a concentration on formal problems in isolation; while he himself may talk about the expressive qualities of line or colour, he almost never talks about them in isolation from the larger context of emotion, feeling, imagination or reality in which they occur. For Van Gogh, reality and truth mean what they meant to the Realists; they have not been transvalued. In 1888, he writes to Bernard: 'In the matter of form, I am too afraid of departing from the possible and the true. . . . My attention is so fixed on what is possible and really exists that I hardly have the desire or the courage to strive for the ideal as it might result from . . . abstract studies.'

Observations & Reflections

Nochlin underscores the cultural tensions that existed in Paris at the time this letter was written and upon which she elaborates throughout her book. She reveals how "the larger content of emotion, feeling, imagination, or reality," and art as a vocation, was exchanged by visual artists for concentration on "formal problems in isolation." For instance, rather than abandoning his commitment to "the larger context of emotion . . . or reality," Van Gogh followed, the vocational and artistic example of Charles Dickens in creating a body of work that communicates common public messages, beliefs, and ideas rooted in daily life.

In late 2003 through 2004, The Metropolitan Museum in New York mounted a major exhibition of the ecstatic, religiously inspired paintings of the sixteenth-century Spanish painter, El Greco. In 2005, the Metropolitan opened another long-awaited blockbuster, this time of Van Gogh's drawings. The accompanying catalog states: "A self-taught artist, he [Van Gogh] succeeded between 1881 and 1890, in developing an inimitable graphic style . . . [the exhibition highlights] the diversity of his technical invention and the striking continuity of his vision" (www.metmuseum.org).

Up to that time, there has never been a large-scale exhibit of Van Gogh's drawings, and it has revealed just how important Vincent's religious views were in shaping his sacred aesthetic. In the exhibition catalog, Colta Ives (2005) wrote: "Van Gogh built a career on the acuity of his vision and the profundity of his faith. His most closely held beliefs were rooted in the religion of his father, a Dutch Reformed pastor . . . ."

There were however important and notable exceptions to these developments. These included the views of painters such as Millet and Van Gogh and writers such as Dostoevsky, Hugo, and Dickens for whom the artistic and spiritual realms remained inseparably united. Each of these painters or writers maintained the view that art's primary purpose was to reflect the sacred wholeness of things. Art had value because it mediated truths from beyond time into a rapidly changing world in

OBSERVATIONS & REFLECTIONS

need of eternal assurance and hope. Van Gogh's artistic consciousness was an outgrowth of the small village where each individual had a measurable impact on the whole. It was a place where earnest, earthy labor and Christian charity were inseparable. As Vincent wrote:

What I have done is a rather hard and coarse reality beside their abstractions, but it will have a rustic quality, and will smell of the earth.

...art is something which although produced by human hands, is not created by these hands alone, but something which wells up from a deeper source in our souls.

The personal and public realms of selfhood were not separate for Van Gogh, which is why he said art made by human hands is not created by [or for] the artist's hands alone. Van Gogh's meaning is clear: art is not made for the artist alone but is designed with others in mind. Van Gogh passionately desired to uplift others through his work, caring deeply how the work would impact his viewer. The social broadcast of his work was modeled by the "good news" emphasis of the Gospel as it flowed outward through Western art and literature.

In our time, moral and religious themes are being widely discussed. Perhaps these discussions have always taken place; but with expanded communications systems and network television broadcasting, we are far more aware of them.

For instance, Roth's (1997) Private Needs, Public Selves: Talk about Religion in America articulated the important roles religion has always played in America, especially following national disasters such as the extensive flooding of the Mississippi River in the Midwest in the 1990s or the recent hurricanes in the South. He also demonstrated the varied ways religious thought is expressed in popular musical themes and in movies. His research has shown how essential religion has been to America's identity and history.

282

OBSERVATIONS & REFLECTIONS

The thirst for spiritual solace is, in part, a response to the myriad fears and uncertainties that shadow our troubled world. It is a quest for inner peace in sea of noise and confusion and hope for an unseen eternity.

A sampling of articles appearing from 2002 to 2005 in The Journal of Aesthetics and Art Criticism reveals an intense interest in moral and ethical themes in art: "The Wheel of Virtue: Art, Literature, and Moral Knowledge" (Carroll, 2002), "Moral Judgments and Works of Art: The Case of Narrative Literature" (Devereaux 2004), "Moral Defects, Aesthetic Defects, and the Imagination" (Mullin 2004), "The Ethics of Exhibitions: On the Presentation of Religious Art" (Worth 2004), "Intrinsic Value and the Notion of a Life" (Levinson 2004), and "Toward a Metaphysical Historicism" (Bacharach 2005).

Thousand-year segments have a sobering impact on humankind, provoking many to soul search and reexamine life's purposes. This often leads to the belief in God and the sense that time is somehow consecrated; the random is rendered providential and promising, rather than bleak and meaningless. Historians and aestheticians have demonstrated the resurgence in spirituality at the beginning of the first millennium, manifested in Romanesque and Gothic art and architecture.

In tandem with recent interest in moral concerns, an article by Richard Wolin about Jürgen Habermas (who is widely regarded as the world's most influential living philosopher) appeared in the September 23, 2005 issue of The Chronicle of Higher Education. The article explained that Habermas is encouraging the practice of "discourse ethics," a form of international discussion in which the covenant tradition—which he demonstrates is at the core of Western political and legal practices—is manifested in human discourse.

Habermas found inspiration for this covenantal format in the philosopher Immanuel Kant's categorical imperative. Through discourse, one is asked to examine various points of view, seeing if they can pass

OBSERVATIONS & REFLECTIONS

the categorical test of universality. Here something is deemed moral, if it can be demonstrated that it would benefit humankind if it were made into universal law. One must prove that anyone in a similar situation should act the same way: "According to Kant, lying and stealing are immoral insofar as they fall beneath the universalization threshold; only at the price of grave self-contradiction could one will that lying and stealing become universal laws" (Wolin).

Considered in the light of the above, we can see how well Van Gogh's artistic beliefs and practices fit into Habermas's ethical discourse. This is because Van Gogh's art and letter writing were a form of discourse embodying covenantal ideals and processes which gave his art the sacred character we have noted. In this way, the reappraisal of Van Gogh presently underway can be understood as part of a much larger reappraisal (and part of an ethical discourse) taking place within Western culture more generally.

Proceeds from the sale of this book are donated to PROGENY—an international organization dedicated to the rescue, safety, treatment, and rehabilitation of exploited and endangered children, and the pursuit of justice on their behalf.

For more information, please visit www.EndangeredChildren.org

A dynamic, interactive, digital version of this book is available with links to vibrant imagery, online video, audio, and other interactive resources. To obtain the digital version of this book, please e-mail the publisher using the message form at the following Internet address:

www.CreativeStorytellers.com